AFTER ABU GHRAIB

Exploring Human Rights in America and the Middle East

This book traverses three pivotal human rights struggles of the post–September 11th era: the American human rights campaign to challenge the Bush administration's "War on Terror" torture and detention policies, Middle Eastern efforts to challenge American human rights practices (reversing the traditional West to East flow of human rights mobilizations and discourses), and Middle Eastern attempts to challenge their own leaders' human rights violations in light of American interventions. This book presents snapshots of human rights being appropriated, promoted, claimed, reclaimed, and contested within and between the American and Middle Eastern contexts. The inquiry has three facets: First, it explores intersections between human rights norms and power as they unfold in the era. Second, it lays out the layers of the era's American and Middle Eastern encounter on the human rights plane. Finally, it draws out the era's key lessons for moving the human rights project forward.

Shadi Mokhtari is an independent scholar and human rights attorney. She currently works with a domestic violence nonprofit organization in the Washington D.C. area and serves as the managing editor of the *Muslim World Journal of Human Rights.* She holds PhD and LLM degrees from Osgoode Hall Law School, York University; a JD from the University of Texas School of Law; a master's in international affairs from Columbia University; and a BA from American University. She has taught as an adjunct professor at Osgoode Hall Law School and has contributed chapters to books, including *Islamic Law and International Law* ("The Iranian Search for Human Rights within an Islamic Framework") (2007), *Islamic Feminism and the Law* ("Towards a New Agenda for Islamic Feminism: Clearing the Human Rights Minefield") (2008), and *Migrant Women's Search for Social Justice* ("Migrant Women's Interests and the Case of Shari'a Tribunals in Ontario") (2009). In 2006, she was selected as a "new voices" panelist at the American Association of International Law Conference and was awarded honorable mention for the John Peter Humphreys Fellowship from the Canadian Council on International Law.

CAMBRIDGE STUDIES IN LAW AND SOCIETY

Cambridge Studies in Law and Society aims to publish the best scholarly work on legal discourse and practice in its social and institutional contexts, combining theoretical insights and empirical research.

The fields that it covers are: studies of law in action; the sociology of law; the anthropology of law; cultural studies of law, including the role of legal discourses in social formations; law and economics; law and politics; and studies of governance. The books consider all forms of legal discourse across societies, rather than being limited to lawyers' discourses alone.

The series editors come from a range of disciplines: academic law; socio-legal studies; sociology; and anthropology. All have been actively involved in teaching and writing about law in context.

Series editors

Chris Arup *Monash University, Victoria*
Martin Chanock *La Trobe University, Melbourne*
Pat O'Malley *University of Sydney*
Sally Engle Merry *New York University*
Susan Silbey *Massachusetts Institute of Technology*

Books in the Series

Diseases of the Will
Mariana Valverde

The Politics of Truth and Reconciliation in South Africa
Legitimizing the Post-Apartheid State
Richard A. Wilson

Modernism and the Grounds of Law
Peter Fitzpatrick

Unemployment and Government
Genealogies of the Social
William Walters

Autonomy and Ethnicity
Negotiating Competing Claims in Multi-Ethnic States
Yash Ghai

Constituting Democracy
Law, Globalism and South Africa's Political Reconstruction
Heinz Klug

The Ritual of Rights in Japan
Law, Society, and Health Policy
Eric A. Feldman

Continued on page following the index

After Abu Ghraib

EXPLORING HUMAN RIGHTS IN
AMERICA AND THE MIDDLE EAST

Shadi Mokhtari

CAMBRIDGE
UNIVERSITY PRESS

CAMBRIDGE UNIVERSITY PRESS
Cambridge, New York, Melbourne, Madrid, Cape Town, Singapore, São Paulo, Delhi

Cambridge University Press
32 Avenue of the Americas, New York, NY 10013-2473, USA

www.cambridge.org
Information on this title: www.cambridge.org/9780521767538

First published 2009

Printed in the United States of America

A catalog record for this publication is available from the British Library.

Library of Congress Cataloging in Publication data
Mokhtari, Shadi
After Abu Ghraib : exploring human rights in America and the Middle East /
Shadi Mokhtari.
    p.   cm. – (Cambridge studies in law and society)
Includes bibliographical references and index.
ISBN 978-0-521-76753-8 (hardback)
    1. Human rights – United States.   2. Human rights – Middle East.   3. Abu Ghraib Prison.
4. War on Terrorism, 2001 – Law and legislation – United States.   I. Title.   II. Series.
K3249.M65   2009
341.4'8 – dc22   2008045107

ISBN 978-0-521-76753-8 hardback

To my father, Rahim Mokhtari, and my mother, Guiti Assadi, for their burning passion for the realization of justice and human dignity in their native Iran, in their adopted United States, and throughout the world.

Contents

Acknowledgments

I am greatly indebted to family, friends, colleagues, and mentors for their support and assistance in the completion of this book. First and foremost, I would like to thank Susan Drummond for her enduring encouragement and invaluable input throughout the process. At every point at which I felt the project was simply too ambitious and impossible to complete, it was Susan who convinced me to get back in front of my computer and start the next chapter. I also thank Obiora Okafor and Annie Bunting for their guidance and feedback throughout my tenure at Osgoode Hall Law School.

I must also express my gratitude to all the people who assisted me throughout my fieldwork. This project would not have been possible without the tremendous insights provided by the American and Middle Eastern human rights activists, journalists, and government officials who graciously offered me their time, experiences, and perspectives. I would also like to thank Anbara Abu Ayyash, David Cole, Gregory Dean Johnson, Galil Noaman, Wendy Patten, and Charles Schmitz, who each provided valuable leads and assistance with some aspect of the field research. My work in Yemen also benefited immensely from the interpretation assistance of Baraa Shiban.

Finally, I would like to thank my husband, Peyman Khalichi, for his immense enthusiasm for my work and for his willingness to always engage with the issues and ideas encompassed in this project. I am also grateful for the support of my brother Rohmteen Mokhtari, who never ceases to amaze me with wisdom beyond his years. His spirit serves as inspiration for the optimism and hope weaved into this work.

Abbreviations

ACLU – American Civil Liberties Union (American NGO)
CAT – Convention Against Torture
CEDAW – Convention on the Elimination of All Forms of Discrimination against Women
CERD – Convention on the Elimination of All Forms of Racial Discrimination
HOOD – The National Organization for Defending Rights and Freedoms (Yemeni NGO)
IAF – Islamic Action Front (Jordanian Islamist Party)
ICRC – International Committee of the Red Cross
INGO – international nongovernmental organization
IO – international organization
LCCR – Leadership Conference on Civil Rights (American NGO)
MCA – Military Commissions Act
MEPI – Middle East Partnership Initiative
NAACP – National Association for the Advancement of Colored People
NCHR – National Center for Human Rights (Jordanian quasi-governmental organization)
NGO – nongovernmental organization
NPR – National Public Radio
PDF – Political Development Forum (Yemeni NGO)
SAF – Sisters' Arab Forum for Human Rights (Yemeni NGO)
UNDP – United Nations Development Programme

Introduction

If the post–September 11th era is to bear the imprint of a succession of setbacks to the human rights paradigm epitomized by Abu Ghraib's arresting images, the era should also be marked by human rights' reemergence at the fore of local and global contests and consciousness. This study traverses three pivotal human rights struggles of the era: the American human rights campaign to challenge Bush administration "War on Terror" torture and detention policies, Middle Eastern efforts to challenge American human rights practices (in effect, reversing the traditional West-to-East flow of human rights mobilizations and discourses), and Middle Eastern attempts to challenge their own leaders' human rights violations in light of American post–September 11th interventions in the Middle East. The snapshots that emerge are of human rights repeatedly being appropriated, invoked, promoted, claimed, reclaimed, and contested within and between the American and Middle Eastern contexts. By placing these deployments side by side and highlighting the myriad of contradictions they encompass and produce, this book brings to light human rights' role as both an emancipatory and hegemonic force following September 11th. There are thus several facets to the present inquiry. First, it explores the era's key intersections between international human rights norms and power as they unfold in post–September 11th era. Second, it lays out the many interconnections and layers of the era's American and Middle Eastern encounters within the human rights realm. Finally, it draws out the primary lessons of post–September 11th developments for moving the human rights project forward.

THE FIELD

This largely empirical study incorporates field research conducted in Washington, DC, Amman, Jordan, and Sana'a, Yemen. Semistructured interviews of American and Middle Eastern human rights advocates, government

1

officials, and journalists are combined with content analysis of select media
coverage, governmental records, human rights nongovernmental organization (NGO) reports, and public forums and conferences. The research
extends through more than one locale to capture not just a sense of human
rights dynamics within one country but the transnational linkages and inter-
relationships encompassed.

Jordan and Yemen present fascinating case studies. Both countries were
(at least officially) engaging with human rights discourses prior to September
11th and both governments were less likely to label human rights norms
as Western or foreign impositions than other governments in the region,
particularly those in the Persian Gulf. Both countries also maintained close
relations with the United States throughout the post–September 11th era,
albeit for slightly different reasons. Beyond these similarities, however, the
two locales stand largely in contrast to each other.

Jordan's human rights discourses are highly influenced by its geography. The country's location between Israeli-occupied Palestinian lands and
American-occupied Iraq colors the worldviews of the population and even
human rights forces. In the same manner, its sizable Palestinian population
and growing Iraqi refugee population affect human rights discourses and
consciousness significantly. Its reputation as a stable and Western-friendly
country whose monarch frequently espouses a commitment to human rights
(at least in rhetoric) has attracted many international human rights and
humanitarian initiatives targeting the Middle East region. The state's control reaches deep and wide in Jordan. Despite leaders' propensity to adopt
human rights discourses and assemble various royal human rights initiatives
(mostly limited to women's rights and children's rights), civil and political
human rights violations such as torture and detentions spurred by criticism
of the state are regularly reported, and there is universal consciousness of
the existence of red lines around speech and opposition, even as the lines are
continuously being redrawn. International human rights groups have also
uncovered numerous cases of torture and illegal detentions emerging from
Jordanian assistance in American "War on Terror" rendition cases.

I chose to conduct field research in Jordan to gain insight into the
Hashemite Kingdom's own intriguing human rights trajectory following
September 11th and to get a small window into Iraqi human rights developments from the considerable presence of Iraqi activists, refugees, and official
delegations either exiled in or frequently traveling to Jordan following the
U.S. invasion of Iraq. I arrived in Amman at the end of May 2006. Just a few
days into my trip, news of the wanton killings of twenty-four Iraqi civilians
by U.S. Marines in Haditha and its cover-up by high-ranking U.S. marine
officials broke.

Before arriving, I had collected a handful of names and phone numbers
of Jordanian, Iraqi, and American activists involved in various human rights

initiatives and I had scheduled an interview with the director of the Amman Center for Human Rights Studies, a Jordanian NGO that from its relatively extensive Internet presence seemed like a major player. I had made a contact at the NGO and hoped it could serve as my primary source for further contacts. After a very frank and elucidating interview with Nizam Assaf (presented extensively in Chapter 4) on my first full day in Amman and after obtaining a valuable list of contacts from the Amman Center for Human Rights Studies' staff, I ran into some unexpected obstacles. My contact at the NGO resigned soon after I had arrived, and after a few days of digesting my line of interview questions that had focused extensively on U.S. human rights practices and promotion policies in the Middle East, Assaf had become somewhat suspicious that I might be more than just an innocuous researcher, prompting him to refuse me permission to sit in on the NGO's activities. A few minutes after sitting in on a training session for Iraqi human rights activists who were in the midst of a heated discussion about the impact of the Haditha massacre on their work, Assaf asked me to leave, explaining, "these are sensitive topics." He later refused to extend an invitation to a regional conference on criminal justice the center was hosting.

Although I was disappointed to miss these events, which no doubt would have enhanced my research, the experience did in some ways underscore the level of apprehension of both domestic and foreign sources with which Middle Eastern human rights activists have come to operate. Fortunately, I did not provoke as much suspicions in further contacts and successfully secured a number of revealing interviews with other Jordanian human rights activists, journalists specializing in human rights coverage in Jordan's major reform-oriented media, associates of the quasi-governmental National Center for Human Rights, UN officials, several Iraqi activists exiled in Jordan, and Americans involved in various human rights promotion projects. I left Amman on July 1, 2008, just a few days after the U.S. Supreme Court had announced what was considered one of its landmark detainee rights decisions in *Hamdan v. Rumsfeld*[1] and a few days before the start of the war between Hezbollah in Lebanon and Israel.

Whereas in Jordan the state is strong, in Yemen it is weak. The country is also by far the poorest in the region and the tenth poorest country in the world. This makes all sectors (governmental and nongovernmental) highly reliant on foreign aid. As a result, the government has been particularly responsive to American interventions, on the one hand revolving around who it should detain and with what semblance of due process within the context of the "War on Terror," and on the other hand revolving around pressure to adopt and institute various human rights and democratization reform measures. For most of the September 11th period, Yemen has had the second

---

[1] *Hamdan v. Rumsfeld*, 126 S. Ct. 2749 (2006).

largest number of Guantanamo detainees and by the time I visited, human rights advocates sarcastically joked it had gained the honor of achieving the number one ranking. The confluence of pressure and aid to institute human rights reforms with American treatment of Yemeni detainees in Guantanamo and pressure for corresponding treatment of suspected terrorists at home has bred fascinating discourses and consciousness around human rights amid international power asymmetries.

Assisting with the United States' counterterrorism efforts was not much a matter of choice but one of necessity. Particularly, in the period immediately following the September 11th attacks, the Yemeni government's "cooperation" was propelled by a real fear that if it did not, it could suffer the same fate as Afghanistan. In recent years, with growing popular anger at American policies in the region, the government has occasionally put forth scathing criticism of the United States but has failed to act by changing its relationship with the global power. As one American embassy official put it, "From time to time, the government will organize a demonstration or march from one innocuous location to another innocuous location to protest American policies."[2]

Interestingly, Yemeni human rights discourses are among the most rooted in the region and certainly predate September 11th. The reunification of the country following a drawn-out civil war provided important openings for the institutionalization of certain human rights norms, for example, a mandate for multiparty elections and the articulation of a number of key rights in the constitution. The initial growth of Yemeni human rights NGOs began in 1999, and most human rights activists consider the past seven years a very productive era for the development of Yemeni civil society. As a result, Yemen is considered one of the region's most progressive in its upholding of civil and political rights and democratic reforms.

I had not considered Yemen as a possible site for field research when I embarked on this project in May 2004. However, several months after beginning the research, my interest in the unique Middle Eastern locale was sparked after hearing the country's then-human rights minister and several researchers speak. As I heard them describe Yemen's complex relationship with the United States within the post–September 11th human rights context and the centrality of the country's 100-plus Guantanamo detainees within its vibrant human rights engagements, I realized how valuable a Yemeni case study might be. I arrived in Sana'a in early January 2007, just after the *eid al-adha* (the Muslim festival of sacrifice at the conclusion of the *haj* pilgrimage to Mecca), which had this year coincided with the execution of Saddam Hussein in Iraq. A few days following my arrival also marked the fifth anniversary of the arrival of the first prisoners at Guantanamo Bay.

---

[2] Interview with U.S. embassy official (I), in Sana'a, Yemen (Jan. 23, 2007).

Again, I entered the country with a list of contacts gleaned from various sources and the hopes that HOOD (The National Organization for Defense of Rights and Freedoms), the Yemeni NGO active in both local human rights issues and Guantanamo detainee cases, would serve as a primary contact. I also met a U.S.-based physician on my flight to Sana'a who took an interest in my research and offered to assist me in making government contacts. As a result, I had an interview with the foreign minister on my first full day and a meeting two days later with the Supreme Court justice who had received considerable Western media attention for his faith-based dialogs with Islamic extremists imprisoned in Yemen.

The interviews (particularly the former) offered little that added substantively to my research. By contrast, an extensive interview with the two primary lawyers at HOOD, Mohammad Najji Allaw, the experienced head of the organization, and Khaled Alanesi, its amicable director, proved extremely valuable and is presented in pieces throughout much of the book. At one point during the interview, Allaw, who posed an extremely cogent third-world critique of global human rights dynamics but occasionally slipped into conspiracy theories, mentioned that he never knows when a foreign visitor posing as a human rights activist or researcher like me is actually there for intelligence purposes. But judging from the duo's fairly warm reception, they did not plan to hold the possibility against me. After the interview Alanesi supplied me with a lengthy list of names to contact. Another highly revealing interview was one conducted with Amal Basha, the spirited and reflective director of the Sisters' Forum for Human Rights who was referred to me by an American women's rights contact working in Jordan. Like Basha, virtually every other Yemeni activist and journalist I encountered was extraordinarily open about the challenges, opportunities, and enigmas of Yemen's post–September 11th human rights predicament. The director of the American Institute for Yemeni Studies also assisted me in making a contact at the U.S. embassy in Sana'a and, after a number of e-mail exchanges, I was able to arrange interviews and discussions with several officials with varying ranks at the embassy. I left Sana'a's enveloping mountains, stunning ancient architecture, traditional attire, and immense poverty at the end of January 2007.

Both case studies provide a wealth of insight into the flux of American and Middle Eastern human rights dynamics in the post–September 11th era; however, the post–September 11th paths of other Middle Eastern countries have also contained abundant material relevant to the present inquiry. Egypt has always been a pivotal player in the region, has a civil society with broad and deep, yet still limited, roots, and has been flagged and funded as a key American ally in the region. It experienced smatterings of progress in the realm of political reforms but whatever inroads were made were quickly pushed back. The Persian Gulf states such as Saudi Arabia also present a fascinating wrinkle; despite their close political and economic ties to the United States, their financial independence allows them to answer American calls for reforms differently than an impoverished country like Yemen. Within the Gulf, Kuwait and Bahrain are notable both for their dynamic struggles for political reform and their elaborate state and civil society efforts to free Guantanamo detainees. Morocco, which is a bit further removed (at least geographically) from post–September 11th events (notwithstanding its involvement with American renditions and its extremist pockets), is another fascinating study in light of its institution of at least some notable human rights and women's rights reforms in recent years. Thus, to the extent possible, post–September 11th developments emerging from other Middle Eastern locales are also woven into the study via secondary sources.

The American case study serves as the fulcrum of this book, as most of its analysis is set against some aspect of American governmental or non-governmental action. Because the complex American disposition toward the human rights paradigm and the international framework institutionalizing it serve as the backdrop for the larger study in this way, Chapter 1 is devoted entirely to the subject. The choice of the United States as a central site of field research was the most obvious given both the United States' overwhelming power and central role in post–September 11th human rights discourses and contests. I spent most of my time between January 2006 and January 2009 in Washington, DC. Most of my interviews of American human rights activists, congressional staffers, and journalists took place in the winter of 2006. I was rather surprised to find some of the American human rights activists I sought to interview highly inaccessible – standing in contrast to most Middle Eastern activists' eagerness to discuss their experiences with post–September 11th human rights developments, but perhaps also reflecting the seeping of Washington's "most powerful city of the most powerful country in the world" culture into the human rights sector. Still, because of my extended stay in the locale, I was able to eventually secure interviews with a majority of the American actors I hoped to reach. I also relied heavily on observation at forums and secondary sources in the American case study. However, tying down the case study proved a formidable task. There was simply so much activity – so many congressional debates, so many interviews with key actors in publications, ranging from The New York Times to Esquire, and so many conferences and forums – that from the onset it was clear that I could incorporate only a small sampling in the study. The same can be said of the Middle Eastern side of the research as well. As a result, the book lays no claim to being exhaustive in its ethnographic inquiry. Instead, it simply lays out different layers and dimensions of the post–September 11th human rights problematic in order to inaugurate the line of inquiry. This is done with the hope that this project can offer new analytical tools and insights for others to take up and further develop, expand, and complicate in the future.

INTERNATIONAL HUMAN RIGHTS AND POWER

It is important to note from the onset that in this project power is conceived in particularly broad terms as the capacity to shape outcomes impacting individuals' or groups' predicaments. The definition encompasses a range of both material and constitutive manifestations of power, including economic pressure, military force, imprisonment, and subjection to violence within detention, as well as the production, constitution, and deployment of norms and knowledge. Although what is known within the social science literature on power as "power over," namely, through the imposition of one's will over others, is central to the book's analysis, gradients of "power to" are implicit in discussions of resistance to power over and the role of social forces. Finally, power is presented as generally relative rather than absolute, multidimensional, fluid, dynamic, and capable of being possessed by individuals, movements, institutions, or states.

The view of human rights adopted is equally expansive and multifaceted. It is one that weaves back and forth between, and integrates, the paradigms' interconnected normative, political, and legal dimensions. At its core, human rights are a set of norms laying out a particular emancipatory vision. Legalization within the international legal framework is considered an important means for realizing that vision, ostensibly by infusing human rights norms with greater authority and capacity to bind states. Yet, since its inception, the international human rights framework has been confronted with questions regarding the regime's ability to fulfill its emancipatory promise in the face of both state power and powerful states. Legal positivists discount human rights law because of the lack of any sovereign power charged with its enforcement and rationalists associate human rights norms with material pursuits of "power" or "interests," viewing them as no more than instruments strategically deployed by actors to further or justify interests.

The post–September 11th era appeared only to solidify critics' skepticism and human rights advocates' anxieties about international human rights' captivity to power. The era has been, to a large extent, defined by "extraordinary renditions" that often sent suspects to be interrogated in countries known to have few qualms or real restrictions on torture, the graphic depictions of humiliation, abuse, and torture at Abu Ghraib, the real prospects of indefinite detention without the most basic of due process guarantees faced by detainees at Guantanamo Bay, Bagram, and other detention facilities, the "disappearing" of suspects the United States deemed of high value into the abyss of secret CIA black sites, Bush administration efforts to reshape domestic and international law prohibition on torture, and few prospects of high-ranking officials being directly held accountable for any of these policies.

At the same time, during this period the United States also consistently enlisted and co-opted human rights norms by linking justifications of its various military and political interventions in the Middle East to pervasive oppression and authoritarianism in the region. The human rights lexicon presented the United States with the opportunity to veil pursuits of interests and power with the veneer of nobility, sacrifice, morality, and justice. It proceeded to deploy human rights norms in such instrumental ways by tapping into and reproducing categories that designated the United States as a human rights promoter and Middle Eastern governments, cultures, and religions as human rights violators. Middle Eastern governments in turn often followed (or continued) suit, both through their use of counterterrorism as renewed license for curtailing rights and through calculated forays into the reform, democracy, and human rights lexicon.

As these dynamics unfolded, decades-old questions surrounding international law and particularly the human rights regimes' capacity to constrain states' (and especially militarily and economically powerful states') behavior in accordance with the normative framework, resurfaced. Observers revisited questions of whether the framework should be considered autonomous or subservient to international power asymmetries and whether it was disingenuous to continue designating international human rights law as "international" or as "law."[3] In short, the era was gripped by an overwhelming sense that human rights norms and the international legal regime that codified it were in the midst of an existential crisis in the face of American power and its post–September 11th global policies. With no apparent force to compel compliance and damage from the delegitimizing effects of human rights norms' instrumentalization on such a grand scale, the human rights project was increasingly considered "weak" and its future uncertain.

As revealing as they were, however, post–September 11th developments could provide only a partial account of the operation of power vis-à-vis the international human rights regime. There were invariably other layers to the Abu Ghraib story as there were to the Guantanamo epic and efforts to co-opt human rights by American and Middle Eastern governments alike. Viewed through different lenses, each of these post–September 11th human rights phenomena also revealed the elusiveness, clumsiness, and vulnerability of power, the way it is apt to trap itself through its reliance on the morality

---

[3] Doris E. Buss, *Keeping Its Promise: Use of Force and the New Man of International Law, in* EMPIRE'S LAW: THE AMERICAN IMPERIAL PROJECT AND THE WAR TO REMAKE THE WORLD 87 (Amy Bartholomew ed., 2006).

of the human rights regime, the way it is trapped by human rights forces it seeks to co-opt, and the way it is resisted from within and abroad. Such dynamics stand as testament to the proposition that although governments could go to great lengths to veil their intentions to abide by human rights standards, there is no guarantee that they will succeed, laying the foundation for challenging power through a framework that it had already designated as legitimate.

Thus, a central thesis of this study is that in the post–September 11 era, human rights have simultaneously manifested and transcended power and international hierarchies. The era is not necessarily exceptional in its positioning of human rights between hegemony and emancipation. Several recent studies considering earlier periods have recognized that international law or human rights are neither entirely paralyzed by power nor entirely divorced from it but occupy a complex space in between.[4] The era does, however, provide a wealth of material for a rich empirical study, because of the concentration and sheer volume of discourse, funding, and contestation centered around human rights it has engendered. In this sense, it presents a unique opportunity to add depth and nuance to understandings of human rights as simultaneously manifesting and transcending power relations or, as Amy Bartholomew has observed, conceptualizing human rights as a "site of struggle."[5]

The empirical research undertaken draws from and brings together two emerging literatures within the international law and human rights scholarship. The first is the Third World Approaches to International Law (TWAIL) literature and corresponding critical scholarship that highlight the ways in which power relations among states, cultures, races, or "civilizations" can be assembled around and built into international human rights dynamics. The second is the international law and compliance, particularly constructivist-inspired scholarship, which tends to focus on the potential of norms and identities to foster compliance with human rights standards, notwithstanding power. Each framework illuminates important aspects of the human rights dynamics at play but takes the analysis only so far before it displays its limitations. The two optics are of greatest value when applied in concert as one's strengths often serve to remedy the other's limitations.

Adopting a research agenda in which power or hegemony figures so prominently can be fraught with its own trappings as it leaves an impression

---

[4] See, for example, Nico Krisch, *International Law in Times of Hegemony*, 16:3 EUR. J. INT'L L. 369 (2005), or Oona Hathaway, *Between Power and Principle: A Political Theory of International Law*, 71 U. CHI. L. REV. (2005). The argument is also generally basic to constructivism, although constructivists tend to place greater emphasis on emancipatory openings.

[5] Amy Bartholomew aptly uses the term in her work on human rights following September 11th. *Empire's Law and the Contradictory Politics of Human Rights supra* note 3, at 180.

of a totalizing conception of power. However, the focus on human rights' emancipatory potential is intended to signal a willingness to look beyond power to its unsettling through internal contradictions and to the various other social and political phenomena with which it intersects. In other words, this book is equally concerned about the relevance of power in the human rights context as it is with the irrelevance of power to the same. If the analysis takes as its starting point the many ways in which power is manifested through human rights, it concludes with a discussion of recommendations for further enhancing the emancipatory potential of the human rights framework.

The New Era's Inherited East/West Human Rights Geography

To understand the operation of power through human rights in the post–September 11th era, it is critical to identify one of the key ways in which power had been infused into global human rights dynamics long before September 11th. Since the regime's inception, the human rights project has been imbued with an entrenched hierarchy. Because of its unmistakable geographic demarcations, the hierarchy is referred to as the "East/West geography of human rights" in this project. At its core, the geography assumes Western liberal contexts' commitment to universalism and the furtherance of the human rights project while it conceives of non-Western countries, cultures, and races as inherently incapable of fully understanding or achieving rights on their own.

In recent years, a body of critical scholarship, much of it articulated within TWAIL literature, has mapped out the key elements of the East/West geography of human rights. This scholarship has interrogated the bifurcation of countries or cultures into human rights champions/guardians/leaders and human rights nightmares/burdens/projects and brought to light the designations' linkages to power, particularly in its constitutive or knowledge-based forms. Makau Mutua has written of the "savage-victim-savior" metaphor of human rights, in which non-Western states and/or cultures are cast in the role of savages, their population or segments of their populations (often women) are cast as victims, and Western liberal states and institutions take on the role of saviors.[6] Similarly, Obiora Okafor and Shedrack Agbakwa have written of three problematic constitutive orthodoxies of mainstream human rights education promoted by international organizations and international non-governmental organizations (INGOs): (1) a "heaven-hell" binary in which the West is presumed a model of human rights compliance while the developing world is presumed to be a human rights nightmare," (2) "a consequent

---

[6] Makau Mutua, *Savages, Victims, and Saviors: The Metaphor of Human Rights*, 42 HARV. INT'L L. J. 201 (2001).

unidirectional traffic of human rights teaching from the West to the Rest,"
and (3) the existence of an abolitionist paradigm that locates the source of
the developing world's human rights predicament in its culture, which it
in turn targets.[7] Powell has offered valuable insights about similar tendencies in the cultural relativism versus universalism debate so central to global
human rights politics, identifying several false underlying assumptions. First,
Western states are culturally neutral and thus devoid of the primitive cultural practices that lead to human rights violations in non-Western states.
Second, relativism cannot be ascribed to the behavior of Western states in
the way it can be ascribed to that of non-Western states. Finally, "the only
relativism which poses any real threat to universalism is cultural relativism,
in contrast to other relativisms that are reflected in the selective enforcement
and invocation of human rights in and by Western and non-Western states
alike."[8]

The East/West geography of human rights encompasses important facets
of the notion of orientalism developed by the renowned Arab-American
literary theorist Edward Said. As Said sketched the phenomenon emerging
from centuries of Western imperialist forays into the East, orientalism is a
Western tendency to imagine and to construct the East (Orient) in ways that
allow it to define itself in favorable contrasting terms.[9] The approach encompasses a Western license to judge, scrutinize, study, represent, enlighten, and
govern the East. Although orientalism is clearly characterized by a power
relationship and web of hierarchies between the orient and occident, the
West's power over the East is taken for granted as scientific truth. Each of
these elements has been widely present in global human rights dynamics
throughout the regime's tenure.

Several insights emerging from the TWAIL and corresponding critical literature are particularly relevant to the analysis that ensues. First, the hierarchy at the root of the East/West geography renders Western violations invisible or easily dismissible as mere aberrations, whereas it makes non-Western
violations ever present and highly visible, often through demonizing, sensationalist, and decontextulized accounts. Second, the construction lends itself
to Western states (which are so inclined) to appropriate the moral authority
of international human rights norms to justify military or economic interventions. Third, the categories have a semiotic relationship with racism and
cultural hierarchy. When the stigma of human rights violations is associated

[7] Obiora Chinedu Okafor and Shedrack C. Agbakwa, *Re-Imagining International Human Rights Education in Our Time: Beyond Three Constitutive Orthodoxies*, 14 LEIDEN J. INT'L L. 563 (2001).
[8] Catherine Powell, *Locating Culture, Identity, and Human Rights*, 30 COLUM. HUM. RTS. L. REV. 201 (1999), at 202–4.
[9] EDWARD SAID, ORIENTALISM (1979).

with the dark-skinned and "backward" cultures of the East, in a circular fashion it can serve as a justification for violating those populations' rights. For example, what is viewed as a particular race, religion, or culture's incapacity to grasp notions of rights serves to dehumanize its population in a way that make the deprivation of their rights more acceptable in the eyes of a Western soldier, politician, or citizen. Finally, conceptualizations of human rights violations flowing from the geography tend to coalesce around internal sources of oppression and injustice and overlook international sources.

Mapping this East/West human rights geography from the onset is critical because much of the analysis presented in the rest of the book relates to how this geography comes to be simultaneously reinforced and challenged through the unfolding of post–September 11th dynamics. For example, both trends are seen in the strategies and arguments posited by human rights advocates challenging the Bush administration's torture and detention policies. It is necessary to note that the geography has become so engrained that even Middle Eastern human rights advocates who are attuned to it, and inclined to pose challenges to it on one front, are also prone to reproduce it on another front. For example, at one point in our interview, HOOD's Khaled Alanesi facetiously asserted that Western human rights experts often viewed Yemeni counterparts as "monkeys" to be trained in the language of human rights without an independent capacity to determine what human rights policies are best for their societies. Extending the analogy, Alanesi also noted that these same Western experts often praised Yemen through comparisons to neighboring Somalia or Saudi Arabia rather than countries with better human rights records, something he saw as an underlying tendency to apply lower human rights standards to the Middle Eastern contexts or to see all non-Western countries as the same in their capacity to achieve rights. Yet at the same time that he criticized the presence of some East/West human rights delineations, roles, and hierarchies, he clearly adhered to others:

About the question of who learns from who, now I see that the West is learning from the developing countries. In a negative way, they have learned how to violate human rights. The human rights violations that happened in the U.S., Britain, or Australia they picked it up from the Arab world; the Arab intelligence have been capable of influencing the Western intelligence forces on how to violate human rights. So the West is learning how to violate human rights from the East. Not only in the practice of violations but also in their law.[10]

Although the assertion is made as part of a tongue-and-cheek rebuke of Middle Eastern governments' undeniably deplorable human rights practices and is even on some level factually correct,[11] the fact that Alanesi frames the

[10] Interview with Khaled Alanesi, executive director, HOOD, in Sana'a, Yemen (Jan. 15, 2007).

[11] *The New York Times* has reported that the CIA consulted Egyptian and Saudi intelligence officials in developing their interrogation techniques. Scott Shane, David Johnston, and

rebuke in terms that portray Western states as essentially unknowledgeable of even how to go about committing human rights violations while Arab states are their traditional architects is indicative of the extent to which the human rights geography unearthed by critical scholars has been internalized by governmental and nongovernmental forces, Western and Middle Eastern alike.

Still, although TWAIL and related critical scholarship play a pivotal role in alerting those promoting the human rights enterprise to the operation of power through human rights and its contemporary hierarchies, they generally offer little beyond this important critique. By placing such substantial emphasis on manifestations of power and injustice embedded within human rights dynamics, scholars often either overlook or choose not to consider the many ways in which power can in fact be challenged, curtailed, or transcended through the same human rights enterprise. Moreover, although it is rarely explicitly articulated, some of the literature can leave one with a sense that the only way to escape the human rights regimes' failings is to abandon the framework altogether, an unattractive prospect given the regimes' formidable achievements and the lack of viable alternatives in the foreseeable future. These shortcomings are in large part remedied by integrating this critical scholarship with a constructivist outlook.

The Human Rights Challenge to Power

An underlying premise adhered to in this book is that power should not be conceived of in static or zero-sum terms. Categories of powerful and powerless are fluid and dynamic, not discrete or absolute. It is not that these categories do not exist, particularly in relative terms. In fact, the operation of power relations within American/Middle Eastern human rights dynamics is a key analytic adopted in the study. Instead, it is best argued that the dichotomy is untidy and porous. The research presented illustrates how domestic forces come to challenge American policies from within, how Middle Eastern forces can challenge and subvert American attempts to co-opt human rights, and how local civil society forces exploit cleavages and contradictions to challenge Middle Eastern states from within during the post–September 11th period. Each instance demonstrates how emancipatory manifestations of the human rights framework envisioned by human rights proponents can overlap, meet, or eclipse hegemonic manifestations deployed by American and Middle Eastern governments. No doubt, those with power attempt to at once co-opt and contravene human rights and in

James Risen, *Secret US Endorsement of Severe Interrogations*, N.Y. TIMES, Oct. 4, 2007, http://www.nytimes.com/2007/10/04/washington/04interrogate.html?_r=2&pagewanted=print&oref=slogin&oref=slogin. For a discussion of American involvement with torture prior to September 11, see Jamie Mayerfeld, *Playing by Our Own Rules: How U.S. Marginalization of Human Rights Led to Torture*, 20 HARV. HUM. RTS. J. 89 (2007).

many ways they do so successfully. However, they can exploit the moral regime for only so long and to only such lengths before they are in some way answerable to it. Thus, in the post–September 11th era, at the same time that human rights serve to structure and define American and Middle Eastern power relations (through state as well as nonstate hierarchies), they also serve to mediate, restructure, and redefine these very relationships, frequently turning them on their heads.

Within the international law and compliance literature, constructivist theory provides a useful analytical framework for understanding human rights' potential to transcend power in these ways. The theory's major strength lies in its capacity to go beyond top-down models of coercive enforcement and strict notions of compliance in shedding light on the effectiveness and potential impact of international legal norms. The theory can emphasize human rights' importance as a normative order with the capacity to shape policymakers' and other relevant actors' views of appropriate behavior. This outcome is realized when human rights advocates engage those reluctant to comply through debate, dialog, persuasion, deliberation, and shaming. Applied to questions of international human rights norms' effectiveness and potential impact, constructivism's core assertions include the following. First, leaders' decisions regarding whether to uphold human rights are shaped not only by material considerations relating to power or interests but also by many subjectivities, including beliefs, understandings, knowledge, expectations, and norms.[12] Second, the norms and normative frameworks, like human rights are particularly critical because they encompass a sense of "shared moral assessment" or evaluation of what good people or good states ought to do.[13] Thus, leaders can become attuned to the stigma and negative judgment encompassed in human rights violations because they care about their reputation and will accordingly try to distance themselves from the "human rights abuser" label. Finally, identities, interests, and even power are dynamic and "socially constructed products of learning, knowledge, cultural practices and ideology";[14] they are not determined or fixed. This

[12] Martha Finnemore and Kathryn Sikkink, *Taking Stock: The Constructivist Research Program in International Relations and Comparative Politics*, 4 AM. REV. POL. SCI. 391 (2001), at 392–3.

[13] Martha Finnmore and Kathryn Sikkink, *International Norm Dynamics and Political Change*, 52 INT'L ORG. 887 (1998); and Thomas Risse and Katheryn Sikkink, *The Socialization of International Human Rights Norms into Domestic Practices: Introduction, in* THE POWER OF HUMAN RIGHTS 8 (Thomas Risse, Stephen Ropp, and Kathryn Sikkink eds., 1999). Constructivists widely hold that ideational factors (including international norms) are intersubjective, meaning that, at some level, they are shared or commonly held and understood.

[14] Harald Koh, *Why Do Nations Obey International Law? Book Review of The New Sovereignty: Compliance with International Regulatory Agreements by A. Chayes and A. Handler Chaynes, and of Fairness in International Law and Institutions by T. M. Frank*, 106 YALE L. J. 2599, 2650 (1997).

fact presents human rights activists with opportunities to promote identity constructions as well as notions of interests and power that are compatible with the observance of human rights, for example, by arguing that torture is un-American or that Islamic notions of justice encompass gender equality.

As noted, the theory places particular emphasis on communicative processes social interaction, including persuasion, argumentation, deliberation, framing, and shaming. The post–September 11th era has encompassed innumerable occasions for such interactions – when Condoleezza Rice addresses students at the American University in Cairo and the audience questions her about Abu Ghraib, when the State Department brings Middle Eastern human rights advocates to the United States to learn from the American model for upholding rights and participants request access to Middle Eastern detainees, when a Bush administration official is challenged by rights advocates at an American law school forum, when a secular women's rights activist and an Islamist who have come together in their opposition to American policies in Guantanamo then proceed to tackle divergences surrounding women's personal status laws, and when a U.S.-based human rights INGO communicates with an Islamist Party whose members have been detained by the local government. All of these interactions and countless others have provided opportunities for human rights to gain ground within American and Middle Eastern consciousness, demonstrating the regime's normative impact.

A relevant debate within the constructivist field surrounds the question of whether the most important interactions are those taking place internationally or domestically and whether it is other governments, international organizations, INGOs, or domestic actors who have the greatest capacity to influence governments' human rights attitudes and policies. The traditional state-centric approach considers interactions between states in the international plane to be most significant. A second strand of constructivist scholarship privileges the role played by liberal Western governments and networks built between transnational advocacy groups and domestic social movements.[15] Recently, a third model, premised on how human rights norms are incorporated primarily through the efforts of domestic human rights advocates bridging international and domestic norms, discourses, and identity constructions, has also sprung up.[16]

---

[15] See Risse & Sikkink, *supra* note 13.

[16] See, for example, Obiora Chinedu Okafor, THE AFRICAN HUMAN RIGHTS SYSTEM, ACTIVIST FORCES AND INTERNATIONAL INSTITUTIONS (2007); Balakrishnan Rajagopal, *The Role of Law in Counter-hegemonic Globalization and Global Legal Pluralism: Lessons from the Normada Valley Struggle in India*, 18 LEIDEN J. INT'L L. 345–87 (2005); and Shadi Mokhtari, *A Constructivist Analysis of the Impact of International Human Rights Norms: The Case of Women's Rights under Islamic Law in Iran* (2005) (unpublished LLM thesis, York University).

Clearly, none of the interactions privileged in each model is mutually exclusive, and, often, they work in tandem to reinforce each other. Moreover, which interaction is most significant will vary from cases to case. In the study of the American engagement with human rights in relation to its torture and detainee treatment policies, the most vital interactions are those that occur at the domestic realm and between domestic actors, mainly because nationalist discourses and identity constructions tend to marginalize and delegitimize foreign critics. This is best captured by the "we must be doing something right if we've got the French upset" caricature alluded to by an American human rights advocate interviewed.[17] But this disposition has slowly changed over time. As it turns out, international interactions were in some respects quite pivotal in the United States following Abu Ghraib. In the Middle East, the picture is just as complex. International interactions and pressure have varying levels of impact. When governments have close ties with the United States or other Western countries, international pressure can be more effective than domestic pressure, particularly in relation to civil and political violations committed by the state. However, these same governments can also join governments like Iran's to exploit converging nationalist, anti-imperialist, and Islamist discourses to justify skirting international human rights standards.

Despite its significant contribution to uncovering the normative ways in which international law can reign in state power, the core constructivist literature is largely blind to the ways in which power relations among states can also be assembled around and built into international norm dynamics.[18] Mirroring assumptions of the East/West geography detailed by critical scholars, within much of the constructivist literature the West's commitment to universalism and furtherance of the human rights project is largely assumed, and it is widely accepted that the most serious human rights challenges lie beyond Western borders. For example, the most important constructivist work on human rights, *The Power of Human Rights*, edited by Thomas Risse, Steven C. Ropp, and Kathryn Sikkink, develop a model that places Western-based human rights INGOs and Western liberal governments as agents of human rights promotion in non-Western states.[19] Not surprisingly, of the ten case studies presented in the book, none are of Western contexts.

Further, constructivism has faced criticism that its emphasis on the constitutive power of norms favors "good norms," such as the promotion of

---

[17] Interview with human rights NGO representative, in Washington, DC (Feb. 24, 2006).

[18] To the extent that international power asymmetries are taken into account, it is through the assertion that powerful states and their leaders are not beyond the reach of international norms' influence.

[19] See Risse & Sikkink, *supra* note 13.

peace and human rights rather than the rise of antithetical norms such as militarism or anti-Muslim sentiment. More important, constructivist accounts rarely dissect the composition of frames and arguments employed to foster compliance with international human rights norms to identify whether they contain any problematic or power-laden elements. Instead, it is often assumed that the framing and shaming deployed by human rights advocates are consistent with the aims of the human rights project. As Michael Barnett and Raymond Duvall have noted, "Although constructivists have emphasized how underlying normative structures constitute actors' identities and interests, they have rarely treated these normative structures themselves as defined and infused by power, or emphasized how constitutive effects also are expressions of power."[20] Thus, it is important to combine the constructivist insight that production of knowledge, identities, and status around compliance with international human rights norms can be an indispensable tool for advancing the human rights project, with critical human rights scholars' warnings that such productions can also be intimately linked to the (re-)production of international power asymmetries.

HUMAN RIGHTS DIMENSIONS OF THE AMERICAN/MIDDLE EASTERN ENCOUNTER

Middle Eastern and American human rights conditions are traditionally viewed as occupying separate spheres. Academics or activists who are generally specialists in Middle Eastern or American rights issues rarely cross over into each other's terrain, even while working within the same institutions. There are many reasons for this compartmentalization, including the widespread belief that Middle Eastern human rights violations stem exclusively from internal factors and a corresponding notion that American human rights dynamics are so exceptional that they have little connection to what lies beyond American borders or the West. However, in presenting the American and Middle Eastern contexts side by side and in interaction, this study attempts a departure from this traditional insular approach. In essence, it endeavors to paint a canvas, recount a narrative, dissect a dialectic, and trace the two contexts' interwoven trajectories. As the reader (whether he or she was drawn to the book as a result of a commitment to American or Middle Eastern human rights trajectories) works his or her way toward the conclusion of the book, he or she should gain a greater sense of the many linkages, parallels, and entanglements of the two contexts and their human rights predicaments.

---

[20] Michael Barnett and Raymond Duvall, *Power in International Politics*, 59 INT'L ORG. 39 (Winter 2005).

The text also endeavors to go beyond the often decontextualized and essentializing portrayals of the era's American/Middle Eastern encounter by highlighting both actual points of contention and the vast array of demarcations invoked that are in essence constructed. To accomplish this, the analysis considers prevailing identity constructions, often formed in opposition to the other, contrasting narratives and lived experiences and sometimes divergent and sometimes convergent sensibilities surrounding notions of justice, morality, and human suffering. In posing and juxtaposing each of these elements, the study places a primary focus on the various forms of "othering" inscribed within and around post–September 11th era human rights discourses and contests. Further, the case studies presented also bring out the overlap between identity constructions and beliefs about "the other" ascribed to by government officials, human rights advocates, and other social forces, demonstrating their continuity and symbiotic relationships.

Although most of the analysis is built around American/Middle Eastern engagements and sense of self in relation to the other, international law, and post–September 11th dynamics, this work also recognizes that an infinite number of other, mainly internal factors have also impacted human rights outcomes in each context but will inevitably be left out of the analysis presented here. Still, despite the obvious fact that American/Middle Eastern relational politics and perceptions were not the sole determinant of how human rights dynamics unfolded in each context, this focus is adopted because these relational aspects of post–September 11th human rights dynamics remain underexplored relative to their widespread presence within the era.

STRENGTHENING THE HUMAN RIGHTS PROJECT

At the same time that the text considers the impact and influence of human rights norms in a post–September 11th context, it is also heavily invested in exploring the implications of post–September 11th developments for advancing the human rights project. To this end, a central aspect of the book is a critical assessment of human rights advocates' achievements and shortcomings in contending with the era's profound human rights challenges. A critique of traditional human rights assumptions and strategies forms much of Chapter 5's analysis of the human rights lessons of the post–September 11th era as in many respects, it draws to a close with the assumption of the U.S. presidency by Barack Obama. Among the key lessons of the era identified are that human rights forces should part with identity constructions and frames that portray the United States as ontologically committed to upholding rights and they must refine the terms for seeking out American human rights leadership.

At several key junctures, the analysis approaches the relativism/universalism debate that has occupied human rights promoters and detractors alike since the regime's inception. Within this project, human rights is treated as a regime largely constructed through human agency but rooted in principles with potential for broad universal appeal. The research presented demonstrates this by detailing instances in which Middle Eastern groups traditionally inclined to dismiss human rights as Western impositions turn to the discourse to counter abuses they endure following September 11th. Still, it is clear that the meaning accorded to human rights by the myriad of actors invoking the language between and within the two contexts are varied and at times in conflict. Finally, this argument that the human rights framework has some universal appeal does not imply that recourse to the human rights framework is devoid of power dynamics or that human rights does not frequently serve, as critical scholars contend, as a hegemonic discourse. In many ways, it has traditionally been the only accessible emancipatory discourse because Western governments and Western activists have designated it as such. However, this fact precludes neither the regime's potential emancipatory effects nor the existence of agency on the part of those invoking it outside of the West.

The content of the international human rights regime and within the existing regime, what rights are emphasized and which are relegated to the realm of "aspirations," has also been an extremely contentious issue often taken up by critical human rights scholars. Although it is not a central focus, the analysis touches on contemporary debates surrounding what is designated an actionable or enforceable human rights violation and what is not. Clearly, the primary human rights discourses of the post–September 11th era have revolved around torture and due process rights, both falling within the civil and political rights category long privileged by Western states. At a few junctures, the book also touches on the implications of September 11th developments for local efforts to promote social and economic rights through the human rights rubric. It also makes an argument for the adoption of an expanded human rights vision that takes the human rights dimensions and consequences of American militarism, beyond the torture and detainee rights struggles so prominently placed on Western human rights agendas in the post–September 11th period, more seriously.

THE BOOK FROM HERE

As has already been foreshadowed, the book is organized to move the reader through the post–September 11th era not chronologically but thematically. Chapter 1 lays out the contours of the American disposition toward the international human rights regime in the post–September 11th era. In so doing, it underscores the tremendous continuity between the United States' legal, political, and ideological treatment of human rights before and after the era and brings to light the many elements of the East/West geography of human rights encompassed in the American disposition. Chapter 2 presents a composite of an unprecedented American human rights campaign challenging administration policies in two specific instances: the Senate confirmation of Alberto Gonzales (a chief facilitator of the administration's "War on Terror" torture and detainee rights policies) as Attorney General and the so-called McCain Anti-Torture Amendment legislation designed to reassert international law obligations prohibiting torture by the United States government. It then goes on to assess the human rights gains of the campaign, including the increased legitimacy and presence of the international human rights framework within American political discourses and consciousness, as well as offer a critique of the more power-laden aspects of the strategies employed by the campaign. Serving as a bridge between the Middle Eastern and American case studies investigated in the book, Chapter 3 presents the various Middle Eastern mobilizations and challenges to U.S. human rights practices that emerge during the era. Chapter 4 focuses on the impact of American post–September 11th era experiments with both human rights violations and human rights promotion in the Middle East on the region's own human rights landscape. A discussion of the era's key lessons for advancing the human rights project forms the focus of Chapter 5.

ONE

American Imaginings of Human Rights and the Middle East

The post–September 11th era provided an extraordinarily lucid view of the many intersections of American power with human rights. Thus, it is only fitting to begin the book's analysis by laying out and linking the most power-laden aspects of American interactions with the human rights paradigm following September 11th. Although the chapter draws considerably from the host of invaluable reports, investigations, and articles dedicated to dissecting the American "road to Abu Ghraib," its intent is not simply to recount the facts and legal formulations at the heart of the Bush administration's human rights practices and policies. Instead, it hopes to move the discussion further by incorporating two additional dimensions of the American treatment of human rights after September 11th. First, it seeks to shed light on the ways in which the East/West geography of human rights facilitated American power during the era. Second, it attempts to highlight the continuity of the Bush administration's legal, political, and ideological doctrines vis-à-vis human rights, with human rights's place in the American imagination prior to September 11th. Within the overall layout of the book, this chapter's positioning of American power serves as the backdrop to the various challenges and mobilizations against American post–September 11th human rights policies as well as the traditional operation of the East/West geography to be taken up in subsequent chapters.

HUMAN RIGHTS, POWER, AND PARADOX IN AMERICAN IDENTITY POLITICS

Throughout the United States' history, upholding individual rights and civil liberties has been a central tenet of dominant American identity constructions. Nationalist discourses are frequently built on a narrative of the United States as unique in its commitment to the preservation of rights and freedom. In this account, the United States is not just a member of a community of states with an entrenched liberal rights-based tradition; it serves as a model to which others generally aspire. Quoting Ian Johnstone, "US 'nationalism' is rooted not in land or people, but in a set of values that, in principle, everyone can embrace. This is a defining feature of American 'exceptionalism', and it has defined the country's relationship with the rest of the world, situating the US as the 'city on the hill' for others to follow."[1]

Accordingly, important aspects of American identity pertaining to human rights are relational and dialogical. In the American imagination, serious human rights violations are always to be found in non-Western locales thought to be paralyzed by the grips of backward cultural and religious contexts and perpetual political and economic crises. Thus, the United States' inherent respect for universal rights is often conceptualized in opposition to the East's violence, chaos, and inherent disregard for notions of rights. The convergence of nationalist and Orientalist discourses fosters the conception of international human rights law as a regime largely designed to regulate the behavior of developing states and not that of the United States. As American activist Loretta Ross has written, the media, international human rights organizations, and the American government all perpetuate the view that international human rights are to be associated with the "the lack of freedom in other countries. This portrayal often prevents the (Americans) from seeing injustices in the United States as human rights violations."[2]

Further, several critical scholars have pointed to the fact that American rights-based identity constructions are viewed in ontological terms. This tendency is brought out in the work of social theorist Susan Buck-Morss, who lays out the essentialist assumptions at the core of American identity formulations and self-image vis-à-vis human rights:

Because the U.S. is a civilized nation, it does not violate human rights.

The implication in this example is that whatever the U.S. does as a nation *by definition* cannot be a violation of human rights – even if the same action done by an uncivilized nation *would* be a violation. Here the truth-claim has left the (epistemological) realm of judgment and moved to the (ontological) realm of identity. To *be* the United States is to *be* civilized.[3]

In other words, something inherent in – perhaps lying in the spirit of – the United States' being renders its actions consistent with human rights ideals. Thus, within the human rights realm, American behavior simply cannot be judged through the same standards applied to other contexts.

---

[1] Ian Johnstone, *US-UN Relations after Iraq: The End of the World (Order) as We Know It?* 15 EUR. J. INT'L. L 813, 817 (2004).

[2] Loretta J. Ross, *Beyond Civil Rights: A New Vision for Social Justice in the United States*, 2:1 HUM. RTS. DIALOGUE (1999), http://www.cceia.org/resources/publications/dialogue/2_01/articles/607.html.

[3] SUSAN BUCK-MORSS, THINKING PAST TERROR: ISLAMISM AND CRITICAL THEORY ON THE LEFT 64–65 (2003).

Closely linked to these relational identity constructions has been a dualistic view of culture. Although there are explicit and implicit assumptions of Middle Eastern societies' human rights "nightmares" being linked to the trappings of a conservative religion and culture, the United States is viewed as standing in a space that is essentially free of culture and religion or culturally and religiously neutral. Sally Engle Merry has argued that in this equation, adherence to modernism, rationality, and capitalism are seen in opposition to, rather than themselves manifestations of, culture.[4] Yet American positions on international human rights instruments or treatment of domestic rights issues often encompass the same cultural dimensions attributed to human rights engagements in Eastern contexts. For example, Deborah Weissman has discussed the way some conservatives' opposition to the United States' ratification of the UN Convention on the Elimination of All Forms of Discrimination against Women has been based on concerns that the instrument advanced a feminist agenda and threatened traditional motherhood and child-rearing roles.[5] These objections only serve to mirror American discussion of women's reproductive rights and the rights of sexual minorities, both of which are deeply entangled in religious and cultural discourses.

The American self-image relating to rights and liberties also colors the way Americans understand their own power. Yes, America is powerful, but this power is largely benign and rooted in idealism. If, through the deployment of its power, rough edges are displayed, they are not to be taken as seriously or placed in the same category as the more vile and ill-intentioned exercises of power witnessed throughout history elsewhere. This is because at its core, beneath layers of what may be politics or even decision-makers' incompetence, some underlying aspect of the American deployment of power is in pursuit of freedom, liberties, and other moral ends. Thus, American power is, in its essence or even in some teleological way, more benign than other forms of power, and, as a result, there is less room for concern over its exercise.

In relation to the international human rights regime, these constructions have been invoked to paint international human rights norms as redundant or irrelevant to the American experience. This worldview in turn has provided a rationale for repeated refusals to take on international human rights obligations in any meaningful way. Within American political and legal discourses, the rights framework provided in the Constitution has routinely been portrayed as above and beyond that offered by the international human rights regime, thus rendering America's commitment to human rights

---

[4] Sally Engle Merry, *Human Rights Law and the Demonizing of Culture (and Anthropology along the Way)*, 26:1 POL. LEGAL ANTHROPOLOGY REV. 55 (2003).

[5] Deborah Weissman, *The Human Rights Dilemma: Rethinking the Humanitarian Project*, 35 COLUM. HUM. RTS. L. REV. 259, 326 (2004).

implicit in the sanctity accorded to its Constitution. The American jurist Hans A. Linde has observed that

It is largely taken as an article of faith that the United States provides the best protection for human rights in the world. If there are any rights recognized in international law that are not recognized in U.S. law, [American] people may assume that there is a good reason for that non-recognition.[6]

In other words, although the American rights regime has much to offer the world, the international human rights regime has little worth considering to offer the United States.

Further, American policymakers have traditionally not only subscribed to realist/positivist understandings of international law as powerless because of its lack of coercive enforcement mechanisms, particularly in relation to American power and preeminence, but also actively strived to keep the international human rights legal regime, and their legal obligations under it, weak to minimize the regime's constraints on American power. As international law scholar Nico Krisch has argued, in the case of international legal institutions applicable to the United States, successive American governments have opted for more "flexible" soft law rather than concrete legal obligations and "pushed for an international legal order with weak centralized enforcement and adjudication."[7] In a manner that in essence mirrored the approach taken by their Middle Eastern counterparts, American leaders have largely performed a delicate dance of affirming human rights in principle but registering broad reservations and exceptions in the name of autonomy in legal, political, and security domains. Reservations to human rights instruments such as the International Convention on Civil and Political Rights (ICCPR) and the Convention Against Torture (CAT) have construed American obligation pursuant to the treaties as limited to definitions and doctrines existing in American law and refused the jurisdiction of the International Court of Justice for settling disputes arising from its adherence to human rights treaties. Accordingly, as human rights scholar David Forsythe has observed, taken together, the reservations, declarations, and understandings to the few international human rights instruments to which the United States has legally bound itself "have amounted to a statement that the United States would not change any of its existing practices."[8]

---

[6] Hans A. Linde's comments on P. L. Hoffman, *The Application of International Human Rights Law in State Courts: A View from California*, 18 INT'L. L. 16 at 77 (1984).

[7] Nico Krisch, *International Law in Times of Hegemony*, 16:3 EUR. J. INT'L. L 369, 392 (2005).

[8] David P. Forsythe, *US Foreign Policy and Human Rights in an Era of Insecurity: The Bush Administration and Human Rights after September 11th, in* WARS ON TERRORISM AND IRAQ: HUMAN RIGHTS, UNILATERALISM AND U.S. FOREIGN POLICY, 91 (Thomas G. Weiss et al. eds., 2004).

Similarly, over the past three decades the United States has slowly moved toward developing U.S.-based human rights mechanisms encompassing litigation, evaluation, and sanction that are applied almost exclusively to the rest of the world. The State Department's Country Reports on Human Rights Practices assess human rights conditions throughout the world. As noted by Weissman, in and of itself, "the act of observation implies a hierarchy of power."[9] Further, rules and regulations are implemented to influence other countries' human rights practices. For example, the well-intentioned "Leahy Law" prevents American aid to foreign military or security forces who have committed gross human rights violations with impunity. As Krisch explains, such regulations

often – though by no means always – mirror international legal rules, but through unilateral application the US retains far greater control over their content and also avoids being scrutinized itself.... [I]t is unsurprising that the US prefers the proactive unilateral enforcement of human rights to the establishment of effective international bodies.[10]

Finally, using domestic laws such as the Alien Torts Claims Act and the Torture Victim Protection Act of 1991, American courts took up the adjudication of international human rights cases occurring outside of the United States. In this way, "US courts assume the function of global appeals court, especially in human rights matters."[11] Although American human rights and civil rights activists have made numerous attempts to bring domestic litigation on international human rights law grounds, these efforts have made little headway in American courts. Efforts to sue American companies operating abroad have been slightly more successful. The American tendency to create mechanisms parallel to the international human rights regime to monitor, regulate, and litigate human rights violations outside its borders while refusing to apply international human rights standards domestically have effectively placed large parts of American action above and beyond the international human rights order.

When extended, these dynamics produce two critical paradoxes. First, at the same time that the dominant narrative positions American behavior beyond the province of the international human rights order, it qualifies the United States to assess other states' adherence to human rights and, if deemed necessary, intervene to further human rights and freedom beyond its borders. Second, at the same time that dominant American identity constructions marginalize the international human rights regime, important aspects of American identity and self-image are tied up with an assumption of American behavior adhering to human rights norms (at least within the civil and

[9] See Deborah Weissman, *supra* note 5, at 259, 316.
[10] See Nico Krisch, *supra* note 7, at 369, 403.
[11] Id. at 369, 403–404 (2005).

political rights categories). Sitting in his office in Yemen's Human Rights Ministry, the Canadian-Sudanese law professor who moved to Sana'a to head up the United Nations Development Programme (UNDP)'s primary human rights initiative in the country, El Obaid El Obaid observed this paradox, which he termed the United States' "schizophrenic" disposition. "There's a sense of 'we'll do it our way' on the one hand and [a] yearning for some rubber stamping from the outside on the other hand."[12] In other words, at some level the moral evaluations and international reputation to which constructivist analysis gives so much weight does come to play in the American context.

To varying degrees both American and Middle Eastern human rights advocates adhere to these constructions despite also holding genuine aspirations for the United States to join and comply with the international human rights regime. In several interviews in Yemen, I encountered this internalization of the notions that American action is inherently compatible with human rights and that the American regime of rights was an unblemished model for others to follow. For example, although he had no shortage of criticism for the United States' post–September 11th human rights practices, when the issue came up in our interview, Jamal Abdullah al Shami of Yemen's Democracy School explained to a young volunteer sitting in on our meeting that the reason Americans do not need a Human Rights Ministry is that rights are sufficiently enshrined in their Constitution.[13] American advocates' propensity to adhere to notions that the United States is the world's natural human rights leader or guardian and that its human rights violations are somehow not as tainted as similar violations committed by others are discussed at the end of Chapter 2.

The various facets of the paradoxical American disposition toward the international human rights regime laid out have been examined extensively in the vast literature on "American exceptionalism(s)." Sometimes calling it "American exemptionalism," scholars have attributed the phenomenon to American culture, power, institutional makeup, and dominant strands of political conservativism.[14]

Many of the constructions at the heart of the American disposition come to the fore of political discourse in the post–September 11th period, where they converged with new domestic norms and nationalist discourses centered around what are termed "War on Terror" imperatives and national security, on the one hand, and the American mission to spread freedom, human rights,

---

[12] Interview with El Obaid El Obaid, Chief Technical Advisor of United Nations Development Program Strengthening Human Rights Project, in Sana'a, Yemen (Jan. 24, 2007).
[13] Interview with Jamal Abdullah al-Shami, Chairman of the Democracy School, in Sana'a, Yemen (Jan. 23, 2007).
[14] See Michael Ignatieff, Introduction: American Exceptionalism and Human Rights, in AMERICAN EXCEPTIONALSISM AND HUMAN RIGHTS (Michael Ignatieff ed., 2005).

and democracy, on the other. The rest of the chapter details how the Bush administration took these identity constructions and construals of human rights and international legal obligations as a point of departure for its post–September 11th human rights policies and practices. As a number of scholars have observed, American exceptionalism after September 11th was in many ways only a more extreme version of the American exceptionalism in operation in prior periods.[15]

HUMAN RIGHTS AND THE MIDDLE EAST AS AMERICA'S CALLING

After September 11th, the human rights paradigm was positioned as an important cornerstone of American interventions in the Middle East. As the Bush administration styled it, the September 11th terrorist attacks had demonstrated the imperative for America as "the leader of the free world" to take up an agenda of promoting human rights, democracy, and liberty in the ailing region. The Middle East clearly suffered from widespread tyranny, oppression, and rights violations. These deprivations of rights and freedom rendered the region a "breeding ground" for terrorists and their sympathizers. Thus, as the American president declared in a 2003 speech at the National Endowment for Democracy, American power was to be placed at the service of freedom in the Middle East – this was not only in America's strategic and security interests, it was "America's calling":

The advance of freedom is the calling of our time; it is the calling of our country. From the Fourteen Points to the Four Freedoms, to the Speech at Westminster, America has put our power at the service of principle. We believe that liberty is the design of nature; we believe that liberty is the direction of history. We believe that human fulfillment and excellence come in the responsible exercise of liberty. And we believe that freedom – the freedom we prize – is not for us alone, it is the right and the capacity of all mankind.[16]

Thus, almost immediately following September 11th, the "War against Terrorism," American military intervention in the region, and amorphous evocations of freedom, justice, and human rights became entwined, the boundaries between each notion fluid and shifting. Examples of human rights being deliberately linked to American militarism and geopolitical ambitions abound. From the outset, the war in Afghanistan was named Operation Enduring Freedom and the war in Iraq was named Operation Iraqi Freedom by the U.S. government. In his 2002 State of the Union address

---

[15] *See*, for example, STANLEY HOFFMAN, CHAOS AND VIOLENCE: WHAT GLOBALIZATION, FAILED STATES AND TERRORISM MEAN FOR U.S. FOREIGN POLICY 120 (2006).

[16] The White House, *President Bush Discusses Freedom in Iraq and Middle East: Remarks by the President at the 20th Anniversary of the National Endowment for Democracy*, Nov. 6, 2003, http://www.whitehouse.gov/news/releases/2003/11/20031106-2.html.

(the same speech that introduced the term *Axis of Evil*), Bush put forth the following while showcasing the new Afghan Minister for Women's Affairs, Sima Samar:

The last time we met in this chamber, the mothers and daughters of Afghanistan were captives in their own homes, forbidden from working or going to school. Today women are free, and are part of Afghanistan's new government. And we welcome the new Minister of Women's Affairs, Doctor Sima Samar. Our progress is a tribute to the spirit of the Afghan people, to the resolve of our coalition, and to the might of the United States military. When I called our troops into action, I did so with complete confidence in their courage and skill. And tonight, thanks to them, we are winning the war on terror. The men and women of our Armed Forces have delivered a message now clear to every enemy of the United States: Even 7,000 miles away, across oceans and continents, on mountaintops and in caves – you will not escape the justice of this nation.[17]

Following a similar pattern, as the evidence of weapons of mass destruction in Iraq failed to materialize, the Bush administration increasingly gravitated toward an emphasis on Iraq's mass graves and rape chambers under Saddam Hussein. In fact, virtually every address or statement by Bush administration officials with regard to either the Afghan or Iraqi wars was accompanied by direct or indirect references to Americans introducing the dawn of human rights or women's rights (usually both) to the region. The message was not abandoned even in the American president's primary speech addressing the photos evidencing American soldiers' abuse and torture of Iraqi detainees at Abu Ghraib.[18] American interventions thus held out the promise of freeing the oppressed – including those withering away in the Middle East's prison cells:

[A]nd, one day, from prison camps and prison cells, and from exile, the leaders of new democracies will arrive. Communism, and militarism and rule by the capricious and corrupt are the relics of a passing era. And we will stand with these oppressed peoples until the day of their freedom finally arrives.[19]

The discourse focused exclusively on the limitations of freedom and injustice suffered at the hands of Middle Eastern culture, extremist renditions of Islam, or the region's repressive governments. There was no room for or grasp of the connections between Middle Eastern aspirations for freedom, justice, and rights and U.S. power and politics in the region.

It is difficult to miss key elements of the preexisting American identity constructions presented above in the new post–September 11th narrative put

---

[17] U.S. Government Printing Office, *George W. Bush, State of the Union Address*, Jan. 29, 2002, http://www.whitehouse.gov/news/releases/2002/01/20020129-11.html (last visited Dec. 18, 2008).

[18] The White House, *George W. Bush, President, Outlines Steps to Help Iraq Achieve Democracy and Freedom: Remarks by the President on Iraq and the War on Terror*, May 24, 2004, www.whitehouse.gov/news/releases/2004/05/20040524-10.html (last visited Aug. 1, 2005).

[19] *See* U.S. Government Printing Office, *supra* note 17.

forth by the Bush administration. The era's American military interventions were presented as in essence part of a long tradition of "sacrifice for liberty," that, although "not always... recognized or appreciated," is nonetheless "worthwhile."[20] The United States' power continued to be portrayed as rooted in its superior values and good intentions. As the president would frame it, America's strength lies in its heart.[21] As Stanley Hoffman has observed, the "War on Terror"

... flattered the exceptionalists of all tendencies by emphasizing the indispensable role of the United States, and it appealed especially to the more idealistic ones by stressing that the defense against terror, America's cause, was also the world's cause; self-interest and morality, power and values, and the sheriff and the missionary were back together again.[22]

Further, the Bush administration clearly enlisted and evoked the human rights geography critical scholars have mapped out, building on assumptions of inherent or ontological American commitments to universalism and the furtherance of the human rights project as well as corresponding conceptions of Middle Easterners as inherently incapable of fully understanding or achieving rights on their own. Thus, in the final analysis, aware of the negative moral evaluation and lack of legitimacy stemming from the unmasked employment of power and force, the United States enlisted morally rooted human rights and democracy norms to legitimate its various interventions in the region. Although, as later chapters detail, this instrumentalization of human rights did not stand unchallenged, it was nonetheless in large part facilitated by the preexisting East/West geography of human rights. Its place atop the hierarchy created by the prevailing human rights geography afforded the United States considerable relative access to human rights discourses, meaning it was more acceptable and natural for the United States to frame geopolitical conflicts and its own role in them using human rights discourses than for a state like Iran, Syria, or Egypt to do so. This privileged position vis-à-vis human rights discourses in turn could more easily be used to facilitate human rights' instrumentalization in furtherance of American power.

INTERNATIONAL HUMAN RIGHTS LAW AS AMERICA'S PERIL

As Julie Mertus has noted in reference to invocations of human dignity and freedom in George Bush's 2003 State of the Union address, in identifying America's calling, the American president clearly placed the impetus for

---

[20] Id.
[21] See The White House, supra note 16.
[22] See STANLEY HOFFMAN, supra note 15, at 122.

U.S. interventions in an inherent (at times religiously ordained) American character, not international human rights law:

Deploying military troops based on a sense of a "calling" and of being "blessed" with "God's gift to humanity" represents a departure from appeals to action based on a sense of obligation grounded in international standards and enforced by multilateral institutions.[23]

As the ensuing discussion lays out, in the post–September 11th era, at the same time that American power is purportedly rooted in its adherence to broad principles of upholding human rights, international human rights institutions are constructed as a threat. Although the United States is an exceptionally good and morally motivated nation in a fight against "evil," "injustice," and "tyranny," forces "resisting freedom" have posed a constant threat to the United States and could, at any time, use international norms and institutions to engage in "asymmetrical warfare" against the United States. A March 2005 Department of Defense National Defense Strategy brief found that "our strength as a nation-state will continue to be challenged by those who employ a strategy of the weak using international fora, judicial processes, and terrorism."[24]

Additionally, U.S. military and government officials frequently argued that al Qaeda–trained detainees would either take advantage of the American tradition of upholding certain rights guarantees (i.e., by assuming they would not be tortured, would be provided with a lawyer, etc.) or would wrongfully claim human rights violations, such as torture and abuse, to taint American operations. In this way, human rights came to be seen as an instrument of the terrorists. This view of human rights as a threat or unnecessary constraint on the broader post–September 11th American mission comes through in a speech by the U.S. president officially announcing the CIA's use of "alternative interrogation techniques" against high-value terrorism suspects:

We knew that Zubaydah had more information that could save innocent lives, but he stopped talking. As his questioning proceeded, it became clear that he had received training on how to resist interrogation. And so the CIA used an alternative set of procedures. These procedures were designed to be safe, to comply with our laws, our Constitution, and our treaty obligations. The Department of Justice reviewed the authorized methods extensively and determined them to be lawful. I cannot describe the specific methods used – I think you understand why – if I did, it would help the terrorists learn how to resist questioning, and to keep information from us that we need to prevent new attacks on our country.[25]

[23] JULIE MERTUS, BAIT AND SWITCH: HUMAN RIGHTS AND U.S. FOREIGN POLICY, 52 (2004).
[24] National Defense Strategy of the United States of America, Department of Defense (Mar. 2005).
[25] The White House, *President Discusses Creation of Military Commissions to Try Suspected Terrorists*, Sept. 2006, http://www.whitehouse.gov/news/releases/2006/09/20060906-3.html.

In tandem with the view of international human rights constraints as a threat, characterizations of international human rights law as ill-equipped, outdated, and inferior to the domestic legal order were used in turn to justify weakening human rights limits and restrictions on American action.

Detailed below are a sampling of post–September 11th attempts to thwart, reinvent, and marginalize international human rights norms, primarily by considering arguments devised in the now infamous web of memos and reports drafted by White House, Department of Justice, and Department of Defense officials, lawyers, and advisors. Collectively, the memos sought to place American action beyond the reach of any law or court – domestic or international – and eliminate any liability for U.S. agents involved for war crimes.

Translating their constructions of international law and human rights norms into official and unofficial policy on behalf of the United States, the Bush administration claimed the authority to unilaterally designate "enemy combatants," denying them POW status and the accordant protections for humane treatment under the Geneva Conventions, indefinitely imprison any foreign national it deemed necessary, operate secret prisons in which ghost detainees would be held with no record of their presence in such U.S. custody, practice "alternative" and "coercive" interrogation techniques, send individuals to countries known to torture through "extraordinary renditions," and do all of this through either grossly unfair procedures or no internationally sanctioned due process procedures at all.

The series of "counterresistance" interrogation techniques considered by the Department of Defense in the fall of 2002 included the following:

a. Category I techniques....
   (1) Yelling at the detainee (not directly in his ear or to the level it could cause physical pain or hearing problems)
   (2) Techniques of deception:
       (a) Multiple interrogator techniques.
       (b) Interrogator identity. The interviewer may identify himself as a citizen of a foreign nation or as an interrogator from a country with a reputation for harsh treatment of detainees.
b. Category II techniques....
   (1) Stress positions (like standing), for a maximum of four hours.
       . . .
   (3) Use of the isolation facility for up to 30 days
       . . .
   (5) Deprivation of sound and auditory stimuli
   (6) The detainee may also have a hood placed over his head during transportation and questioning....
   (7) Use of 20 hour interrogations

(8) Removal of all comfort items (including religious items)
...
(10) Removal of clothing
(11) Forced grooming (shaving of facial hair, etc.)
(12) Using detainees individual phobias (such as fear of dogs) to induce stress.

c. Category III... These techniques required for a very small percentage of the most uncooperative detainees (less than 3 percent).

(1) The use of scenarios to convince detainee death or severely painful consequences are imminent for him and/or his family.
(2) Exposure to cold weather or water (with appropriate medical monitoring).
(3) Use of a wet towel and dripping water to induce misperception of suffocation.
(4) Use of mild, non-injurious physical contact such as grabbing, poking in the chest with the finger, and light pushing.[26]

A Department of Defense legal brief deemed all techniques legal, advising caution only in the use of threats of imminent death because the act was stipulated in the U.S. statute implementing the UN Convention Against Torture. The American secretary of defense approved the Category I and II techniques as well as the use of mild physical contact on December 2, 2002, adding a handwritten note, "I stand for 8 to 10 hours. Why is standing limited to 4 hours"? On January 15, 2003, he rescinded his approval, yet many of the techniques had already made their way into the culture of American detention facilities from Guantanamo to Abu Ghraib to Bagram and many stops in between. The blurred line between official and unofficial policies, as well as the pervasive climate in which they materialized, is best captured in the following description of Camp Nama in *The New York Times*:

The Black Room was part of a temporary detention site at Camp Nama, the secret headquarters of a shadowy military unit known as Task Force 6-26. Located at Baghdad International Airport, the camp was the first stop for many insurgents on their way to the Abu Ghraib prison a few miles away. Placards posted by soldiers at the detention area advised, "NO BLOOD, NO FOUL." The slogan, as one Defense Department official explained, reflected an adage adopted by Task Force 6-26: "If you don't make them bleed, they can't prosecute for it."[27]

---

[26] Memorandum from Diane Beaver, Staff Judge Advocate, Department of Defense, Joint Task Force 170, Guantanamo Bay, Cuba, to General James T. Hill, Commander, Joint Task Force 170 (Oct. 11, 2002), *reprinted in* THE TORTURE PAPERS: THE ROAD TO ABU GRAIB 227–228 (Karen J. Greenberg and Joshua L. Dratel eds., 2005).

[27] Eric Schmitt and Carolyn Marshall, *Before and After Abu Ghraib, A U.S. Unit Abused Detainees*, N.Y. TIMES, Mar. 19, 2006.

Human rights organizations later uncovered evidence that the methods listed as Category III were used by the CIA in its network of secret prisons, so-called CIA black sites. On the ground, the line between official and unofficial policy was increasingly blurred. In February 2006, Human Rights First put out a report documenting ninety-eight deaths of detainees in U.S. custody in Iraq and Afghanistan, forty-five of which were confirmed or suspected homicides and at least eight of which were cases of detainees being tortured to death.[28] Details of the torture endured by those transferred to countries like Syria, Jordan, and Morocco included brutal beatings, use of electric shock, and cutting of the genitals.

Through the military commissions it eventually instituted and Congress approved, the administration sought to try select detainees for war crimes in a legal process in which detainees could be convicted based on secret evidence they were not permitted to see or evidence obtained through torture or so-called coercive means, yet detainees' recourse for appeal was limited to findings of law, not findings of fact that would exclude consideration of evidence supporting their guilt or innocence beyond the military commissions.

Although previous administrations had gone to great lengths to simultaneously maintain American privilege, preference, and influence in international norm development and to marginalize and carve out American exceptions once they were developed, by and large, on the surface, they proclaimed deference to international law. The Bush administration, on the other hand, was more openly hostile to international norms and institutions, a disposition that was evident before September 11, most notably in Bush administration decisions to withdraw the United States from both the Kyoto Protocol and the Rome Statute of the International Criminal Court. After September 11th, the trend only intensified. Still, despite their deviations from the traditional American posture toward international human rights law, it is important to recognize that the Bush administration policies did not develop in a vacuum. As the final part of this section argues, they were simply built on the foundation of American exceptionalism already firmly in place.

Exceptional Times

A fundamental pillar of the Bush administration's justification for their blatant violations of established international human rights law was that the War on Terrorism was a new or "novel" type of conflict, presenting exceptional or unprecedented circumstances for which the existing human rights paradigm and the international legal order institutionalizing it was

[28] Human Rights First, *Command's Responsibility: Detainee Deaths in U.S. Custody in Iraq and Afghanistan*, Feb. 2006, http://www.humanrightsfirst.org/command.

ill equipped. In an interview with journalist Tim Russert a few days after September 11th, the American vice president first signaled the need to transcend previously held human rights constraints and commitments stating, "We also have to work, through, sort of the dark side, if you will.... That's the world these folks operate in...." He went on to more explicitly paint his vision of the place of human rights within the dangerous new post–September 11th world:

MR. RUSSERT: There have been restrictions placed on the United States intelligence gathering, reluctance to use unsavory characters, those who violated human rights, to assist in intelligence gathering. Will we lift some of those restrictions?

MR. CHENEY: Oh, I think so. I think the ... one of the by-products, if you will, of this tragic set of circumstances is that we'll see a very thorough sort of reassessment of how we operate and the kinds of people we deal with. There's – if you're going to deal only with sort of officially approved, certified good guys, you're not going to find out what the bad guys are doing. You need to be able to penetrate these organizations. You need to have on the payroll some very unsavory characters if, in fact, you're going to be able to learn all that needs to be learned in order to forestall these kinds of activities. It is a mean, nasty, dangerous dirty business out there, and we have to operate in that arena. I'm convinced we can do it; we can do it successfully. But we need to make certain that we have not tied the hands, if you will, of our intelligence communities in terms of accomplishing their mission.[29]

It would not take long for the "exceptional times and cirumstances" argument to push American foreign policy and its approach to international law into an even more unilateral, direction This trend was perhaps most famously exemplified in a January 25, 2002, memo from then–White House Counsel Alberto Gonzales, when he advised the U.S. president not to extend Geneva Convention protections to al Qaeda and the Taliban:

As you have said, the war against terrorism is a new kind of war. It is not the traditional clash between nations adhering to the laws of war that formed the backdrop for GPW [Geneva Convention III on the Treatment of Prisoners of War]. The nature of the new war places a high premium on other factors such as the ability to quickly obtain information from captured terrorists and their sponsors in order to avoid further atrocities against American civilians and the need to try terrorists for war crimes such as wantonly killing civilians. In my judgment, this new paradigm renders obsolete Geneva's strict limitations on questioning of enemy prisoners and renders quaint some of its provisions requiring that captured enemy be afforded such things as commissary privileges, scrip (i.e., advances of monthly pay), athletic uniforms, and scientific instruments.[30]

---

[29] The White House, *The Vice President Appears on Meet the Press with Tim Russert*, Sept. 16, 2001, http://www.whitehouse.gov/vicepresident/news-speeches/speeches/vp20010916.html.

[30] Memorandum from Alberto Gonzales, White House Counsel to George W. Bush (Jan. 25, 2002), *reprinted in supra* note 26, at 119.

In this memo Gonzales contends that "it is difficult to predict the need and circumstances that could arise in the course of the war on terrorism."[31] Thus, he recommends not affording Geneva Conventions protections to al Qaeda and Taliban fighters, because such a policy "preserves flexibility" and avoids "foreclosing options for the future, particularly against non-state actors."[32]

On February 7, 2002, following Gonzales's counsel, in a memo to high-ranking officials in his government, Bush declared that the Geneva Conventions apply only to states, and that "terrorism ushers in a new paradigm" requiring "new thinking on the laws of war."[33] This insistence on the post–September 11th era's exceptionalism was widely invoked by Bush administration officials throughout the era. I also encountered it in an interview with an official at the U.S. embassy in Yemen:

> The Guantanamo situation in particular is a dilemma. The new threat to the world order or American national security comes from an international network with which the international world order has not learned to cope yet. There is no way to stop a bin Laden with a group of Arabs camped out in Afghanistan plotting an attack on New York. Under which law do you try them? Where do you incarcerate them and what are the rules of engagement? It's a new threat and it requires new laws, new procedures, a new political arrangements. The UN comes from WWII arrangements. Today we are witnesses a new global configuration that may require a new adjusting of the tools that we have.[34]

The argument that international law is ill suited to confront the new terrorism challenge often coincided with attempts to delegitimize (question the hard law quality of) and effectively marginalize international human rights norms and treaty obligations. Depictions of international human rights law as not real law, more specifically as naïve, advisory, and irrelevant (or, in Alberto Gonzales's words, *quaint* and *obsolete*) were increasingly part of the post–September 11th landscape.[35] In a House Armed Services Committee hearing on military commissions to try Guantanamo detainees in which American obligations to comply with Common Article III of the Geneva Conventions figured prominently, Committee Chair Duncan Hunter states, "We won't lower our standards; we will always treat detainees humanely, but we can't be naive, either."[36] Within the context of the hearing's

---

[31] *Id.* at 120.

[32] *Id.* at 119.

[33] Memorandum from George W. Bush to the Vice President, the Secretary of State, the Secretary of Defense, Attorney General, Chief of Staff to the President, Director of CIA, Assistant to the President for National Security Affairs, and Chairman of the Joint Chiefs of Staff (Feb. 7, 2002), *reprinted in supra* note 26, at 134.

[34] Interview with a senior U.S. embassy official, in Sana'a, Yemen (Jan. 23, 2007).

[35] Memorandum from Alberto Gonzales, White House Counsel to George W. Bush (Jan. 25, 2002), *reprinted in supra* note 26, at 119.

[36] *Transcript of the Hearing on Military Commissions and Tribunal, House Armed Services Committee,* 109th Cong. (July 12, 2006).

discussions, the clear implication of his words is that complying fully with the Geneva Convention protections could be considered proceeding with naiveté.

The Bush administration similarly marginalized international human rights law by repeatedly asserting that it was composed of various legal obligations that were vague or undefined. For example, Common Article III of the Geneva Conventions provides that:

> Persons taking no active part in the hostilities, including members of armed forces who have laid down their arms and those placed hors de combat by sickness, wounds, detention, or any other cause, shall in all circumstances be treated humanely, without any adverse distinction founded on race, colour, religion or faith, sex, birth or wealth, or any other similar criteria.[37]

Among the acts it specifically prohibits are "outrages upon personal dignity, in particular, humiliating and degrading treatment." This provision was frequently rejected by Bush administration lawyers on the grounds that it was open to interpretation. In the previously mentioned memorandum to the president, Alberto Gonzales posited as follows:

> First, some of the language of the GPW is undefined (It prohibits, for example, "outrages upon personal dignity" and "inhumane treatment"), and it is difficult to predict with confidence what actions might be deemed to constitute violations of the relevant provisions of GPW.[38]

Similarly, in an August 1, 2002, memo to Gonzales, Deputy Assistant Attorney General John Yoo refers to the "amorphous concept of mental pain and suffering" adopted in the Convention Against Torture.[39]

Another American strategy to counter the constraints posed by international human rights law consisted of reconstituting established international legal doctrine and interpretations. Amy Bartholomew refers to the United States's disturbing "self-proclaimed right to unilaterally define and to state international law – to constitute it monologically" and an inclination to treat international law "as derivative of its will as a global sovereign."[40] This reconstitution and reinterpretation of international law has taken place at several junctures throughout the post–September 11th era. Perhaps one of the most blatant American attempts to reconfigure international law lies

---

[37] Geneva Convention Relative to the Treatment of Prisoners of War art. 3(1), Aug. 12, 1949, 6 U.S.T. 3316, 75 U.N.T.S. 135 *available at* http://www.unhchr.ch/html/menu3/b/91.htm.

[38] Memorandum from Alberto Gonzales, White House Counsel to George W. Bush (Jan. 25, 2002), *reprinted in supra* note 26, at 120.

[39] Memorandum from John Yoo, Deputy Assistant Attorney General, U.S. Department of Justice, Office of Legal Counsel, to Alberto R. Gonzales, Counsel to the President (Aug. 1, 2002), *reprinted in supra* note 26, at 220.

[40] Amy Bartholomew, *Empire's Law and the Contradictory Politics of Human Rights, in* EMPIRE'S LAW: THE AMERICAN IMPERIAL PROJECT AND THE WAR TO REMAKE THE WORLD, 162 (Amy Bartholomew ed., 2006).

within the realm of use of force. The UN charter recognizes the legitimate use of force only in instances of self-defense or when the use of force is authorized by the Security Council. Yet, as Krisch observes in recent years, the United States has breached prevailing use of force doctrine on several fronts:

The US and its allies have advanced claims for new rights to use force in three main areas: a right to unilaterally enforce security council authorizations in the interventions in the Former Yugoslavia and Iraq; a broadened right to exercise self-defense against terrorist attacks in the missile attacks on Sudan and Afghanistan and later the war in Afghanistan; and a bold right to pre-emptive self-defense, so far only cautiously invoked in the War in Iraq.[41]

Among the areas Krisch delineates, the resort to preemptive war without Security Council authorization has been the most troubling and consequential in the post–September 11th era.

The Bush administration also engaged in a reordering of international norms in denying al Qaeda members Geneva Conventions protections, maintaining that the treaty applies "to conflicts with regular foreign armed forces" and not "to a conflict with terrorists."[42] Accordingly, the administration adopts a policy that applies the Geneva Conventions to the conflict with Afghanistan but holds that none of the provisions of the Geneva Conventions apply to the American conflict with al Qaeda fighters who are categorized as "unlawful combatants" and not afforded POW status. Contrary to the Bush administration's rendition, the Geneva Conventions were drafted to provide minimal levels of protection to all persons involved in international armed conflicts. Even if al Qaeda detainees were to be considered nonprivileged or enemy combatants, they would still be covered by the Fourth Geneva Convention Relative to the Protection of Civilians in Time of War. The Geneva Conventions further require that detainees be presumptively considered and treated as prisoners of war (i.e., privileged or lawful combatants detained by an opposing army) until determined otherwise in proceedings held by a competent tribunal in which each detainee's case is considered separately.

Finally, the Bush administration's tendency to reinvent international human rights norms is also manifested in the definition of torture it adopts – a definition so limited in scope, it effectively strips the concept of its established meaning. Article 1 of the UN Convention Against Torture offers the following definition of torture:

Torture means any act by which severe pain or suffering, whether physical or mental, is intentionally inflicted on a person for such purposes as obtaining from him or a

---

[41] *See* Nico Krisch, *supra* note 7, at 369, 403.
[42] Memorandum from Alberto Gonzales, White House Counsel to George W. Bush (Jan. 25, 2002), *reprinted in supra* note 26, at 220.

third person information or a confession, punishing him for an act he or a third person has committed or is suspected of having committed, or intimidating or coercing him or a third person, or for any reason based on discrimination of any kind, when such pain or suffering is inflicted by or at the instigation of or with the consent or acquiescence of a public official or other person acting in an official capacity. It does not include pain or suffering arising only from, inherent in or incidental to lawful sanctions.[43]

Upon ratifying the Convention Against Torture in 1994, the United States entered some fourteen reservations, declarations, and understandings. Incorporating these stipulations, the definition of torture subsequently adopted in the legislation implementing the Convention, 18 U.S.C. § 2340, states that "'torture' means an act committed by a person acting under the color of law *specifically* (emphasis added) intended to inflict severe physical or mental pain or suffering (other than pain or suffering incidental to lawful sanctions) upon another person within his custody or physical control." Taking vast strides further away from the definition of torture under international law, in a now-infamous August 1, 2002, memo to Alberto Gonzales, Assistant Attorney General Jay Bybee concludes:

For an act to constitute torture as defined in Section 2340, it must inflict pain that is difficult to endure. Physical pain amounting to torture must be equivalent in intensity to the pain accompanying serious physical injury, such as organ failure, impairment of bodily function, or even death. For purely mental pain or suffering to amount to torture under Section 2340, it must result in significant psychological harm of significant duration, e.g. lasting for months or even years . . . the statute, taken as a whole, makes plain that it prohibits only extreme acts.[44]

The memo also states that "because Section 2340 requires that a defendant act with the specific intent to inflict severe pain, the infliction of such pain must be the defendant's precise objective."[45]

Finally, in a March 2004 memo, Jack Goldsmith, a United States assistant attorney general in the Office of Legal Council and conservative international law scholar, finds that Article 49 of the Geneva Conventions, which prohibits the deportation or forced transfer of protected persons in an occupation, does *not* preclude the transfer of detainees from Iraq to other countries for interrogation purposes:

We now conclude the United States may, consistent with article 49, (1) remove "protected persons" who are illegal aliens from Iraq pursuant to local immigration law; and (2) relocate "protected persons" (whether illegal aliens or not) from Iraq

---

[43] Convention Against Torture and Other Cruel, Inhuman or Degrading Treatment or Punishment, G.A. Res. 46, U.N. Doc. A/39/51, at 1(1)(1984) *available at* http://www.unhchr.ch/html/menu3/b/h_cat39.htm.

[44] Memorandum from Jay Bybee, Assistant Attorney General to Alberto Gonzales, Counsel to the President (Aug. 1, 2002), *reprinted in supra* note 26, at 172.

[45] *Id.* at 174.

to another country to facilitate interrogation, for a brief but not indefinite period, so long as adjudicative proceedings have not been initiated against them.[46]

Part of the legal rationale for this conclusion was that the original intent behind the Geneva provision was to counter mass deportations and transfers akin to those undertaken by the Nazis and Japanese in World War II. The limited construal of the provision in effect provides legal cover for subjecting individuals detained in the Iraqi conflict (a conflict to which the United States has agreed the Geneva Conventions do apply) to the "extraordinary rendition" policy adopted by the administration in the immediate aftermath of September 11th.

A Selective Privileging of Domestic Law

A subsequent approach adopted by the United States to limit the reach of international law on U.S. action in the "War on Terror" included the deployment of justifications for violations of international human rights law based on domestic law. Again, drawing on pervasive American identity constructions and beliefs, political elites argued that the United States had little need for international human rights safeguards, as its domestic safeguards themselves sufficiently enshrined the values of which international norms are, and should be, comprised. Discussions surrounding the legality of acts such as detentions and torture were then largely confined to the realm of U.S. constitutional analysis to the exclusion and marginalization of international legal analysis.

Bush administration memos presented the idea of an overriding presidential power to order torture, collapsing the issue of detainee treatment into the U.S. president's constitutional powers to direct military operations.[47] The Bybee torture memo went so far as to equate detention and interrogation decisions to directing troop movement on the battlefield, finding that neither the Convention Against Torture nor Congress could restrict the American president's authority in "War on Terror" detention and interrogation fields.[48] It concludes that prosecution under the U.S. statute implementing the Convention Against Torture "may be barred because enforcement of the statute would represent an unconstitutional infringement of the President's authority to conduct war."[49] This warped analysis held that

[46] Memorandum from Jack Goldsmith III, Assistant Attorney General, Office of Legal Counsel, to William H. Taft IV, William J. Haynes II, John Bellinger, and Scott Mueller (Mar. 19, 2004), *reprinted in supra* note 26, at 368.

[47] Memorandum from John Yoo, Deputy Assistant Attorney General, U.S. Department of Justice and Robert J. Delahunty, Special Counsel, U.S. Department of Justice, to William J. Haynes II, General Counsel, Department of Defense (Jan. 9, 2002), *reprinted in supra* note 26, at 64.

[48] Memorandum from Jay Bybee, Assistant Attorney General to Alberto Gonzales, Counsel to the President (Aug. 1, 2002), *reprinted in supra* note 26, at 207.

[49] *Id.* at 173.

because information obtained through interrogations "may prevent future attacks from foreign enemies," efforts to apply laws prohibiting torture "in a manner that interferes with the President's direction of such core war matter as the detention and interrogation of enemy combatants" would be unconstitutional. Another memo held that the United States was not bound by customary international law because the Supremacy Clause of the U.S. Constitution does not recognize it:

> In other words, customary international law has not undergone the difficult hurdles that stand before the enactment of constitutional amendments, statutes, or treaties. As such it can have no legal effect on the government or on American citizens because it is not law. Even the inclusion of treaties in the Supremacy Clause does not render treaties automatically self-executing in federal court, not to mention self-executing against the executive branch.[50]

In each of these formulations, highly questionable domestic legal arguments (for example, interpreting the executive power delegated to the president in Article II, Section 1, of the American Constitution as vesting sweeping, virtually unchecked, authority in the realm of national defense and warfare) are posited to place U.S. action outside the purview of international human rights law.

Invoking allegiance to the Constitution provided the Bush administration and its allies with a shield against internal criticism: it could be used to produce normative associations with the American tradition of upholding rights to deny noncitizens human right protections. Thus, a systematic attempt to bar detainees from any domestic rights protections accompanies the use of domestic legal analysis to preclude international rights protections. First, the choice of Guantanamo Bay as a primary location for "War on Terror" detentions was an unmistakable attempt to present jurisdictional hurdles for domestic challenges through litigation. Second, a February 26, 2002, memo from Jay Bybee to William Haynes undertook an extensive domestic law analysis of why U.S. constitutional and, particularly, Bill of Rights protections (e.g., Fifth Amendment protection against self-incrimination, Miranda warnings, Sixth Amendment right to counsel prior to initiation of judicial proceedings) do not apply to aliens.[51] That constitutional protections could not be extended to noncitizens was treated merely as a regrettable but unalterable fact by administration officials, who concurrently went to great

---

[50] Memorandum from John Yoo, Deputy Assistant Attorney General, U.S. Department of Justice, and Robert J. Delahunty, Special Counsel, U.S. Department of Justice, to William J. Haynes II, General Counsel, Department of Defense (Jan. 9, 2002), *reprinted in supra* note 26, at 72.

[51] Memorandum from Jay Bybee, Assistant Attorney General, Department of Justice, to William Haynes II, General Counsel, Department of Defense (Feb. 26, 2002), *reprinted in supra* note 26, at 165–171.

lengths to foreclose detainees' ability to put forth writ of habeas corpus petitions in American courts.

Although they were interested in applying constitutional arguments for why international law was to be abrogated, American officials were clearly not willing to provide many of the most basic rights protections derived from domestic law that served as the basis for American claims to being the world's champion for human rights. Joshua Dratel observes that the lawyers and policymakers involved seemed to fear their own federal courts, an independent judiciary – a legitimate, legislated, established system of justice designed to promote fairness and accuracy.[52] Yet, throughout the exercise, there is little sense of a contradiction in the American claim to human rights leadership and its current practice of discrimination based on citizenship, nationality, race, or religion in the rights guarantees it is willing to provide.[53] In fact, as the following exchange at a congressional hearing on detainee rights illustrates, providing domestic rights guarantees, typically portrayed as the universal model for others to follow, is, in the post–September 11th era, considered by many conservatives in power to be providing "a weapon" to the enemy:

REP. TAUSCHER: But that's the challenge of the asymmetry of this fight.

MR. DELL'ORTO: Exactly. And we can't let him use our process, our due process, our legal system, as one of his other weapons as he carries on this fight.

Equally troubling was the emergence of a post–September 11th mainstream debate in the media, among policymakers outside the Bush administration, and within some academic circles over whether the absolute prohibition on torture was appropriate when dealing with the new counterterrorism terrain, with increasing numbers of pundits and experts justifying the use of torture in "the War against Terrorism" as a "lesser evil."[54] As Amy Bartholomew observed, the emerging legal and political discourse threatened "to move torture from the despicable, subterranean, illegal action to which a state responding to crises might illegitimately resort, to one that has legal standing with terrible implications for the rule of law not to mention human rights."[55] On the one hand, there was a near-consensus or assumption that Americans would never engage in the type of torture and inhumane treatment that occurs in other countries. On the other hand, once the Abu Ghraib photos and Guantanamo Bay accounts provided incontrovertible

---

[52] Joshua L. Dratel, *The Legal Narrative, in supra* note 26, at xxi.

[53] For a discussion of the divide between notions of citizens' rights and human rights as well as the formulation of various hierarchies in U.S. policies post–September 11th, *see* Anthea Roberts, *Righting Wrongs or Wronging Rights? The United States and Human Rights Post-September 11*, 15 EUR. J. INT'L L. 721 (2004).

[54] Jim Rutenberg, *Torture Seeps into Discussion by News Media*, N.Y. TIMES, Nov. 5, 2001.

[55] *See* Amy Bartholomew, *supra* note 40, at 5.

evidence to the contrary, mainstream America quickly made the transition to assuming the role of the good cop who had to resort to rough methods to mete out global justice. Aided by Hollywood depictions of "ticking time-bomb" scenarios and FOX News interviews with experts and even academics making the case for torture as a necessary evil, large parts of the U.S. population rapidly gravitated toward the notion that unsavory means may be required to win the fight against evil and tyranny.

In this climate, raising human rights concerns or invoking international law was stigmatized and equated with weakness or with being unpatriotic, and it had a silencing effect on individual policymakers or media voices who may have otherwise raised reservations. Similarly, the voices of human rights advocates were marginalized by both the government and the media. Although they were accorded significant legitimacy with regards to their accounts of human rights violations abroad, in their criticisms of American counterterrorism policies they were labeled as do-gooders who, in blind enthusiasm for defending terrorists, exaggerated the scope and seriousness of U.S. infringements of human rights. As John Sifton of Human Rights Watch recounted, human rights defenders are also frequently painted as naïve about the real risks involved in fighting the "War on Terror":

According to the appeasement view, human rights defenders are naive. We don't understand the reality: that circumstances may arise where torture may be needed.... Also, we who oppose torture are supposed to be apologetic for our position. We're making the world less safe, and we owe it to the rest of our community to admit this.[56]

This situation prompted articles in which members of the American human rights movement contemplated strategies for getting their voices heard.[57]

Exceptional Nation

Again, there is a tremendous degree of continuity between the legal and political discourse of the Bush administration and the legal and political discourses surrounding human rights that prevailed before September 11th, namely, the reproduction of the East/West geography and its various roles and assumptions. Not only were these exceptional times, the United States was an exceptional nation. Its historical and identity-based commitment to rights entitled it to a presumption of compliance – if not to the letter of international human rights law, then within the spirit of the human rights ideals it had historically embraced. In the final analysis, the narrative being advanced held: if the United States' objective was to sustain its own and

---

[56] E-mail from John Sifton, senior researcher at Human Rights Watch, to author (May 2, 2006) (on file with author).

[57] See, for example, Juan Mendez and Javier Mariezcurrena, *Prospects for Human Rights Advocacy in the Wake of September 11, 2001*, 22 LAW & INEQ. 223 (2004).

further others' rights, freedom, and democracy, then it must be assumed that either American means will also be moral and good or, alternately, its means should not be at issue, in light of its purported ends.[58] Robert Keohane and Anne-Marie Slaughter describe what amounts to an ontologically based assumption of adherence to human rights in an *International Herald Tribune* op-ed following Abu Ghraib:

President George W. Bush's efforts to build democracy in Iraq are underpinned by a misguided view of America's own democracy. He believes that American democracy works because Americans are innately good people, believing in values of tolerance and respect for others and guided by religious faith. In his view, Americans don't need checks and balances so much as reminders of basic American values and America's overriding moral mission to bring freedom to the world. Similarly, abuses of power, as at Abu Ghraib prison and beyond, do not represent the failure of the system, but rather the deviant behavior of a few bad people.[59]

The excerpt's concluding reference to the common attribution of exercises of power to "a few bad apples" within the dominant construction is also taken up in a commentary by Phillip Kennicott:

Among the corrosive lies a nation at war tells itself is that the glory – the lofty goals announced beforehand, the victories, the liberation of the oppressed – belongs to the country as a whole; but the failure – the accidents, the uncounted civilian dead, the crimes and atrocities – is always exceptional. Noble goals flow naturally from a noble people; the occasional act of barbarity is always the work of individuals, unaccountable, confusing and indigestible to the national conscience. This kind of thinking was widely in evidence among military and political leaders after the emergence of pictures documenting American abuse of Iraqi prisoners in Abu Ghraib prison. These photographs do not capture the soul of America, they argued. They are aberrant.[60]

Further, by relying on the same assumptions of American behavior as a priori in line with human rights, the Bush administration is largely successful in promoting the use of euphemisms such as "harsh" or "coercive interrogation techniques" to the same behavior it (and the American public) label as torture when conducted in other countries. Although recharacterizing human rights violations in more innocuous terms is hardly unique to the United States, the Bush administration's attempt to do so was aided considerably by the prevailing societal assumptions of American human rights compliance. As a result, throughout the post–September 11th era, within mainstream discourse, there is never a firm consensus that the American government has

[58] Jack Donnelly, *International Human Rights: Unintended Consequences of the War on Terrorism, in supra* note 8, at 103.

[59] Robert O. Keohane and Anne-Marie Slaughter, *Bush's Mistaken View of US Democracy*, INT'L. HERALD TRIB. Jun. 23, 2004.

[60] Phillip Kennicott, *A Wretched New Picture of America: Photos from Iraq Show We Are Our Worst Enemy*, WASHINGTON POST, May 5, 2004, at C01.

in fact committed torture. Instead, debates surround questions of whether specific techniques (e.g., water-boarding) constitute torture. The normative force that propelled the debates over whether acts traditionally understood as torture were to be in fact understood as torture, when committed by Americans, was the embedded belief in the United States' good intentions vis-à-vis upholding human rights.

The discursive case for American exceptionalism and ontological commitment to human rights easily translates to the legal formulations for carving out exceptions for American human rights violations devised by the Bush administration. Namely, based on an assumption of American adherence to human rights, the United States should be trusted to act in accordance with human rights norms. Thus, in the post–September 11th era, the United States takes previously asserted prerogatives to create a human rights order parallel to the international human rights regime to new heights, availing itself of even greater liberty to administer and adjudicate human rights from beyond the international human rights regime. The trend was first manifested in the Bush administration's decision to deny Taliban and al Qaeda detainees POW status under the Geneva Conventions but unilaterally decree that the prisoners will be treated in a manner consistent with the Geneva Conventions. The stance gives the United States the space to qualify its bestowal of rights "to the extent appropriate and consistent with military necessity," as Secretary of Defense Donald Rumsfeld does in a January 19, 2002, memo.[61] In the same spirit, Alberto Gonzales notes the argument put forth by those advocating that the United States should afford Geneva Conventions protections to al Qaeda and Taliban detainees: "concluding that the Geneva Conventions does not apply may encourage other countries to look for technical 'loopholes' in future conflicts to conclude that they are not bound by the GPW either."[62] He, however, goes on to dismiss the scenario, finding that:

It should be noted that your policy of providing humane treatment to enemy detainees gives us the credibility to insist on like treatment for our soldiers. Moreover, even if GPW is not applicable, we can still bring war crimes charges against anyone who mistreats U.S. personnel.[63]

The final sentence of Gonzales's analysis unveils the administration's more astounding claim that it should be trusted not only to act in a manner consistent with universally recognized norms without taking on any legal obligation to that effect but also to mete out justice through its own prosecutions

---

[61] Memorandum from Donald Rumsfeld, Secretary of Defense, to the Chairman of the Joint Chiefs of Staff (Jan. 19, 2002), *reprinted in supra* note 26, at 80.

[62] Memorandum from Alberto Gonzales, White House Counsel, to George W. Bush (Jan. 25, 2002), *reprinted in supra* note 26, at 120.

[63] *Id.* at 121.

based on the same international legal norms to which it refuses to be legally subjected. In his January 2002 memo, Deputy Attorney General John Yoo found that the United States' treatment of applying the Geneva Conventions "as a matter of policy, not law" permits the United States to prosecute based on the Geneva Conventions as customary international law:

To say that the specific provisions of the Geneva and Hague Conventions do not apply in the current conflict with the Taliban militia *as a legal requirement* is by no means to say that the principles of the law of armed conflict cannot be applied as a matter of U.S. Government policy. The President as Commander-in-Chief can determine as a matter of his judgment for the efficient prosecution of the military campaign that the policy of the United States will be to enforce customary standards of the law of war against the Taliban and to punish any transgressions against those standards. Thus, for example, even though Geneva Convention III may not apply, the United States may deem it a violation of the laws and usages of war for Taliban troops to torture any American prisoners whom they may happen to seize. The U.S. military thus could prosecute Taliban militiamen for war crimes for engaging in such conduct. A decision to apply the principles of the Geneva Conventions or of others laws of war as a matter of policy, not law, would be fully consistent with the past practice of the United States.[64]

He goes on to conclude as follows:

Although customary international law does not bind the President, the President may still use his constitutional warmaking authority to subject members of al Qaeda or the Taliban militia to the laws of war. While this result may seem at first glance to be counter-intuitive, it is a product of the President's Commander-in-Chief and Chief Executive powers to prosecute the war effectively.

. . .

We do not believe that these courts (American Military tribunals) should lose jurisdiction to try members of al Qaeda or the Taliban militia for violations of the laws of war, even though we have concluded that the laws of war have no binding effect – *as federal law* – on the President.[65]

The same "trust us" spirit underpins Bush's description of the CIA Secret Detention program in which torture is widely believed to have been practiced:

Many specifics of this program, including where these detainees have been held and the details of their confinement, cannot be divulged. Doing so would provide our enemies with information they could use to take retribution against our allies and harm our country. I can say that questioning the detainees in this program has given

---

[64] Memorandum from John Yoo, Deputy Assistant Attorney General, U.S. Department of Justice, and Robert J. Delahunty, Special Counsel, U.S. Department of Justice, to William J. Haynes II, General Counsel, Department of Defense (Jan. 9, 2002), *reprinted in supra* note 26, at 62.

[65] *Id.* at 76.

us information that has saved innocent lives by helping us stop new attacks – here in the United States and across the world.[66]

Again, the premise of the argument is that the United States is at liberty to determine both the amount of information regarding its treatment of detainees to be divulged and when and to what extent human rights protections are necessary or appropriate. Its action can be shrouded in secrecy because that is what the exigencies of the "War on Terrorism" require and because it is the United States. As the president states, "We do not condone torture. I have never ordered torture. I will never order torture. The values of this country are such that torture is not a part of our soul and our being."[67] In other words, given its identity rooted in rights, it will always intend to further human rights and human dignity. If it pushes the bounds of existing rights regimes, it must be understood that it does so out of some absolute necessity.

In addition to making full use of American identity constructions designating the United States as human rights compliant, the Bush administration makes use of legal products of pre–September 11th exceptionalism, namely, American reservations to the limited number of international human rights instruments to which the United States is a party. The entering of reservations to human rights treaties has always been an issue of great debate and controversy among human rights promoters. Under the Vienna Convention on the Law of Treaties, reservations are allowed "to modify the legal effect of certain provisions of the treaty in their application to that State" unless the treaty explicitly either limits or prohibit reservations or the reservation being entered is contrary to the object and spirit of the treaty.[68] Many international human rights lawyers hold the view that although such provisions for reservations may be appropriate in relation to most other treaties, they are not appropriate or valid in the context of human rights treaties, as most reservations stand contrary to the object and purpose of the conventions. Nonetheless, reservations are often accepted as an undesirable but necessary trade-off for bringing into the regime countries that have demonstrated that they would otherwise likely not join. Thus, historically, human rights treaty bodies have accepted a myriad of sweeping reservations (often made with varying levels of bad faith) to human rights instruments from countries reluctant to fully or seriously take on international human rights obligations, including the United States.

---

[66] See The White House, supra note 25.

[67] Remarks by the president and Prime Minister Medgyessy of Hungary in photo opportunity (Jun. 22, 2004).

[68] Vienna Convention on the Law of Treaties, UN Doc. A/Conf.39/27, at available at 2(1)d (1969), available at http://untreaty.un.org/ilc/texts/instruments/english/conventions/ 1_1_1969.pdf.

The Bush administration's view of previous American reservations to the Convention Against Torture as an accessible avenue to thwart the regulation of the international human rights regime is evidenced in an August 1, 2002, memo by John Yoo to Alberto Gonzales. In this memo, Yoo cites and defends an understanding entered by the Reagan administration that adopts definitions of torture (particularly the level of intent required to constitute it) as well as mental pain and suffering that depart from those found in the international instrument:

Under international law a reservation made when ratifying a treaty validly alters or modifies the treaty obligation. . . .

Thus, we conclude that the Bush administration's understanding created a valid and effective reservation to the Torture Convention. Even if it were otherwise, there is no international court to review the conduct of the United States under the Convention. In an additional reservation the United States refused to accept the jurisdiction of the ICJ. . . . Although the Convention creates a committee to monitor compliance, it can only conduct studies and has no enforcement powers.[69]

As Yoo is all too happy to report, even if one reservation is invalid, another reservation forecloses any possibility for accountability under the international regime.

In his confirmation hearings for Attorney General, Alberto Gonzales invoked another reservation to argue that the Convention Against Torture did not apply to noncitizens. This time the American reservation in question was one that limits the United States' obligations under the convention's Article 16 prohibition of cruel, inhumane, or degrading treatment "only insofar as the term 'cruel, inhuman or degrading treatment or punishment' means the cruel, unusual and inhumane treatment or punishment prohibited by the Fifth, Eighth, and/or Fourteenth Amendments to the Constitution of the United States." Gonzales maintained that because long-standing U.S. jurisprudence and policy confer no constitution rights to foreign nationals, the United States has no legal obligation to ensure that aliens do not suffer cruel, inhuman, and degrading treatment by American authorities.

Similarly, in her October 11, 2002, memo for the Commander of Joint Task Force 170 regarding the Department of Defense's proposed "Counter-resistance" strategies cited above, Diane Beaver notes that in ratifying the International Convention on Civil and Political Rights, the United States registered a reservation on Article 7 of the convention prohibiting inhuman treatment, stating that it was bound only to the extent that the U.S. Constitution prohibits "cruel and unusual punishment." She goes on to state that there is no existing jurisprudence on the Eighth Amendment in the context

---

[69] Memorandum from John Yoo, Deputy Assistant Attorney General, U.S. Department of Justice, Office of Legal Counsel, to Alberto R. Gonzales, Counsel to the President (Aug. 1, 2002), *reprinted in supra* note 26, at 220.

of interrogations but finds that in other contexts, "ultimately the 8th amendment analysis is based primarily on whether the government had a good faith legitimate governmental interest, and did not act maliciously and sadistically for the very purpose of causing harm."[70] From this premise, she concludes that because there is a legitimate government objective in obtaining information and as long as no severe pain is inflicted or prolonged mental harm intended, the techniques are legally permissible.

It can certainly be argued that the Bush administration's treatment distorts American reservations. For example, in a letter to Patrick Leahy, Abraham Sofaer, a State Department legal advisor at the time when the Reagan administration signed the Convention Against Torture, challenges the Gonzales interpretation of the U.S. reservation on Article 16 of the Convention Against Torture, stating that the reservation was meant only to alter the definition of "cruel, inhumane and degrading" punishment being applied and not limit its application exclusively to territories under U.S. jurisdiction.[71] Still, the larger point is that both the existence and particularly permissive formulation of many of the U.S. reservations entered in the previous administration assisted the Bush administration's agenda to exempt its human rights violations from the constraints posed by international law. The Bush administration gladly took previously entered reservations carving out exceptions to international human rights law's regulation of American behavior as a point of departure for claiming further exceptions to the same.[72]

THE MIDDLE EAST AS AMERICA'S PERIL

Nico Krisch argues that the practice of creating categories of states or individuals to which international law does not apply has historically been a common approach adopted by powerful states to circumvent the principles of sovereign equality and universalism embedded in the international legal order. He goes on to brilliantly lay out the United States' use of this strategy in the post–September 11th era:

Today we can observe a somewhat similar phenomenon: a division of the world into a sphere of peace, in which individual rights and democracy flourish, and an area of

---

[70] Memorandum from Diane Beaver, Staff Judge Advocate, Department of Defense, Joint Task Force 170, Guantanamo Bay, Cuba, to General James T. Hill, Commander, Joint Task Force 170 (Oct. 11, 2002), *reprinted in supra* note 26, at 232.

[71] Letter from Abraham Sofaer, Former State Department Legal Advisor, to Patrick Leahy, Senate Judiciary Committee (Jan. 25, 2005), *available at* http://www.humanrightsfirst .org/us_law/etn/pdf/sofaer-leahy-cat-art16-093005.pdf.

[72] A more elaborate discussion of how American reservations, declarations, and understandings of international human rights instruments aided Bush administration torture policies is undertaken by Jamie Mayerfeld. *See* Jamie Mayerfeld, *Playing by Our Own Rules: How U.S. Marginalization of Human Rights Led to Torture*, 20 HARV. HUM. RTS. J. 89 (2007).

lawlessness, characterized by collapsed state structures, dictatorships and widespread violations of human rights. On the level of theory, this is most prominently reflected in John Rawls' conceptions of a *Law of Peoples*, in which only outlaw states enjoy very limited protection, but it finds expression also in the ideas of "liberal international law" that were advanced throughout the 1990s. In the practice of Western states, we can observe such tendencies in the new emphasis on democracy and human rights as conditions for full membership in the international community and for the protection from foreign or international intervention. They are most obvious, however, in US attempts at creating a particular legal regime for so-called "rogue states" who allegedly sponsor terrorism or develop weapons of mass destruction. . . . they have also become the potential objects of pre-emptive self-defense. Similarly, certain "rogue" individuals – alleged terrorists and "unlawful combatants" – have been stripped of many of the rights they enjoy under international human rights and humanitarian law. . . . the US has thus undertaken attempts to create different categories of states and individuals and to limit the reach of international law to some of these.[73]

In its post–September 11th constructions, the United States created the categories of *terrorist, enemy of the United States,* and *enemy of freedom and human rights* as categories to which any strict application of human rights norms were inappropriate. Moreover, each of the three categories was treated as either synonymous with the other or interchangeable. The terrorists who stood as the United States' enemies were thus first and foremost motivated by a disdain for rights and freedom – also dubbed "the American way of life." In his speech advocating legislative approval for military commissions, Bush asserts:

Free nations have faced new enemies and adjusted to new threats before – and we have prevailed. Like the struggles of the last century, today's war on terror is, above all, a struggle for freedom and liberty. The adversaries are different, but the stakes in this war are the same: We're fighting for our way of life, and our ability to live in freedom. We're fighting for the cause of humanity, against those who seek to impose the darkness of tyranny and terror upon the entire world. And we're fighting for a peaceful future for our children and our grandchildren.[74]

The melding of the inscriptions is also apparent in congressional testimony from Bush administration Solicitor General and September 11th widower Theodore Olson:

No issue, I believe, deserves more thoughtful consideration from our elected representatives than ensuring that the American people are defended from a savage terrorist enemy that deliberately targets civilian lives and mutilates our soldiers in an effort to destroy our way of life.[75]

---

[73] *See* Nico Krisch, supra note 7, at 369, 387.
[74] *See* The White House, *supra* note 25.
[75] *Testimony of Theodore Olson, Former Solicitor General of the United States, Standards of Military Commissions and Tribunals, before the House Armed Services Committee* (Jul. 12, 2006).

Further inquiry into the three interconnected components of the categories employed – the dehumanization of detainees, their positioning outside of the purview of legal norms, and the assignment of imputed guilt to those associated with terrorism and in more diffuse ways to the civilian populations and societies of the Middle East who cultivate them – proves illuminating.

Constructing the Enemy as Beyond Human Rights

Representations and categorizations of the enemy as violent and averse to human rights were deployed to dehumanize "War on Terror" detainees to the extent that arbitrary denials of international human rights guarantees would seem natural and justifiable. Early on, the Bush administration incessantly reinforced associations of the Taliban with their human rights and women's rights violations.

Ruling cabals like the Taliban show their version of religious piety in public whippings of women, ruthless suppression of any difference or dissent, and support for terrorists who arm and train to murder the innocent.[76]

Not only did the focus on the Taliban's human rights violations contribute to legitimating the American intervention in Afghanistan, it served to demonize and dehumanize Taliban fighters and sympathizers to the extent that depriving them of basic due process rights or internationally sanctioned guarantees against torture and inhuman treatment took on a less objectionable air.

Characterizations of al Qaeda and Iraqi insurgents' violence and terrorism serve the same function. In the House Armed Services Committee hearings on military commissions, after prefacing her statement with the information she is one of the few members of the House without a college degree but she considers herself a reflection of "middle America," Representative Candice Miller transforms "War on Terror" detainees to the uncivilized and by implication, subhuman while taking exception to any characterization of American actions as falling outside those normally adhered to by civilized nations:

And I will tell you, listening to the Supreme Court ruling, it just struck me as being incredibly counterintuitive. And when we think about the type of enemy that we're facing today, a new type of enemy, one that hides in the shadows, one that preys on the innocent, one that wants to kill us, and they've been categorized as how we need to be civilized, these people do not meet the basic standards of civilized human beings. I think it's very difficult for us as Americans to even get our mind around the concept of a suicide bomber, teaching a young person to be a suicide bomber and what that means. I mean, I don't consider that to be civilized behavior.[77]

The sentiment is echoed by Theodore Olson in the same proceedings:

The point that I think is important is that when you are fighting an enemy like this one, that defies all civilized rules, that intends to be as savage as possible to the most

---

[76] *See* The White House, *supra* note 16.

[77] Testimony of Candice Miller, Republican Representative, Standards of Military Commissions and Tribunals, before the House Armed Services Committee (Jul. 12, 2006).

vulnerable people in the world, and that has no scruples or principles, and that will go back every time to the battlefield – but not to the battlefield, but to a synagogue or a school bus – we have to have some flexibility built into the system so that the president, as commander in chief, and military officials down the line have some flexibility.[78]

Because it was no longer acceptable to officially denigrate particular races, religions, or cultures as inferior or savage to justify denials of rights, American officials justified discrimination in its application of human rights based on individuals' adherence to interpretations or ideologies viewed as infiltrating the Middle East and its broader religion and culture. In other words, the savages and uncivilized undeserving of rights were those who perpetrated violence and rejected notions of rights and freedom. The focus was not on a culture but an "inhuman" subculture.

Another example of American officials' dehumanization of terrorist suspects in its custody emerged in American military official's characterization of the three suicides, forty-one failed suicide attempts, and dozens of hunger strikes by Guantanamo detainees as orchestrated attacks against the United States. Rear Admiral Harry B. Harris, Jr., who commanded Guantanamo Bay when two Saudi and one Yemeni national committed suicide in June 2006, stated the suicides were "not an act of desperation, but an act of asymmetric warfare against us," and General Bantz J. Craddock called the detainees "a determined, intelligent, committed element" who "continue to do everything they can . . . to become martyrs."[79] Again, it is an irrational ideology and not their condition of indefinite incarceration without judicial recourse that prompts the suicides.

Finally, the post–September 11th violence perpetrated by terrorist forces is constructed as unprecedented and exceptional, having no connection to other violent social movement or forms of violence that have materialized in various moments and locales throughout the globe. There is no recognition of any social and psychological dynamics similar or related to those at play in violence undertaken, for example, by the Ku Klux Klan or Black Panthers in the United States. There is also a sharp distinction made between the terrorists and insurgents' violence and its impact on civilians and American violence. Cyra Choudhury describes the duality in place:

U.S. as ontologically civilized, humane, reasonable, and innocent in opposition to Iraqis who resist the U.S. as terrorists and insurgents – which should be read to mean barbaric, irrational, uncivilized, and *a priori* culpable – is used to justify the violence that is done to them. This power of construction allows us to deflect attention away from ourselves and towards the Other. Moreover, because we can construct victims

---

[78] *See* Theodore Olson, *supra* note 75.

[79] Josh White, *Three Detainees Commit Suicide at Guantanamo*, WASHINGTON POST, Jun. 11, 2006, http://www.washingtonpost.com/wp-dyn/content/article/2006/06/10/AR2006061000507.html

as well, it gives us the ability to exclude from that status the vast majority of Iraqis who suffer violence.[80]

Clearly, my argument is not that the Taliban did not commit egregious human rights violations or that the violence perpetrated by al Qaeda and other terrorist movements is not imbued with a slew of alarming implications. Rather, it is imperative to shed light on the ease with which shaming and condemnation of violations of these norms by the United States is transformed into a tool to exempt particular individuals or groups from what are designated as universal human rights protections. In other words, particularly when working from within the framework of the East/West geography of human rights, the move from "they must be condemned for their human rights violations and violence" to "they are barely human, they cannot legitimately lay claim to human rights" turns out to be one that is easily facilitated.

Positioning the "Lawless" beyond the Law

Similar dynamics are present in American post–September 11th legal formulations. To deprive them of the human rights protections provided by international human rights and humanitarian law, the Bush administration categorized Afghanistan under the Taliban as a "failed state" to whom the Geneva Conventions did not apply and the Taliban as a "militia." Al Qaeda was designated a "non-state actor" and therefore ineligible to be a signatory to the Geneva Conventions. As discussed above, according to Bush administration lawyers, the Third Geneva Conventions did not apply to Guantanamo detainees because they were "unlawful combatants." As the era progresses, the "unlawful" in "unlawful combatant" takes on a life of its own in the American political discourses. For example, in congressional testimony, Daniel Dell'Orto, a Department of Defense lawyer puts forth the following:

What we have here are people who don't wear uniforms, they don't carry arms openly, they don't distinguish themselves from the civilian population in any way, they don't follow the laws of war; they are without any discipline in the way they conduct their combat. They deliberately attack civilians. They behead people, they mutilate people. And so they are, in theory, at all levels, unlawful combatants.[81]

In this manner, "Unlawful combatant" is transformed from a questionably applied legal category to a rhetorical encapsulation of the enemy.

---

[80] Cyra A. Choudhury, *Comprehending "Our" Violence: Reflections on the Liberal Universalist Tradition, National Identity and the War on Iraq, Muslim World Journal of Human Rights*, 3.1 BERKELEY ELEC. PRESS 2-1 (2006), http://www.bepress.com/mwjhr/vol3/iss1/art2.

[81] Testimony of Daniel Dell'Orto, Principle Deputy General Counsel, Department of Defense, Standards of Military Commissions and Tribunals, before the House Armed Services Committee (July 12, 2006).

Further, part of the American mission is to counter the enemy's lawlessness. The American president vows, "This nation, in world war and in Cold War has never permitted the brutal and the lawless to set history's course. Now as before, we will secure our nation, protect our freedom and help others find freedom of their own."[82] A White House report "assessing" the progress of the first 100 days of the Iraqi invasion includes the following in its list of "10 Ways the Liberation of Iraq Supports the War on Terror":

Saddam Hussein would not uphold his international commitments, and now that he is no longer in power, the world is safe from this tyrant. The old Iraqi regime defied the international community and seventeen UN resolutions for twelve years and gave every indication that it would never disarm and never comply with the just demands of the world.[83]

Paradoxically, a primary means of countering the enemy's lawlessness is to deprive them of the law, and this is rationalized using a notion of reciprocity, in stark contrast to both the letter and the spirit of international human rights law and its universalist philosophical underpinnings. This stance is most pronounced in discussions of affording Geneva Conventions protections to Guantanamo detainees. Acting Assistant Attorney General Stephen Bradbury argues in front of the House Armed Services Committee:

Of course, the terrorists who fight for al Qaeda have nothing but contempt for the laws of war. They've killed thousands of innocent civilians in the United States and thousands more in numerous countries around the world. They openly mock the rule of law, the Geneva Conventions, and the standards of civilized people everywhere, and they will attack us again if given the chance. When the Geneva Conventions were concluded in 1949, the drafters of the Conventions certainly did not anticipate armed conflicts with international terrorist organizations such as al Qaeda.[84]

In the final analysis, it is their disregard for human rights and the rule of law that places them squarely outside of both. They do not deserve the basic protections of the law because they do not respect, follow, or comprehend them.

Detainees' Ascribed Guilt versus American Innocence
The final element that facilitated the placement of "War on Terror" detainees into a category standing outside human rights protections was a process of ascribing guilt to them. As of November 2005, 83,000 foreign nationals had

---

[82] The White House, *Result in Iraq: 100 Days Towards Security and Freedom*, Aug. 8, 2003, http://www.whitehouse.gov/infocus/iraq/part1.html.
[83] *Id.*
[84] Testimony of Steven Bradbury, Acting Assistant Attorney General, Office of Legal Council, Department of Justice, Standards of Military Commissions and Tribunals, before the House Armed Services Committee (July 12, 2006).

been detained by the United States.[85] Numerous reports and investigations have found that large percentages of those detained were either innocent or guilty of significantly less serious crimes than portrayed by the Bush administration. A February 2004 report by the International Committee of the Red Cross (ICRC) stated that "Certain CF (Coalition Forces) military intelligence officers told the ICRC that in their estimate between 70 and 90 percent of the persons deprived of their liberty in Iraq had been arrested by mistake."[86] Similarly, a 2006 report put out by Seton Hall Law School provided the following statistics regarding Guantanamo detainees:

1. Fifty-five percent (55%) of the detainees are not determined to have committed any hostile acts against the United States or its coalition allies.

2. Only 8% of the detainees were characterized as al Qaeda fighters. Of the remaining detainees, 40% have no definitive connection with al Qaeda at all and 18% have no definitive affiliation with either al Qaeda or the Taliban.

3. The government has detained numerous persons based on mere affiliations with a large number of groups that, in fact, are not on the Department of Homeland Security terrorist watchlist. Moreover, the nexus between such a detainee and such organizations varies considerably. Eight percent are detained because they are deemed "fighters for," 30% are considered "members of," and a large majority (60%) are detained merely because they are "associated with" a group or groups the U.S. government asserts are terrorist organizations. For 2% of the prisoners their nexus to any terrorist group is unidentified.

4. Only 5% of the detainees were captured by United States forces and 86% of the detainees were arrested by either Pakistan or the Northern Alliance and turned over to United States custody.[87]

The final point is crucial. As Human Rights Watch Advocacy Director Tom Malinowsky explains in testimony before the U.S. Helsinki Commission, while the United States derived a right to indefinitely detain individuals at Guantanamo without due process from the laws of war, most Guantanamo detainees "were not captured on anything resembling a traditional battlefield, in a traditional war, in which it is easy to determine who is a combatant and who is not."[88] As he goes on to explain, most were among

[85] The Associated Press, *U.S. Has Detained 83,000 in Anti-terror Effort*, Nov. 16, 2005, http://msnbc.msn.com/id/10071594/.

[86] Report of the International Committee of the Red Cross (ICRC) on the Treatment by the Coalition Forces of Prisoners of War and Other Protected Persons by the Geneva Conventions in Iraq During Arrest, Internment and Interrogation, *reprinted in supra* note 26, at 388.

[87] Seton Hall Law, Mark Dembeaux and Joshua Denbeaux, *Report on Guantanomo Detainees: A Profile of 517 Detainees through Analysis of Department of Defense Data*, Feb. 2006, http://law.shu.edu/news/guantanamo_report_final_2_08_06.pdf.

[88] Testimony by Tom Malinowsky, Washington Advocacy Director, Human Rights Watch, Guantanamo: Implications for US Human Rights Leadership before the U.S. Helsinki Commission (June 21, 2006).

the thousands of foreign nationals fleeing Afghanistan following the American attack. Instead of being captured by American soldiers, they were often sold for bounties by Pakistan or Afghan militias, whereas others were picked up in places as far away as Bosnia, Thailand, and Gambia:

> The United States government has not even claimed most of these men were even fighting the United States; many are accused of little more than living in a house or working for a charity linked to the Taliban. They are part of a broad, amorphous universe of people who are suspected to have had some association with international terrorism.
>
> . . .
>
> What the Bush Administration has done in Guantanamo has been to blur that distinction [between combatants and civilians] – to apply the highly permissive rules governing a military battlefield to anyone anywhere in the world who is suspected of having any association with terrorism.[89]

As Choudhury similarly contends, "it is unclear why precisely the prisoners are incarcerated other than the official designation of criminality based on an assumption that they were involved in some way with nefarious activities that constitute 'terrorism.'"[90]

Despite this predicament, detainees were assigned the "terrorist" or "enemy" label without any semblance of what is generally considered a pinnacle of Western and international due process rights – the presumption of innocence until proven guilty. Yet, to many within the Bush administration and among intelligence officers on the ground, once an enemy was identified, guilt was easily ascribed and often assumed. President Bush, his administration, and U.S. allies repeatedly imputed guilt to the detainees being held at Guantanamo. The notion that those detained by the United States were guilty was repeatedly invoked in speeches by Bush and his administration. One such instance was in his speech promoting military commissions and confirming the existence of CIA black sites:

> It's important for Americans and others across the world to understand the kind of people held at Guantanamo. These aren't common criminals, or bystanders accidentally swept up on the battlefield – we have in place a rigorous process to ensure those held at Guantanamo Bay belong at Guantanamo. Those held at Guantanamo include suspected bomb makers, terrorist trainers, recruiters and facilitators, and potential suicide bombers. They are in our custody so they cannot murder our people. One detainee held at Guantanamo told a questioner questioning him – he said this: "I'll never forget your face. I will kill you, your brothers, your mother, and sisters."[91]

Assumptions of guilt resulted in not only prolonged detentions but also abuse and torture. In his sworn statement, taken in conjunction with

[89] Id.
[90] See Cyra A. Choudhury, supra note 80.
[91] See The White House, supra note 25.

Abu Ghraib investigations, an American soldier who witnessed the abuse recounts, "Every time I said something about how I was worried about the treatment of the detainees, they would ... say they are the enemy and if I was out there they would kill me, so they don't care."[92] In similar fashion, numerous innocent individuals have provided compelling accounts of enduring months of gruesome torture after being illegally detained and transferred by American officials to Middle Eastern countries for "interrogations" through the United States practice of "extraordinary renditions." Their ordeals have frequently stemmed from mistaken identity or inaccurate perceptions of the victim's links to terrorists, among the most publicized cases being those of Canadian citizen Maher Arar and German citizen Khalid el-Masri.

The military commissions the Bush administration instituted and that Congress eventually authorized in 2006 were characterized by human rights advocates as legal proceedings designed to produce a judgment of guilt. In the House of Representatives hearings on the commissions, Rear Admiral John Hutson, a retired Navy Judge Advocate General, correctly describes the proposed commissions as attempts to "reverse engineer" justice by "assuming that everybody is guilty, and then create a commission that is geared to proving that point."[93] He goes on to artfully draw out the surreal due process scenario presented by the commission's rules and procedures.

Let me just say that I think it would be very, very difficult for the United States of America to say to anybody, "We know you're guilty. We can't tell you why, but there's somebody that says you're guilty. We can't tell you who, but we know they're reliable. We can't tell you how we know that, but you're guilty."[94]

In response to questions and statements constantly equating the detainees to terrorists, savages, and perpetrators of beheadings in a congressional hearing held to consider legislation to determine detainees' rights in prosecutions, the Rear Admiral is forced to constantly remind hearing conveners of the "innocent until proven guilty" principle purportedly enshrined in American and international rights guarantees:

But if we decide that we're going to prosecute them, then we have to afford them those rights, which include not presuming that they're cutting everybody's head off, and they're suicide bombers, but that we just buy into this presumption of innocence deal. And if we can do that, then we can create a system in which we will really be able to prosecute.[95]

[92] Sworn statement of Samuel Jefferson Provance, reprinted in *supra* note 26, at 482.
[93] Testimony of Rear Admiral John Hutson, United States Navy, Retired, Former Judge Advocate General, U.S. Navy, Hearing of the House Armed Services Committee on Standards of Military Commissions and Tribunals (Jul. 12, 2006).
[94] *See* Theodore Olson, *supra* note 75.
[95] *Id.*

If Arab and Muslim detainees are afforded a presumption of guilt that places them beyond the protections of human rights law, American soldiers and operatives are afforded an automatic determination of innocence that positions them beyond the sanctions of human rights law. The American president makes the following case for absolving American citizens, namely, CIA agents involved in the "alternative interrogation techniques" from liability in committing torture or war crimes:

In its ruling on military commissions, the Court determined that a provision of the Geneva Conventions known as "Common Article Three" applies to our war with al Qaeda. This article includes provisions that prohibit "outrages upon personal dignity" and "humiliating and degrading treatment." . . . And some believe our military and intelligence personnel involved in capturing and questioning terrorists could now be at risk of prosecution under the War Crimes Act – simply for doing their jobs in a thorough and professional way. This is unacceptable. Our military and intelligence personnel go face to face with the world's most dangerous men every day. They have risked their lives to capture some of the most brutal terrorists on Earth. . . . America owes our brave men and women some things in return. We owe them their thanks for saving lives and keeping America safe. And we owe them clear rules, so they can continue to do their jobs and protect our people. . . . I'm asking that Congress make it clear that captured terrorists cannot use the Geneva Conventions as a basis to sue our personnel in courts – in U.S. courts. The men and women who protect us should not have to fear lawsuits filed by terrorists because they're doing their jobs.[96]

In this formulation, CIA agents' practice of inducing hypothermia or waterboarding – the practice of strapping a prisoner face up onto a table and pouring water into his nose to create the sensation of drowning – is a manifestation of their professionalism and thoroughness in furtherance of the dangerous mission taken on by the United States. They are unmistakably "the good guys." Prohibitions stemming from human rights law are conversely out of touch with the requisite exigencies of the undertaking as well as the inherent location of guilt and innocence on which the mission is built.

Expanding the Enemy

Less than a month after September 11th, there were signs of the expanded view of "the enemy" being conceived and promoted by the Bush administration. In a speech announcing a list of the twenty-two most wanted terrorists at FBI headquarters on October 10, 2001, Bush held:

I say "the first 22" because our war is not just against 22 individuals. Our war is against networks and groups, people who coddle them, people who try to hide them, people who fund them. This is our calling. This is the calling of the United States of

---

[96] *See* The White House, *supra* note 25.

America, the most free nation in the world. A nation built on fundamental values that rejects hate, rejects violence, rejects murderers, rejects evil. And we will not tire. We will not relent.[97]

Such verbiage, coupled with later references to "a terrorist underworld – including groups like Hamas, Hezbollah, Islamic Jihad, Jaish-i-Mohammed" operating "in remote jungles and deserts" and hiding "in the centers of large cities," revealed the undefined and porous boundaries being used in defining the American enemy. First, the emphasis on terrorists hiding in or infiltrating civilian populations renders every Arab or Muslim on the street suspect if not of being a terrorist, of providing them moral or material support, particularly in instances where resistance or resentment toward American power is displayed. In this way, Middle Eastern faces come to signify terrorist sympathizers and potential terrorists and the lines among terrorists, Islamists, Muslims, and Middle Eastern civilians are easily blurred. A sentiment implying that even those who have not committed any crime are somehow not entirely innocent (or deserving of the protection ordinarily to be afforded to the innocent) clearly emerges in American political discourse. For example, Theodore Olson tells members of the House Armed Services Committee in the hearings on military commissions the following:

I don't want a soldier, when he kicks down a door in a hut in Afghanistan searching for Osama bin Laden to have to worry about whether when he does so, and questions the individuals he finds inside, who may or may not be bin Laden's bodyguards, or even that individual himself, to worry about whether he's got to advise him of some rights before he takes a statement.[98]

Although the statement is a reference to reports of concerns over prosecution preventing bin Laden's capture by CIA agents during the Clinton presidency, the way the argument is framed, by highlighting a scenario in which capturing the guilty is sacrificed through the upholding of rights while omitting the possibility of rights offering protection to potential civilians, is telling. Those found "in a hut" are likely guilty through action or association. Even if they are innocent, they can be sacrificed in furtherance of the larger aims of the American mission.

In the documentary *The Ghosts of Abu Ghraib*, one of the soldiers assigned to the prison states that when he first arrived in Iraq, he asked a superior, "What are the rules of engagement?" According to his account, the response he receives from a superior was as follows: "If it looks like the enemy, shoot it." Making another attempt to obtain clear instructions, he responds, "I've never been out of the United States. Everything looks like

[97] The White House, *President Unveils "Most Wanted" Terrorists*, Oct. 10, 2001. http://www.whitehouse.gov/news/releases/2001/10/20011010-3.html.
[98] *See* Theodore Olson, *supra* note 75.

the enemy to me." Again he was told, "If it looks like the enemy, shoot it."[99] In this manner, attributions of guilt are inevitably expanded because, even if they are not terrorists, Arab and Muslim populations share the terrorists' physical attributes, adhere to the same religious beliefs and rituals, and emerge from the same culture marked by violence and antimodernisms (such as nonadherence to women's rights and conservative views of sexuality). Just as labels of *enemy, terrorist,* and *human rights violator* allow for the swooping up of many innocents in one wide net in the detention context, broader labels of *culturally backward, violent,* and *irrational* are imputed to bystanders and civilians in the Middle East.

In the same manner, the violence that has swept Iraq is seen as emerging in a vacuum – the result of the inexplicable or inherent irrationality and cultural traits of Iraqis. Missing is the backdrop and context of converging trauma described by an Arab human rights activist I interviewed in Amman. As she noted, Iraq has suffered from a combination of conditions; coping with any one of these conditions is traumatic for a country. Iraqi society has been shaken by three wars since the late 1970s, a devastating economic embargo affecting wide segments of its population, military occupation, and coming out of an oppressive regime with all of its legacies (disappearances, mass grave, torture, and so on). Because consideration of this context is largely absent from American soldiers' and politicians' understanding of Iraqi society and the violence that has engulfed it, ontological distinctions of civilized versus uncivilized, rational versus irrational, and good versus evil take hold. As Cyra Choudhury has observed, "From this ontological position, our [American] violence, which cannot be a violation of human rights, is a therapeutic corrective applied to a people who must be 'rescued' from their 'backwardness.'"[100] This outlook renders the tremendous suffering of Middle Eastern civilian populations caught up in American military interventions and counterterrorism operations susceptible to being written off as collateral damage; not only are their rights dispensable relative to those of Americans, their lives are virtually dispensable as they are plugged into calculations.

CONCLUSION

As it was repeatedly articulated in justifications for its interventions in the Middle East, the United States embraces a universalist conception of human dignity and human rights. The American president was adamant that the

---

[99] Interview with Sergeant Ken Davis in the documentary film THE GHOSTS OF ABU GHRAIB (2007).

[100] *See* Cyra A. Choudhury, *supra* note 80.

liberal principles of democracy and human rights are as applicable to Middle Easterners and Muslims as they are to Western populations. He makes the point most explicitly in his 2003 speech at the National Endowment for Democracy:

And the questions arise: Are the peoples of the Middle East somehow beyond the reach of liberty? Are millions of men and women and children condemned by history or culture to live in despotism? Are they alone never to know freedom, and never even to have a choice in the matter? I, for one, do not believe it. I believe every person has the ability and the right to be free. Some skeptics of democracy assert that the traditions of Islam are inhospitable to the representative government. This "cultural condescension," as Ronald Reagan termed it, has a long history.

. . .

More than half of all the Muslims in the world live in freedom under democratically constituted governments. They succeed in democratic societies, not in spite of their faith, but because of it. A religion that demands individual moral accountability and encourages the encounter of the individual with God is fully compatible with the rights and responsibilities of self-government.[101]

Yet, despite the asserted endorsement of universalism, in practice the American treatment of human rights in the post–September 11th era was unequivocally contingent in many key respects.

Without any apology, individuals and groups thought to be rogue elements marked by their violence, "ideology of hate," disregard for human rights, and civilian casualties were denied human rights protections. In this way, post–September 11th policies were derived from constructions of human rights as either reciprocal (i.e., owed only when the rights-barer himself had adhered to human rights norms) or treatment to be bestowed, earned, or deserved – not derived from something inherent in the human condition. Once an alleged terrorist stopped talking, "alternative or harsher interrogation techniques" could be applied. As former CIA Head of Counterterrorism Cofer Black stated in a congressional Intelligence Committee meeting, at some point, "the gloves come off." Human rights are universal but also come with prerequisites.

From this point of departure, the Bush administration proceeds to construct a body of law divorced from the spirit and universalist moral foundations of the human rights regime. Human rights treatment is based in legal doctrine and effects on discrimination against noncitizens and between noncitizens through differential treatment and rights guarantees closely linked to nationality, race, or religion.[102] Detainees are widely deprived of the rights protections provided in international instruments, yet they

---

[101] See The White House, supra note 16.
[102] See Anthea Roberts, supra note 53, at 721.

remain subject to prosecution for violations of international norms. Americans agents, however, are exempt from the international regime's sanctions but continue to have legitimate claim over rights protections derived from it.

Further, although the rationale for American exceptionalism post–September 11th was largely couched in material terms through the language of security and assertions of American material power, the lines between material and ideational arguments are also increasingly blurred. In other words, security is progressively seen more in moral, cultural, ideological, and sometimes religious terms.[103] For example, on countless occasions the so-called War on Terrorism has been associated with the cause of combating the terrorists' values such that they may never be imposed on Americans and the rest of the world.[104] As Jack Donnelly explains,

Washington's tolerance for systemic human rights violations, and even state terrorism, when responding to terrorism, has been facilitated by the tendency to see anti-terrorism less as a material interest of U.S. foreign policy than as a crusade against evil. In a struggle against evil in contrast to the pursuit of material interests, victory is all that matters. As the struggle progresses, the end comes to be seen as justifying a growing range of morally and legally problematic means.[105]

As much of the chapter has sought to portray, these American human rights contingencies are in many respects borne out of constructions of American action as presumptively rights adherent and Muslim and Arabs action as presumptively averse to rights and civilization. The East/West geography of human rights provided the United States with a pretext for a slew of military, economic, and political forays into the Middle East, and the formulation provided the global power with substantial universalist cover for what in reality was its own contingent adherence to human rights. Again, this dynamic is not absolute. Much of the rest of the book considers the rejection of the American formulations that emerged in the post–September 11th period. However, when considered in relative terms, the American ability to construct its identity, intentions, and actions as universalist and pro–human rights was a real phenomenon, borne out of not only its material power but

---

[103] Jack Donnelly speaks of the antagonism between human rights and national security when security is seen in moral as opposed to material terms. Jack Donnelley, *International Human Rights: Unintended Consequences of the War on Terrorism, in supra* note 8, at 105.

[104] The White House, *Radio Address by Mrs. Bush*, Nov. 17, 2001, http://www.whitehouse .gov/news/releases/2001/11/20011117.html.

[105] *See* Jack Donnelley, *in supra* note 8, at 103. It is also noteworthy that American human rights interventions in the post–September 11th era take place within an American domestic backdrop in which notions of religious and cultural considerations are at the core of the Bush administration's policies and large segments of the American populations' arguments for curtailing homosexual's and women's reproductive rights.

also its power to construct the contours and terms of global human rights discourses and assumptions.

Finally, in arguing that these post–September 11th developments were in many respects built on America's pre–September 11th human rights dispositions, rather than standing in stark contrast to them, the chapter suggests that the post–September 11th events being considered should not be viewed as an event with a defined temporal beginning and end. Instead, the September 11th era should be viewed as an opportunity to more closely examine the potential impact and consequences of global power asymmetries in international human rights dynamics.

TWO

The Human Rights Challenge from Within

Much has been written about the American "road to Abu Ghraib." This chapter focuses on the road *after* Abu Ghraib. It sketches a composite of an unprecedented American human rights campaign that slowly took shape after the gripping images of torture and abuse at the notorious Iraqi prison first came to light. It begins by focusing on two early manifestations of the campaign, the first being an impressive effort to challenge the confirmation of Alberto Gonzales as Attorney General of the United States and the second a mobilization around the passage of the so-called McCain Anti-Torture Amendment to the 2006 Department of Defense Appropriation Act.[1]

Ultimately, Alberto Gonzales won confirmation and the human rights achievements of the McCain amendment were stripped almost immediately following its passage – first by a tentative U.S. Congress through its coupling of the amendment with a provision that limited habeas corpus appeals for Guantanamo detainees, then by a president intent on preserving the torture option through a signing statement, and later by the two branches in concert through provisions of the Military Commissions Act (MCA). Despite the seemingly bleak outcome, the initiatives reshaped American human rights dynamics and laid an important foundation for human rights contests to come. For this reason, beyond presenting the actors and strategies involved, this chapter is largely devoted to evaluating the two early initiatives introduced and exploring the subsequent evolution of the United States' domestic human rights landscape.

ABU GRHAIB AS AN OPENING

The *Cumberland Times-News*, the local newspaper of the nearest Maryland town housing the reserve military unit implicated in the Abu Ghraib abuses,

---

[1] McCain Amdt. S.AMDT. No. 1977 amends H. R. Rep. No. 2863 (2005).

wrote in an editorial published days after the photos of abuse at the notorious
Iraqi prison came to light: "Visiting journalists search in vain for some dark
local element that gave birth to the monstrous actions in Abu Ghraib. We are
America, for better and worse."[2] Similarly, Susan Collins, a Maine Senator
stated at one of several congressional hearings on Abu Ghraib:

Worst of all, our nation, a nation that, to a degree unprecedented in human history,
has sacrificed its blood and treasure to secure liberty and human rights around the
world now must try to convince the world that the horrific images on their TV
screens and front pages are not the real America, that what they see is not who we
are.[3]

As each of these statements betray, Abu Ghraib forced Americans to reconcile the considerable gulf between their self-image as deploying benign
power in the service of rights and freedom and incontrovertible evidence
of American power instead engendering its opposite, amid an unmistakable
backdrop of racism and cultural hierarchy.

Abu Ghraib also (temporarily) froze the mounting prescriptions for torture as "necessary evil" by pushing the issue out of the realm of the abstract,
theoretical, and hypothetical into the realm of the stark, explicit, and real.[4]
The images were so profoundly unsettling that they did not permit observation from a safe, aloof distance. It was reported that when members of
the U.S. Senate received a private showing of all 1,800 images depicting
sexual abuse and torture, the pictures caused gasps.[5] Inevitably, the photos
drew in the viewer and forced a conclusion that the victims in the pictures
possessed a humanity that had been violated. As one human rights advocate put it, "no one could look at the pictures and say, 'Well those are
bad guys. It's not pretty but that was necessary.' Nobody said that. They
couldn't say it when confronted with the pictures, whereas [members of
the administration] are saying it about the exact same conduct that's not
depicted in pictures."[6] When summoned to testify before the Senate Armed
Services Committee, even Donald Rumsfeld, the characteristically stoic U.S.

---

[2] CUMBERLAND NEWS-TIMES (May 9, 2004) and transcript of May 11, 2004, News-
hour available at http://www.pbs.org/newshour/bb/middle_east/jan-june04/prisoners_5-11
.html.

[3] Comment by Senator Susan M. Collins, Senate Armed Services Committee hearing on Abu
Ghraib prison (May 7, 2004).

[4] The point that Abu Ghraib moved the torture question from the abstract to the concrete
was made by Tom Malinowsky. Interview with Tom Malinowsky, Washington Advocacy
Director for Human Rights Watch, in Washington, DC (Mar. 16, 2006).

[5] Kathy Kiely and William M. Welch, Abu Ghraib Photos Cause Gasp in Congress, USA
TODAY, May 12, 2004, available at http://www.usatoday.com/news/world/iraq/2004-05-
12-congress-abuse_x.htm.

[6] Interview with American human rights NGO representative, in Washington, DC (Feb. 24,
2006).

Secretary of State who, in his review of abusive interrogation techniques, had previously objected to a four-hour limit on forced standing of prisoners, stated "I feel terrible about what happened to these Iraqi detainees. They are human beings."[7] (The American comedian Jon Stewart later showed a clip of the U.S. Secretary of Defense's pronouncement, satirically deeming it the announcement of a major Bush administration policy shift.)

Following Abu Ghraib, it was equally evident to most outside the Bush administration that the policy that had laid the foundation for the degradation being witnessed was, at its core, deeply flawed. Accordingly, for many Abu Ghraib spurred an important realization – that it was increasingly impossible for Americans to credibly profess an authoritative commitment to human rights based solely on their adherence to the domestic constitutional/civil rights order reserved exclusively for Americans while shunning the international regime. In line with constructivist accounts, to varying degrees, the crisis prompted a rejection of previous norms that cast international law as outdated, weak, and ineffective and created a demand for a new set of norms encompassing a more expansive and universal conception of human rights and the international legal order built around it.[8] One of countless editorial and op-ed pieces calling for American compliance with international law in the months following the Abu Ghraib revelations read, "Senators have an opportunity to begin laying the foundation for a new policy, one that reaffirms America's commitment to international agreements that remain relevant in a dangerous world."[9] Throughout the political spectrum, one witnessed widespread condemnation of the violations and rhetorical acceptance of the substance and legitimacy of international norms violated, which stood in stark contrast to its previous characterizations as irrelevant and quaint.

Abu Ghraib also mobilized American human rights proponents and sympathizers, moving key legislators, journalists, and even human rights organizations to take up detainee rights issues to an extent that was unprecedented before Abu Ghraib. Avi Cover of Human Rights First expanded on this point:

What Abu Ghraib revealed or confirmed was if this was going on, then there's other stuff out there. So what do you know? What can you share with us? What do you know about Abu Ghraib? How did Abu Ghraib happen? How do we stop another Abu Ghraib from happening? Abu Ghraib changed things for everyone. It may have

[7] Testimony of Secretary of State Donald H. Rumsfeld before the Senate Armed Services Committee (May 7, 2004), *available at* http://armed-services.senate.gov/statemnt/2004/May/Rumsfeld.pdf.

[8] Martha Finnemore and Kathryn Sikkink, *Taking Stock: The Constructivist Research Program in International Relations and Comparative Politics*, 4 AM. REV. POL. SCI. 391, 407 (2001).

[9] Steve Andreason, *Beyond the Roots of Abu Ghraib*, WASHINGTON POST, Sept. 7, 2004.

been one of Susan Sontag's last pieces, but people have written about the power of that visual image being so arresting and being such a catalyzing factor. I think it's true on all fronts, the media, even NGOs. On some level, NGOs were uncovering only so much of that and it was a wakeup call for NGOs too, certainly for Congress, and even for the Defense department, even though they have a lot more fixing to do.[10]

Beyond a new sense of the magnitude and urgency of the human rights scenario they confronted, the gripping images also provided important openings and discursive spaces from which they could articulate arguments for American compliance with international human rights norms – an opening that did not previously exist. Virtually every policy discussion, public forum, or media piece discussing American detainee policy since May 2004 carried the Abu Ghraib imprint by making some reference to the infamous pictures, with many using the episode as a primary point of departure. It was this extensive exposure to the existence of American abuses that facilitated a public debate in which new frames surrounding values, identity, and the significance of international human rights norms could be evoked.

A BURGEONING AMERICAN HUMAN RIGHTS CAMPAIGN

As detailed in Chapter 1, beyond his own January 2002 memo advising the American president to deny al Qaeda and Taliban detainees Geneva Conventions status, Alberto Gonzales largely oversaw the process of redefinition and marginalization of international human rights law emerging from the White House and Justice Department. When George Bush nominated him as Attorney General at the onset of his second term, American human rights forces began mobilizing an unprecedented campaign against his nomination based almost exclusively on his position on the applicability of international human rights norms in the "War on Terror." Through this campaign, human rights forces made critical inroads toward successfully challenging Bush administration attempts to circumvent international norms and reignited the American debate on torture and detainee rights issues after an extended period (including the 2004 presidential campaign season) in which the topic had virtually disappeared from political discourse.

The McCain amendment was the first viable legislative initiative brought forth to challenge Bush administration legal doctrines and policies relating to abuse and torture of foreign nationals detained by the United States in the post–September 11th era. The amendment comprised two key provisions. The first limited interrogation techniques to those stipulated in the

---

[10] Telephone interview with Avi Cover, Senior Associate at Human Rights First (Jan. 27, 2006).

Army Field Manual, which was assumed to stand largely in compliance with key obligations of the Geneva Conventions. The second provision banned cruel, unusual, and degrading treatment as defined in American reservations, declarations, and understandings entered on ratification of the United Nations Convention Against Torture (CAT). The provision was essentially the reinstitution of a preexisting international legal obligation under the CAT through new domestic legislation. To counter Bush administration contentions that its CAT obligations do not apply extraterritorially, the provision stipulates that the ban on cruel, inhumane, and degrading treatment is not geographically limited. The amendment states:

SEC. __. UNIFORM STANDARDS FOR THE INTERROGATION OF PERSONS UNDER THE DETENTION OF THE DEPARTMENT OF DEFENSE.

(a) IN GENERAL. – No person in the custody or under the effective control of the Department of Defense or under detention in a Department of Defense facility shall be subject to any treatment or technique of interrogation not authorized by and listed in the United States Army Field Manual on Intelligence Interrogation.

. . .

(c) CONSTRUCTION. – Nothing in this section shall be construed to affect the rights under the United States Constitution of any person in the custody or under the physical jurisdiction of the United States.

SEC. __. PROHIBITION ON CRUEL, INHUMAN, OR DEGRADING TREATMENT OR PUNISHMENT OF PERSONS UNDER CUSTODY OR CONTROL OF THE UNITED STATES GOVERNMENT.

(a) In General. – No individual in the custody or under the physical control of the United States Government, regardless of nationality or physical location, shall be subject to cruel, inhuman, or degrading treatment or punishment.

(b) Construction. – Nothing in this section shall be construed to impose any geographical limitation on the applicability of the prohibition against cruel, inhuman, or degrading treatment or punishment under this section.

. . .

(d) Cruel, Inhuman, or Degrading Treatment or Punishment Defined. – In this section, the term "cruel, inhuman, or degrading treatment or punishment" means the cruel, unusual, and inhumane treatment or punishment prohibited by the Fifth, Eighth, and Fourteenth Amendments to the Constitution of the United States, as defined in the United States Reservations, Declarations and Understandings to the United Nations Convention Against Torture and Other Forms of Cruel, Inhuman or Degrading Treatment or Punishment done at New York, December 10, 1984.

Given the relative substance and significance of the McCain amendment at the time, media and human rights forces quickly organized a subsequent initiative to compel passage of the amendment. This second mobilization turned out to be equally critical in shifting the discursive landscape even further such that it became increasingly acceptable and common to invoke international law and evaluate American policies and practices within the parameters of a human rights framework.

In each instance, efforts by human rights NGOs, members of the elite media, and select congressional leaders converged to form the core of a domestic campaign to compel greater American observance of human rights norms in torture and detainee treatment policies within the Bush administration's declared "War on Terror." Although the three forces' linkages were informal and ad hoc, they frequently interacted, collaborated, and adopted overlapping strategies. Human rights activists and journalists often forged personal and professional relationships. They might exchange information and discuss administration policies while visiting Guantanamo or other sites of alleged abuses.[11] In other instances more active efforts at getting human rights groups' own editorials published or persuading editorial boards to take up detainee rights issues took place.[12] For example, in an editorial criticizing the practice of rendition and highlighting the 2003 abduction and rendition of Abu Omar in Milan by CIA operatives, the *Houston Chronicle* cited a visit by the U.S. Chairman of Amnesty International one day prior to the article's publication.

Similarly, human rights groups and the offices of members of Congress taking the lead in challenging the Bush administration's torture policies also developed close ties. Congressional staffers frequently relied on human rights organizations for information, particularly pertaining to specific violations and interpretations of international law as well as for providing "cover" by enlisting political heavyweights such as high-ranking military officials as allies.[13] Two human rights groups in particular, Human Rights First and Human Rights Watch, maintained very close contact with Senator John McCain's office while the McCain amendment was being considered, deliberating on developments and providing extensive legal assistance. At the height of the struggle over the measure, McCain's staffers spoke with associates from these groups every day, sometimes several times a day and sometimes in the middle of the night.

Finally, congressional leaders braving the political minefield of the campaign depended on the media to keep the issue at the fore of public consciousness and political discourse. One striking example of the ties between the media and congressional leaders was seen in the November 21, 2005, issue of *Newsweek*, which featured John McCain's picture with the words "The Truth about Torture by Sen. John McCain" on its cover. The magazine's

---

[11] *Id.*

[12] *The Italian Job: The CIA's Capture and Transport of Terrorist Suspect Must End*, Editorial, HOUSTON CHRONICLE, Jun. 28, 2005, 8.

[13] During the Gonzales confirmation process, congressional staffers of allied congressmen relied on human rights groups to assist them in formulating questions to be posed in the hearings.

decision to feature a several-page essay by an American politician advocating a particular policy position was extraordinary.

Before detailing the course taken by the campaign, a brief introduction to each actor's point of entry and distinct role within the mobilization is presented. The sketches are meant to lend context vital to understanding the campaign's composition, significance and limitations.

Human Rights NGOs

Throughout the world, domestic human rights NGOs are generally known for their attempts to pursue social justice agendas by weaving together international and domestic norms and discourses. Placing American social justice and advocacy groups in the "domestic human rights NGO" rubric can be challenging. Prior to September 11th, most domestic "civil rights" advocacy groups, largely as a result of their experience with the boundaries of the domestic landscape in which they operated, iterated their rights claims using the American constitutional rights framework almost exclusively. At the same time, U.S.-based human rights groups focused predominately on rights violations occurring abroad and traditionally lobbied the U.S. government less in relation to American human rights violations than in relation to human rights conditions in other countries within a foreign policy context. In response to critiques posed by Asian and African human rights advocates in the 1990s, these international nongovernmental organizations (INGOs) increasingly lent scrutiny to American human rights practices, taking up campaigns highlighting violations in U.S. prisons or the rise of racial profiling in America. Still, the scope of their efforts were generally limited because of what was largely viewed as an international mandate and an underlying sense that the most pressing human rights violations took place beyond American borders. Thus, prior to September 11th, inwardly focused (civil rights) NGOs were less inclined to engage with the international human rights framework and human rights INGOs were less invested in engaging with the American political landscape and domestic discourses in relation to American practices than human rights NGOs in other parts of the world. Despite this starting point, since September 13, 2001, when a coalition of civil rights and human rights groups gathered in a meeting called "In Defense of Freedom" to discuss their new terrain and the challenges it posed, the two groups coalesced around a domestic rights agenda that increasingly incorporated the international human rights framework.[14]

A number of American civil rights groups joined U.S.-based INGOs in either opposing or publicly raising questions about Alberto Gonzales's nomination for Attorney General based primarily on his position on international

---

[14] Carnegie Council on Ethics and International Affairs, *U.S. Civil Liberties in September 11th's Wake: A Roundtable Discussion with Jamie Fellner, Elisa Massimino, and Michael Ratner* (2002), http://www.cceia.org/viewMedia.php/prmTemplateID/8/prmID/807.

law and the rights of foreign detainees located abroad. Their decision is notable because Gonzales's nomination as the United States' first Latino Attorney General and his moderate record on traditional civil rights issues relative to other Bush nominees to judicial positions, and relative to his predecessor, otherwise rendered him an acceptable candidate at the time. These groups, which included the Leadership Conference on Civil Rights (LCCR), the Alliance for Justice, and the American Civil Liberties Union (ACLU), put out numerous press releases, reports, and Internet alerts to mobilize their grassroots membership and push Democratic Senators to challenge the Gonzales nomination.[15] On November 29, 2004, thirty civil society groups, ranging from the National Council of Jewish Women to the National Council of the Churches of Christ of the United States and the United Steelworkers of America to the National Association for the Advancement of Colored People, signed a letter to the chairman and ranking member of the Senate Judiciary Committee to raise concerns about the Gonzales nomination and to ask the committee to closely scrutinize his record on detainee policies in Iraq and Afghanistan.[16] These groups coordinated similar letters, signed by religious groups and legal professionals, while Human Rights First embarked on a groundbreaking collaboration with high-ranking retired military leaders who signed a letter opposing the nomination and proclaiming their support for American compliance with the Geneva Conventions. As Avi Cover of Human Rights First observed, the impact of the INGOs and domestic advocacy groups' efforts was to define the Gonzales confirmation as a referendum on the Bush administration's detainee rights policies:

When his name was announced, his name had not been identified in the way we were able to identify it with the torture policies. What was critical was that it became a debate about these issues. It essentially became a hearing about these issues and do

---

[15] Generally, these publications started with a declaration of support for the nomination of a Hispanic for the position, but then went on to discuss in some detail Gonzales's record on torture and detainee rights policies within the administration.

[16] CivilRights.org, *Letter from thirty human rights and civil rights organizations to Orrin Hatch, Senate Judiciary Committee Chairman, and Patrick Leahy, Senate Judiciary Committee Ranking Member* (Nov. 28, 2004), http://www.civilrights.org/issues/enforcement/ details.cfm?id=26423. The first substantive point made in the letter reads as follows:

Mr. Gonzales' role in setting the administration's policy on detention, interrogation, and torture: As White House Counsel, Mr. Gonzales oversaw the development of policies that were applied for handling prisoners in Afghanistan, Iraq, and elsewhere. He wrote a memo disparaging the Geneva Conventions and arguing that they do not bind the United States in the war in Afghanistan. He was warned by U.S. military leaders that this decision would undermine respect for the law in the military, but he advised the President to reject that advice, with catastrophic results. He requested and reviewed legal opinions that radically altered the definition of torture and claimed U.S. officials were not bound by laws prohibiting torture. Changes made as a result to long-established U.S. policy and practice paved the way for the horrific torture at Abu Ghraib.

we want this to be our policy and how does the administration defend these policies. That was an important conversation to have.[17]

The media quickly picked up the debate, and more and more Democratic Senators followed suit.

Although domestic civil rights groups played an important role in the Gonzales confirmation processes, when it came to the McCain amendment, they maintained a lower profile. Instead, two prominent American human rights INGOs led social justice groups' efforts to push for the antitorture legislation. The smaller of the two, Human Rights First, was more inclined to take on engaging with domestic discourses and enlisting domestic intermediaries. The other leading player, Human Rights Watch, also pursued these avenues but to a lesser degree, displaying more of a tendency to engage in traditional INGO strategies of shaming and centering arguments around international legal obligations.

Throughout the campaign, the ACLU's extensive and relentless efforts to force the release of FBI, Department of Defense, and Army documentation that shed further light on the scope of abuses and lack of accountability through Freedom of Information Act requests and litigation and the Center for Constitutional Rights' groundbreaking lawsuits on behalf of Guantanamo detainees were also very instrumental.

The Media

In virtually every interview, the centrality of the media's role was underscored. Many of the actors interviewed believed that without the media's extensive coverage of the abuses taking place and forceful editorials to carry and maintain detainee rights issues in the public sphere, it would have been impossible to get the McCain amendment off the ground.[18] As one congressional staffer emphasized, the week-in/week-out media reports of prisoner abuse in Guantanamo Bay, Iraq, the CIA black sites, and Bagram served as a major catalyst for Senate leaders' decisions to take up the antitorture legislation.[19]

Because the Bush administration had gone to such lengths to withhold information about detainee policies from Congress, legislators relied almost exclusively on the media for information with which to put the pieces of the puzzle together.[20] Media articles, particularly coverage by the *The Washington Post* and *The New York Times*, were regularly referred to in congressional proceedings and debates. One by one, aided by internal dissenters, the media exposed policy documents the administration had withheld. Alberto

[17] *See* Avi Cover, *supra* note 10.
[18] *See* human right NGO representative, *supra* note 6; interview with congressional staffer, in Washington DC (Feb. 24, 2006).
[19] Interview with congressional staffer, in Washington, DC (Feb. 17, 2006).
[20] *See* congressional staffer, *supra* note 19.

Gonzales's January 25, 2002, memo to George W. Bush regarding Geneva Conventions protection for al Qaeda and Taliban members was first made public by *Newsweek* in the weeks following the release of the Abu Ghraib photos.[21] The August 1, 2002, Justice Department memo in which the definition of torture had been limited "to pain equivalent in intensity to the pain accompanying serious physical injury such as organ failure, impairment of bodily function or even death" was first made public by the *The Washington Post*.[22] Finally, particular media outlets were relentless in exposing behind-closed-doors political maneuvering by administration officials and congressional allies designed to undermine the McCain amendment.[23]

Despite, human rights NGOs' increased credibility following Abu Ghraib, the media's coverage of the various human rights violations associated with "the war on terrorism" still had a far more significant impact, both reaching a substantially larger audience and benefiting from a greater assumption of independence and neutrality. For example, Human Rights Watch put out a report about "ghost detainees" being held in secret facilities in October 2004;[24] however, it was not until the *The Washington Post* broke the story through their own sources that the issue provoked elaborate domestic and international responses and outcry.[25] As Katherine Newell Bierman of Human Rights Watch described, "The media was able to report the story in a way that made the story new and more pressing for people than if it had been us."[26] For the same reasons of perceived independence, the media had access to sources human rights NGOs did not. Thus, in the CIA secret detention facilities story, for example, *The Washington Post* was able to reference CIA informants rather than human rights organizations and that made the story more credible and thus more politically salient. The increased access also meant that the media were sometimes in a better position to uncover human rights violations than the human rights organizations themselves.

Beyond shedding light on administration human right policies and making the case for reform, the media made repeated references to international law and accorded the international framework increasingly greater legitimacy and authority, regularly placing it on par with the domestic legal

[21] Michael Isikoff, *Memos Reveal War Crimes Warnings*, NEWSWEEK, May 19, 2004, http://www.newsweek.com/id/105057/page/2.

[22] Dana Priest, *Justice Dept. Memo Says Torture May Be Justified*, WASHINGTON POST, Jun. 13, 2004, http://www.washingtonpost.com/wp-dyn/articles/A38894-2004Jun13.html.

[23] *See*, for example, Liz Sidoti, *House GOP May Try to Weaken Detainee Rules*, ASSOCIATED PRESS, October 7, 2005.

[24] Human Rights Watch, *The United States' "Dissapeared": The CIA's Long-Term Ghost Detainees* (October 2004), http://www.hrw.org/backgrounder/usa/us1004/.

[25] Dana Priest, *CIA Holds Terror Suspects in Secret Prisons*, WASHINGTON POST, Nov. 2, 2005, at A01.

[26] Interview with Katherine Newell Bierman, Counterterrorism Council, U.S. Program, Human Rights Watch, in Washington DC (Feb. 1, 2006).

order. Finally, since the Abu Ghraib scandal unfolded, the media began to introduce, describe, and reprint provisions of international human rights instruments for American policymakers and the public.[27]

Although the media effort to uncover American human rights violations and related administration policies was primarily led by the elite media, namely, *The Washington Post* and, to a lesser extent, *The New York Times*, at the height of the debate over the McCain amendment, media coverage of the issue became extremely widespread. The issue prompted national network and cable news coverage and was picked up by a wide range of local newspapers. According to a list provided by McCain's office, between July 26, 2005, and August 5, 2005, editorials in favor of the McCain amendment appeared in *The Salt Lake City Tribune*, the *Minneapolis Star Tribune*, the *Lansing State Journal*, the *Palm Beach Post*, *The Baltimore Sun*, the *Milwaukee Journal Sentinel*, *The State* (South Carolina), *The Houston Chronicle*, the *St. Petersburg Times*, *The Oregonian*, the *Bangor Daily News*, *The Patriot-News*, the Louisville *Courier-Journal*, and *The Barre Montpelier Times Argus*.

Congressional Leaders

A small group of Republican senators, several with elaborate military credentials, posed a considerable challenge to the Bush administration's detainee rights policies and put their weight behind the McCain amendment. Undoubtedly the most central figure in the group was John McCain himself. His reputation as both a hawk and a principled "maverick" combined with the fact that he had endured torture as a POW during the Vietnam War positioned him as a rare spokesperson with an "in-group" status essential to facilitating processes of persuasion and deliberation with other Republicans in power. At a time when congressional Republicans had fully consolidated their power with the Bush administration, such a challenge to the White House would have been unimaginable without the leadership of McCain and the handful of other Republicans taking on the issue.

McCain and other congressional leaders could hardly be credited with any consistent, comprehensive, or unwavering allegiance to the broader human rights project. Their commitment to securing human rights outcomes was instead partial and fluid. Their motivations were rooted in the desire to, on the one hand, uphold what they viewed as American ideals rooted in a tradition of rights and, on the other, safeguard American interests and power they considered to be tied to and bolstered by these ideals. Within the first realm, the senators' apprehensions about administration abuses were clearly normative as they were born out of a concern with how the United

---

[27] John Barry, Michael Hersh, and Michael Isikoff, *The Roots of Torture*, 163:21 NEWSWEEK 12 (2004) in which provisions of the Geneva Conventions are introduced.

States was perceived and evaluated through moral standards, particularly human rights norms and norms associated with democratic societies. For example, as one interviewee noted, McCain had "the idea that Americans are a nation of ideals and the fear of losing that and the impact that would have on our ability to make the world a better place was very key."[28] At the same time, they were not only concerned about the nation's reputation but also clearly troubled by the disrepute that Abu Ghraib and other revelations of torture and prisoner abuse had brought to the United States military as an institution that to them was a symbol of national pride. Intertwined with the sense of loss of ideals was the fear that declined moral stature would result in a decrease in America's influence and ability to pursue foreign policy objectives and, on the military front, negatively affect the military's recruitment numbers and the safety of troops currently in combat.

Accordingly, international interactions played a prominent role in developing the senators' sense of urgency for gravitating toward international human rights norms. In every trip abroad, particularly to Europe or the Middle East, the senators were confronted by questions and harsh criticisms of American human rights practices in Iraq and Guantanamo.[29] The questioning pursued by Lindsay Graham, another key Republican senator and former Air Force Judge Advocate, at the Gonzales confirmation hearings, is revealing.

Abu Ghraib has hurt us in many ways. I travel throughout the world like the rest of the members of the Senate, and I can tell you it is a club that our enemies use, and we need to take that club out of their hands. Guantanamo Bay – the way it's been run has hurt the war effort. So if we're going to win this war, Judge Gonzales, we need friends and we need to recapture the moral high ground.[30]

In short, as much as the Bush administration's apparent indifference to international evaluations of its human rights policies was an anomaly given constructivist precepts, other congressional leaders' clear concern about how the world perceived them, their country, and the institution with which they had close ties fit into the constructivist calculus.

A POST–SEPTEMBER 11TH ERA STRATEGY

The strategies pursued by the campaign in the Gonzales confirmation and passage of the McCain amendment were, to a large extent, colored and

---

[28] *See* human rights NGO representative, *supra* note 6.

[29] *See* congressional staffer, *supra* note 18.

[30] Questions and comments by Lindsay Graham, nomination of Alberto Gonzales as U.S. Attorney General before the Senate Judiciary Committee (Jan. 6, 2005), *available at* http://www.nytimes.com/2005/01/06/politics/06TEXT-GONZALES.html.

shaped by the confines of the post–September 11th era's climate, which was dominated by militarism, nationalism, and a sense of perpetual threat from the world that lay beyond American borders. Consequently, campaign strategies weaved together arguments and symbols rooted in legality and morality with evocations of patriotism and American preeminence, or, as Avi Cover of Human Rights First offered, they embarked on a project to "cite the law, but as a point of principle and honestly sing apple pie, the star-spangled banner and baseball, to some extent."[31] Tom Malinowsky was even more direct about what lay at the heart of the strategy pursued: "our side had to wrap itself in the flag."[32]

Shaming

Shaming is the quintessential tool of human rights advocacy worldwide. A form of social sanction, it endeavors to associate an individual's or government's behavior with the stigma of violating a morally rooted normative order. In their efforts to counter torture and abuse policies, human rights NGOs and the media make extensive use of this strategy, although Republican congressional leaders pushing the McCain amendment largely stayed clear of overt forms of shaming because of their party ties with the administration. Given that, prior to Abu Ghraib, outside of human rights NGOs and the military, most elites largely overlooked and disregarded the international legal order, the resort to human rights norms and international law as a primary normative framework used to stigmatize Bush administration policies is striking.

Naturally, shaming figured prominently in the campaign against Alberto Gonzales's nomination as Attorney General. An editorial in *The Washington Post* following his testimony at the confirmation hearings typifies the approach:

Mr. Gonzales was clearer – disturbingly so, as it turns out. According to President Bush's closest legal adviser, this administration continues to assert its right to indefinitely hold foreigners in secret locations without any legal process; to deny them access to the International Red Cross; to transport them to countries where torture is practiced; and to subject them to treatment that is "cruel, inhumane or degrading," even though such abuse is banned by an international treaty that the United States has ratified. In effect, Mr. Gonzales has confirmed that the Bush administration is violating human rights as a matter of policy.[33]

The editorial then goes on to say, "Senators who supported the amendment consequently face a critical question: If they vote to confirm Mr. Gonzales as the government's chief legal authority, will they not be endorsing the

---

[31] *See* Avi Cover, *supra* note 10.
[32] *See* Tom Malinowsky, *supra* note 4.
[33] Editorial, *A Degrading Policy*, WASHINGTON POST, Jan. 26, 2005, A20.

systematic use of 'cruel, inhumane and degrading' practices by the United States?"[34] In the same way, a series of editorials written as the political struggle over the McCain amendment progressed attempted to shame members of the Bush administration by identifying them as supporters of abuse and torture. On October 10, 2005, *The New York Times* featured a column titled, "Who Isn't against Torture?" asserting:

> Some people get it. Some don't. Senator John McCain, one of the strongest supporters of the war in Iraq, has sponsored a legislative amendment that would prohibit the "cruel, inhuman or degrading treatment" of prisoners in the custody of the U.S. military. Last week the Senate approved the amendment by the overwhelming vote of 90 to 9. . . . Joining Senator McCain in his push for clear and unequivocal language banning the abusive treatment of prisoners were Senator John Warner of Virginia, the Republican chairman of the Armed Services Committee, and Senator Lindsey Graham of South Carolina, a former military lawyer who is also a Republican and an influential member of the committee. Both are hawks on the war. Also lining up in support were more than two dozen retired senior military officers, including two former chairmen of the Joint Chiefs of Staff, Colin Powell and John Shalikashvili. So who would you expect to remain out of step with this important march toward sanity, the rule of law and the continuation of a longstanding American commitment to humane values? Did you say President Bush? Well, that would be correct. The president, who has trouble getting anything right, is trying to block this effort to outlaw the abusive treatment of prisoners.[35]

Finally, perhaps one of the most forceful examples of the media employing shaming was evidenced by an editorial in *The Washington Post* entitled, "Vice President for Torture," that condemned Dick Cheney's repeated attempts to prevent the passage of the McCain amendment:

> Vice President Cheney is aggressively pursuing an initiative that may be unprecedented for an elected official of the executive branch: He is proposing that Congress legally authorize human rights abuses by Americans. "Cruel, inhuman and degrading" treatment of prisoners is banned by an international treaty negotiated by the Reagan administration and ratified by the United States. The State Department annually issues a report criticizing other governments for violating it. Now Mr. Cheney is asking Congress to approve legal language that would allow the CIA to commit such abuses against foreign prisoners it is holding abroad. In other words, this vice president has become an open advocate of torture.[36]

---

[34] *Id.*

[35] Bob Herbert, *Who Isn't against Torture?* N.Y. TIMES, Oct. 10, 2005, http://query.nytimes.com/gst/fullpage.html?res=9F03E2D61F30F933A25753C1A9639C8B63. Another editorial, in the Washington Post, employed a similar shaming technique:

> Let's be clear: Mr. Bush is proposing to use the first veto of his presidency on a defense bill needed to fund military operations in Iraq and Afghanistan so that he can preserve the prerogative to subject detainees to cruel, inhuman and degrading treatment. In effect, he threatens to declare to the world his administration's moral bankruptcy.

Editorial, *End the Abuse*, WASHINGTON POST, Oct. 7, 2005, at A22.

[36] Editorial, *Vice President for Torture*, WASHINGTON POST, Oct. 26, 2005, at A18.

Although it did not prompt the American vice president to budge in his staunch support for the American executive to reserve a right to engage in torture and seriously curtail detainees' due process rights, in a subsequent interview, he refers to the "vice president for torture" designation with disdain – a sign that it did not entirely escape his attention.

Not surprisingly, Human Rights NGOs used similar shaming techniques in which the stigma of being "a human rights violator" or an "advocate of torture" was used to influence policymakers' positions.[37] However, as the backlash from many American politicians and facets of the media to Amnesty International president Irene Khan's labeling of Guantanamo as the "gulag of our times" revealed that shaming strategies had their limits.[38] In the end, much of the task before advocates involved maintaining a delicate balance between often opposing normative forces, a task pursued even more vigorously through the framing strategies that formed another major pillar of the campaign's efforts.

BRIDGING NORMATIVE DIVIDES

In accordance with constructivist precepts highlighting attempts by those pressing a human rights agenda to communicate arguments, persuade, and deliberate, any analysis of the emergence of the American campaign must consider how international norms are fashioned by domestic proponents. As Cortell and Davis suggest, "in situations where the match between international norms and the prevailing domestic understandings is partial, proponents of the international norm face a political and rhetorical struggle that will require them to argue convincingly for the priority of one set of domestic understandings over others."[39] This is largely accomplished through framing:

Norm entrepreneurs are critical for norm emergence because they call attention to issues or even "create" issues by using language that names, interprets and dramatizes them. Social movement theorists refer to this reinterpretation or renaming process as "framing." The construction of cognitive frames is an essential component of norm entrepreneurs' political strategies, since, when they are successful, the new frames resonate with broader public understandings and are adopted as new ways of talking about and understanding issues. In constructing their frames, norm entrepreneurs face firmly embedded alternative norms and frames that create alternate perceptions of both appropriateness and interest.... new norms never enter a normative vacuum,

[37] See Human Rights Watch, *Introduction, World Report 2006* Jan. 1, 2006, *available at* http://www.hrw.org/sites/default/files/reports/wr2006.pdf.
[38] See, for example, the *Washington Post* editorial criticizing the analogy; Editorial, *American Gulag*, WASHINGTON POST, May 26, 2005, at A26.
[39] Andrew Cortell and James Davis, *Understanding the Domestic Impact of International Norms: A Research Agenda*, 2 INT'L. STUDIES REV. 65, 77 (2000).

but instead emerge in a highly contested normative space where they must compete with other norms and perceptions of interest.[40]

Further, persuaders frequently frame norms in ways that connect emerging norms with existing and established norms to bolster the credibility of their claims.[41]

Framing became the most important component of the rights coalition's overall strategy, particularly with regard to persuading tentative senators. Over coffee in a Senate building cafeteria, one staffer explained the imperative of the approach:

There's a million good reasons why you should not torture people, but it's critical you choose the right ones when you're trying to persuade people. That's something that our friends in Europe have not understood very well. The Germans, for example, we agree with them on the substance of (the idea that) we should stick to international law..., but that doesn't cut it in the United States, you can't make those arguments... politically because people don't put a whole lot of faith in international law *qua* international law. Ask the average person on the street and he says, "well, there's no enforcement mechanism and international law doesn't even matter and the United States is the most powerful country in the world and plus we are exceptional; we can do things that other countries can't."[42]

The view was reiterated by an activist who held that what made all the difference in the campaign was whether human rights norms were framed as constraints in responding to terrorism or as lying at the core of American values and standing in opposition to terrorists' values.[43]

The use of framing by human rights NGOs, the media, and congressional leaders took several forms. To varying degrees, each invoked American identity constructions, existing symbols of nationalism and patriotism, and utilitarian arguments relating to interests and security to make the case for American adherence to human rights norms.

Identity Politics, American Values, and the "This Is about Us, Not about Them" Formulation

A large portion of the campaign's efforts was invested in bringing out the cognitive dissonance caused by Bush administration policies that violated detainee rights and a widely held self-image as global human rights leader, without being labeled "anti-American."[44] Thus, all three forces involved elected to frame the debate as one centered around the essence of American

[40] Martha Finnmore and Kathryn Sikkink, *International Norm Dynamics and Political Change*, 52 INT'L. ORG. 887, 897 (1998).
[41] *Id.* at 887, 908 (1998).
[42] *See* congressional staffer, *supra* note 18.
[43] See human rights NGO representative, *supra* note 6.
[44] *Id.*

values and identity. John McCain's assertion, "This is about us, not about them" becomes the essential message of the campaign:

Let me close by noting that I hold no brief for the prisoners. I do hold a brief for the reputation of the United States of America. We are Americans. We hold ourselves to humane standards of treatment of people, no matter how evil or terrible they may be. To do otherwise, undermines our security, but it also undermines our greatness as a nation. We are not simply any other country. We stand for something more in the world, a moral mission, one of freedom and democracy and human rights at home and abroad. We are better than these terrorists, and we will win. The enemy we fight has no respect for human life or human rights. They don't deserve our sympathy. But this isn't about who they are; this is about who we are. These are the values that distinguish us from our enemies.[45]

The argument adopts the fundamental premises of the East/West human rights dichotomy. However, instead of appropriating human rights to justify American interventions as the Bush administration is apt to do, it invokes the American tradition of rights to make the case for increased American compliance with human rights obligations. For example, McCain adopts the Bush administration's "they hate us for our freedom" rhetoric by saying "it (the proposed legislation) is consistent with our laws and, most importantly, our values. Let's not forget that al-Qaida sought not only to destroy American lives on September 11, but American values, our way of life, and all we cherish."[46] Another common variation of this line of argument is reflected in a column in *The New York Times*:

Some argue that since our actions are not as horrifying as Al Qaeda's, we should not be concerned. When did Al Qaeda become any type of standard by which we measure the morality of the United States? We are America, and our actions should be held to a higher standard, the ideals expressed in documents such as the Declaration of Independence and the Constitution.[47]

---

[45] 190 Cong. Rec. 17, 147 (daily Ed. Oct. 5, 2005) (statement of John McCain) *available at* http://frwebgate.access.gpo.gov/cgi-bin/getdoc.cgi?dbname=2005_record& docid=cr05oc05-19. This line of argument appeared immediately in response to the Abu Ghraib photos and was made throughout the debate over Gonzales's confirmation. For example, during those confirmation hearings, Senator Patrick Leahy made the following statement:

We are the most powerful nation on Earth – actually the most powerful nation Earth has ever known. The country that is great promise. We are blessed with so much. And we're a country that cherishes liberty and human rights. We've been a beacon of hope and freedom to the world. Certainly, it was that hope and freedom that brought my grandparents to this country not speaking a word of English, but coming here for that peace and freedom. We face vicious enemies in the war on terrorism. But we can and will defeat them without sacrificing our values or stooping to their levels.

[46] *Id.*
[47] See Bob Herbert, *supra* note 35.

The appeal to a more morally attuned, more authentic, essential American self is also made in an exchange between Lindsay Graham and Alberto Gonzales during Gonzales's confirmation hearings:

GONZALES: I would respectfully disagree with your statement that we're becoming more like our enemy. We are nothing like our enemy, Senator. While we are struggling, mightily, trying to find out what happened at Abu Ghraib, they are beheading people like Danny Pearl and Nick Berg. We are nothing like our enemies, Senator.

GRAHAM: Can I suggest to you that I didn't say that we are like our enemies; that the worst thing we did when you compare it to Saddam Hussein was a good day there? But we're not like who we want to be and who we have been. And that's the point I'm trying to make, that when you start looking at torture statutes and you look at ways around the spirit of the law, that you're losing the moral high ground. And that was the counsel from the Secretary of State's office that once you start down this road that it's very hard to come back. So I do believe we have lost our way. And my challenge to you as a leader of this nation is to help us find our way without giving up our obligation and right to fight our enemy.[48]

Human rights groups also largely adopted the "it's about us" message but generally delivered it with less of an air of cultural and civilizational hierarchy than did congressional leaders.

Despite their disparate starting points and worldviews, a key factor that generally linked the three forces within the campaign was that, to varying degrees, they ascribed to the "this is about us" values argument. In other words, although they consciously crafted it as an effective rhetorical device, most also adhered to it as a deeply held conviction and personal identity construction. I have already referred to the dynamic in relation to the congressional leaders involved, but it was also apparent in my interviews with Dana Priest, the reporter for *The Washington Post* who won the Pulitzer Prize for her story uncovering the existence of CIA black sites, Jackson Diehl, the member of the editorial board of *The Washington Post* who was largely responsible for the newspaper's scourging editorials condemning torture and other detainee rights abuses, and several of the human rights advocates interviewed. All of them shared a sense that the policies they were challenging were quintessentially un-American.

Fashioning International Law as Not Un-American

Similarly, to set the foundations for the argument that the United States must comply with international human rights norms and treaty obligations, advocates recast international law as consistent with American values, identity, and interests rather than a constraint on American interests and security. Incorporating all of these dimensions, one senator argued, "We instill in our people as much as possible that, 'You're to follow the law of armed conflict,

---

[48] See Lindsay Graham, *supra* note 30.

because that's what your nation stands for, that's what you're fighting for, and you're to follow it because it's there to protect you.'"[49] Another senator linked the roots of the international human rights and humanitarian regime with the American experience:

The prohibition on torture and other cruel treatment is deeply rooted in the history of America. Our Founding Fathers made it clear in the Bill of Rights that torture and other forms of cruel treatment are prohibited.

These principles have even guided us during the times of great national testing. During the Civil War, President Abraham Lincoln asked Francis Lieber, a military law expert, to create a set of rules to govern the conduct of U.S. soldiers in the Civil War. The result was the Lieber Code. It prohibited torture and other cruel treatment of captured enemy forces. It really was the foundation for the Geneva Conventions.

After World War II, the United States took the lead in establishing a number of treaties that banned the use of torture and other cruel treatment against all persons at all times. There are no exceptions to this prohibition.[50]

In a similar manner, John McCain argued in his November 21, 2005, *Newsweek* essay that international law enshrines American values.[51] Although the argument is similar to preexisting American constructions of the relationship between the Constitutional framework and the international framework as commensurate, here it is invoked as a reason to comply with international norms rather than a reason to dismiss them.

Centering Domestic Law

A related practice consisted of campaign members invoking domestic law either in lieu of or in conjunction with international law to tap into the greater authority and legitimacy accorded to the domestic legal framework by those they sought to persuade. Although human rights groups always invoked the authority of international law, in many cases, domestic and military law was also invoked in parallel, depending on the audience. In some cases, this was a conscious tactical decision, and in other cases, it was an inevitable consequence of having to engage with dominant political discourses. In either scenario, a largely pragmatic approach was adopted. This is reflected in the views of Human Rights First's Avi Cover.

If some individual is going to be more compelled by (the argument that) the Fifth Amendment requires them to do this as opposed to Article 16 (of the CAT), in a lot of respects, I'm OK with this. Obviously there's the greater issue of saying we don't care what our treaty obligations are and that's vastly problematic.[52]

---

[49] *Id.*

[50] Senate floor debate on McCain amendment (Oct. 5, 2005) (speech by Senator Dick Durbin).

[51] John McCain, *Torture's Terrible Toll*, 146:21 NEWSWEEK 35 (Nov. 21, 2005).

[52] *See* Avi Cover, *supra* note 10.

As I discuss in later sections, as the campaign progressed, international norms became more and more self-standing, and it becomes increasingly "safe" to invoke its authority without necessarily having to resort to parallel domestic provisions.

Security-Based and Utilitarian Arguments for Human Rights Compliance

Along with the various frames referencing American values, the case for taking American human rights obligations seriously were made through an array of military, security, and interest-based arguments, many of which had both ideational and material dimensions. For example, it was argued that "standing up for the troops" meant giving them clear guidelines.[53] This would not only uphold their reputation and integrity but also ensure their safety and security.[54] The notion of reciprocity also figured prominently in congressional leaders' attempts to persuade their colleagues: "What happens in the next conflict when American military personnel are held captive by the enemy and they make the argument, with some validity, that we have violated the rules of war? What happens to our men and women in the military then?"[55] According to one interviewee, the turning point for the McCain amendment came only when the issue was framed in these terms.[56]

Another line of argument asserted that American human rights violations fostered greater anti-American sentiment worldwide and particularly among Muslims, further endangering American national security. In McCain's words, "What should also be obvious is that the intelligence we collect must be reliable and acquired humanely, under clear standards understood by all our fighting men and women. To do differently would not only offend our values as Americans but undermine our war effort, because abuse of prisoners harms, not helps, in the war on terror."[57] In other words, there was not only a moral imperative to refrain from cruel, inhuman, and degrading treatment but also a (perhaps more pressing) strategic imperative to follow such a human rights course.

Finally, the argument that torture had been proven ineffective because a detainee subjected to it would say anything to end the mistreatment was regularly floated around along with the normative and morally based contentions being advanced. Some human rights advocates made extensive and proactive use of the utilitarian and security-based arguments regularly made by congressional leaders, military intermediaries, and, to a slightly lesser

---

[53] See *supra* note 45 (Statement by Lindsay Graham).
[54] See *supra* note 30. Questions and comments by Joseph Biden.
[55] *See* John McCain, *supra* note 45.
[56] *See* human rights NGO representative, *supra* note 6.
[57] *See* John McCain, *supra* note 45.

extent, the media.[58] Others were less comfortable using the line of arguments but were often drawn into and forced to engage with these arguments, invoking them cautiously but generally attributing them to others. Advocates believed that the arguments simply could not be ignored within "an environment where people were feeling insecure."[59] Katherine Newell Bierman of Human Rights Watch echoed this view:

I've seen debates over whether using the national security framework is overly accepting of the administration's position and that if you start from the standpoint that these are national security issues, you've already sold out your first resistance, which would be "no, this is not a national security issue, this is about our communities." A lot of the D.C.-based organizations say, you hear national security, that's bad. We don't want national security. In the end Americans are concerned about national security and Americans are afraid and if you're not addressing that, then you are not addressing the core barrier to your message. You're not going to get through to people.[60]

The statement poses revealing questions about how domestic NGOs are forced to grapple with normative aspects of the strategies and means they employ when they opt to enter the fray of domestic political discourse.

Enlisting the Military as Powerful Intermediary and Victim

Beyond shaming and framing, a third strategy adopted in the campaign was that of enlisting intermediaries. Although domestic NGOs facilitated letters from a number of civil society groups, including religious organizations and legal professionals, by far the most important intermediaries recruited were those affiliated with the military. As is already evident, to a large extent, after September 11th, mainstream political discourse had placed detainee rights issues within the purview of national security and human right groups were often marginalized by being labeled "out of touch" with what was considered the era's new security imperatives. Human Rights First sought an intermediary who would be more compelling to the legislators they were targeting. As a result, one of their most important strategies involved convincing elite members of the U.S. military (as high up as a former Joint Chiefs of Staff) to write letters to the Senate urging it to consider detainee rights in its votes. The group started out by pursuing particular military figures and once they had one member on board, they were able to tap into his networks and have him vouch for Human Rights First as a legitimate

---

[58] *See*, for example, Human Rights First Washington Advocacy Director Elisa Massimino's contribution on the future of human rights. Elisa Massimino, *Fighting from Strength: Human Rights and the Challenge of Terrorism*, in THE FUTURE OF HUMAN RIGHTS (William F. Schultz ed., 2008).

[59] *See* human rights NGO representative, *supra* note 6.

[60] *See* Katherine Newell Bierman, *supra* note 26.

and politically safe affiliation. Their letters and public positions taken by
the generals on the matter became a major focus both during the Gonzales
confirmation hearings and the fight over the McCain amendment, changing
the tenor of both debates.[61] "Anybody who didn't want to appear soft on
terrorism could say, look, I'm just following the advice of all these military
guys."[62] This was largely applicable to Democrats in the case of the Gonzales
confirmation and Republicans in the case of the McCain amendment. One
human rights NGO representative referred to the letters as providing "cover"
and "ammunition."[63]

Another military figure brought into the public spotlight by human rights
groups and John McCain was Captain Ian Fishback. In contrast to the high-
ranking officers appearing in the letter campaign, he represented the brave
and morally motivated servicemen forsaken by Bush administration policies
and, as such, also played a prominent role in the debate surrounding the
McCain amendment. Fishback's letter to Senator McCain was repeatedly
referenced by supporters of the legislation in the Senate floor debate. His
compelling story of a seventeen-month search for a clear answer regarding
which guidelines were to be followed in the treatment of detainees from his
superiors resonated widely and received considerable media attention.

Mediating Boundaries

All the actors involved in the debate were aware of the boundaries of
the existing political landscape and security-based normative framework.
Although they pushed the boundaries inch by inch, they were all also keenly
aware of a delicate balance that had to be maintained for their human rights
agenda to go forward. This often meant coordination between the various
actors involved around who would speak and who would stay in the background and, as already discussed, how arguments would be formulated.

Although they were instrumental in pushing the majority of Senate
Democrats to vote against Gonzales, when it came to the McCain amendment, it was understood by many of the rights advocacy groups involved
that it was necessary for Human Rights First and Human Rights Watch to
take the lead publicly and for domestic civil rights traditionally viewed as
committed to the left to keep a lower profile:

On the McCain amendment, we were very careful to make sure this didn't look like
a left-wing driven agenda to embarrass the White House. People were very savvy.
[Human Rights First] was the only group that could mobilize the military officials
like [it] did. . . . if you are focused on the result and not the credit, you have to be
strategic about what the public face of the initiative is. [For the McCain amendment],
the retired military felt very strongly about it and [Human Rights First was] able

---

[61] See Avi Cover, *supra* note 10.
[62] See congressional staffer, *supra* note 18.
[63] See Avi Cover, *supra* note 10.

to help channel that feeling into something useful. Many of them would not have felt comfortable if it had looked like an ACLU-driven agenda and even an Amnesty International agenda. It's neither right or wrong, it's just the way it was.[64]

In many instances human rights groups themselves preferred to work behind the scenes through a less public profile. When they collaborated with other legislators or military officials, their names would generally not appear in the public statements that resulted.[65] When there was media coverage of their investigations of detainee abuse, they tried to ensure the story was more about the facts than about a human rights organization as the source.[66] Because they were so concerned about avoiding labels of political partisanship, they were extremely cautious in the framing and formulation of the initiatives:

When we decided to oppose Gonzales, he was only the second cabinet appointee we had decided to oppose. That in and of itself was a significant decision being made.... We understood that as a very significant undertaking and an important statement.... In everything we did and in all the advocacy work we did, we were not going to be political and even though it would be perceived as a political statement and we were entering the political fray, we're going to be about substantively these issues and not any other issues.... We were going to talk about enemy combatants and not applying the law faithfully or fairly, denying the Geneva Conventions and issues of torture. We're not talking about his views on abortion. We're not talking about his views on criminalization of drug use, or the Patriot Act. And we remained faithful to that.[67]

Not surprisingly, similar calculations were present on the Senate side of the equation. Part of the overall (and, again, unspoken but understood) strategy for garnering Republican support for the McCain amendment was to keep Democrats off to the sides. Republican senators from conservative states supporting the measure constantly had to establish that their hearts were not bleeding for "the terrorists" to constituents and colleagues who questioned their stance. This dynamic plays out in Lindsay Graham's need to assure his colleagues and constituents of his strength in a statement during the Gonzales confirmation hearings: "Nobody wants to coddle a terrorist. And if you mention giving rights to a terrorist, all of a sudden you're naive and weak. I can assure you, sir, I'm not naive and weak."[68]

By and large, the strategic paths taken by the campaign were rooted in pragmatism, a desire to obtain immediate and short-term results, and a perception of the necessity to sometimes make less than palatable compromises in what was largely seen as a crisis for global rights conditions and American

[64] See human rights NGO representative, *supra* note 6.
[65] See Avi Cover, *supra* note 10.
[66] See Katherine Newell Bierman, *supra* note 26.
[67] See Avi Cover, *supra* note 10.
[68] See Lindsay Graham, *supra* note 30.

leadership within them. Given the myriad of real and perceived constraints faced by the campaign as well as its virtually unprecedented nature, the following assessment of the campaign's gains and achievements produced a mixed review.

TAKING STOCK

By creatively deploying international human rights norms, domestic forces in many respects transformed American human rights discourses and consciousness and moved the country in a direction in which international human rights norms were increasingly seen as posing constraints on American behavior and policy options, particularly relating to torture. Despite the unprecedented openings it presented, however, the progress achieved by the campaign has to date received scant recognition. There are several reasons for this. First, the gains made remained in the seemingly distant and intangible level of human rights discourses and infrastructure, whereas advocates were naturally focused on the here and now of preventing Bush administration attempts to carve out legal avenues for torture, closing down Guantanamo, guaranteeing detainees meaningful due process rights – none of which materialized in any definitive form. Second, the progress made varied considerably in terms of how far it reached and how much it impacted disparate forces. Thus, it was easy for the modest signs of change to be overshadowed by the sometimes overwhelming signs of continuity, particularly those emanating from the Bush administration. Finally, indicators of progress appeared as diffuse and scattered pieces; their significance becomes apparent only once assembled together. In this section I attempt such a synthesis.

Legislative and Policy Outcomes: Modest Inroads toward American Human Rights Compliance

By August 2008, the campaign's legislative and policy victories had been modest and virtually every hard-fought gain of the campaign had quickly been matched by a new Bush administration attempt to circumvent it. Still, some of these modest victories are worth briefly recounting and their significance considered in light of the constructivist insight that incremental concessions, no matter how seemingly insignificant, can accumulate over time and result in an eventual turning of the tide or "tipping point."[69]

On December 30, 2004, just days before Alberto Gonzales's confirmation hearings were set to commence, the Department of Justice replaced the controversial Bybee torture memo with a new memo written by Daniel Levin. The new memo repudiated the earlier memo's limited definition of

---

[69] *See* Finnmore & Sikkink, *supra* note 40, at 887.

acts constituting torture and its assertion that under certain circumstances a torturer can escape criminal liability. The changed tone of the new memo was notable. It began as follows:

Torture is abhorrent both to American law and values and to international norms. This universal repudiation of torture is reflected in our criminal law, for example, 18 U.S.C. §§2340-2340A, international agreements; exemplified by the United Nations Convention Against Torture (the "CAT"); customary international law; centuries of Anglo-American law; and the longstanding policy of the United States; repeatedly and recently reaffirmed by the President.[70]

Moreover, the Senate vote on the Gonzales confirmation produced surprising results, with thirty-five Democratic senators and one Independent senator voting against Gonzales's nomination solely based on his involvement with the Bush administration's detainee rights and torture policies. Gonzales received the fewest minority party votes for the Attorney General position since 1925.[71]

Following the hearings, Senate Democrats renewed calls for the establishment of an independent commission to investigate detainee abuse. The proposal received support from the elite media and ultimately served as leverage to get some Republicans on board with the McCain amendment.[72] On November 3, 2005, the Department of Defense issued a new directive that instructed soldiers to treat detainees humanely and banned the use of dogs in interrogations.[73]

Without a doubt the biggest success of the rights initiative considered in this study was to be found in the developments surrounding the passage of the McCain amendment. First, despite the threat of a presidential veto, the amendment passed the Senate by a remarkable vote of ninety to nine. Few involved in the process had imagined such a dramatic result. Second, despite repeated efforts by Dick Cheney and congressional allies to abort or alter the legislation in the conference committee, efforts by human rights groups, the media, and congressional leaders ensured that the back-door dealings were made as public as possible. Eventually, the measure was sent to the White House in its original form and George Bush signed the legislation on December 30, 2005, in a public ceremony with McCain at his side. However, the success was sobered by its coupling with legislation spearheaded by Lindsay Graham (whose commitment to upholding detainee rights was largely confined to his stance against torture) to limit Guantanamo detainees' access to habeas corpus appeals as well as news that Bush had signed the

---

[70] Daniel Levin, Memorandum for James B. Comey (December 30, 2004), *available at* http://files.findlaw.com/news.findlaw.com/hdocs/docs/terrorism/dojtorture123004mem.pdf.

[71] Charles Babbington and Dan Eggen, *Senate Confirms Gonzales 60 to 36, Vote Reflects Concerns over Detainee Policy*, WASHINGTON POST, Feb. 4, 2005, A01.

[72] *See* Avi Cover, *supra* note 10.

[73] Department of Defense, Directive No. 3115.09 (Nov. 3, 2005).

legislation with a presidential signing agreement that stripped the legislation of its intended purpose.

Following the McCain amendment, one of the campaign's biggest victories was a judicial one: the Supreme Court decision in *Hamdan v. Rumsfeld* holding that Guantanamo military commissions violated the Geneva Conventions. The decision left an opening for the military commissions the Bush administration favored but required they be authorized by statute, forcing another legislative battle just before the 2006 elections. The measure that curtailed detainee due process rights on numerous fronts and left the door open for the use of evidence obtained through torture ultimately passed, serving a major blow to the campaign whose congressional supporters, including John McCain, largely deflected at the eleventh hour. However, given the tone and unprecedented presence and legitimacy accorded to international treaties and human rights considerations within the widespread debates over the legislation, the measure could just have easily passed in a form that incorporated many of the human rights campaign's demands. The reasons why it did not are complex and largely attributable to factors beyond the campaign's control. Almost immediately after taking over Congress, a number of Democrats developed legislation that attempted to reverse provisions of the MCA and mandate compliance with international human rights obligations and ban the practice of "extraordinary renditions." However, none of the efforts materialized as substantive human rights gains until Barack Obama assumed the presidency in January 2009.

A New Era of American Human Rights Awareness, Engagements, and Consciousness

Constructivists look at several indicators for evidence of a progressive displacement of existing norms with emerging norms. Most relevant to discussions of the emergence of international human rights norms are three stages identified by constructivist scholars Thomas Risse and Kathryn Sikkink. Noting that they do not necessarily follow sequentially and that overlap is common, the authors point to (1) adaptation and strategic bargaining that entail some strategic or instrumental concessions and the beginnings of actors engagement with human rights discourse; (2) moral consciousness raising that is characterized by processes of persuasion, argumentation, dialog, and shaming, often leading to actor's acceptance of human rights norms in their discursive practices; and, finally, (3) full institutionalization and habitualization.[74] Cortell and Davis add that the legitimacy and salience of international norms within domestic contexts can be measured by changes in overall national discourse, state institutions (e.g., norm conflicting

---

[74] Thomas Risse and Katheryn Sikkink, *The Socialization of International Human Rights Norms into Domestic Practices: Introduction, in* THE POWER OF HUMAN RIGHTS (Thomas Risse, Stephen Ropp, and Kathryn Sikkink eds., 1999).

institutions being weakened or eliminated), state policies, certain behaviors being ruled out of the set of acceptable alternatives, and actors feeling a strong need to justify or apologize for violations.[75] As the authors note and the present case study displays, the entry of international norms into domestic discourse is perhaps the most important of the indicators listed.[76]

Arguably, the most consequential advance of the American campaign profiled stems from the moral consciousness-raising and overall changes in American political discourse on international human rights norms it set in motion. Increasingly, international norms and treaty obligations were introduced into the public domain, accorded legitimacy, and referred to as binding law in political and civil society discourse. Many examples are found in the materials presented above. The following statement by Lindsay Graham was typical:

> The Bybee memo was an effort by people at the Justice Department to take international torture statutes that we had ratified and been party of and have the most bizarre interpretation basically where anything goes. It was an effort on the part of the Department of Justice lawyers to stretch the law to the point where the law meant nothing. And early on in this process, those in uniform who happened to be military lawyers stood up and spoke.[77]

Although references to international human rights treaties as "the law" are not groundbreaking from a strictly legal or constitutional standpoint, they do represent a modest discursive shift, a move toward ever-so-slightly reconstituting the balance between domestic law's privilege and international law's "intrusion."

Questions of international law became pivotal in many judicial and executive branch confirmations in a way that they had not before. Just one glimpse into the transformation is illustrated by the questions regarding international law in the Senate confirmation hearings of both of the Bush administration's Supreme Court nominees. Again, in the Senate floor debate on the McCain amendment, Graham recalls his questioning of John Roberts:

> GRAHAM: Do you believe that the Geneva Convention, as a body of law, that it has been good for America to be part of that convention?
>
> ROBERTS: I do, yes.
>
> GRAHAM: Why?
>
> ROBERTS: Well, my understanding in general is it's an effort to bring civilized standards to conduct of war – a generally uncivilized enterprise throughout history; an effort to bring some protection and regularity to prisoners of war in particular. And I think that's a very important international effort.[78]

---

[75] See Cortell & Davis, *supra* note 39, at 65, 70–71.

[76] *Id.* at 71.

[77] See Lindsay Graham, *supra* note 30.

[78] See Lindsay Graham, *supra* note 30.

For a Republican to invoke international law in this way in a United States Supreme Court nominee's confirmation hearing breaks new ground in American political and legal dynamics, even if (or precisely because) it sits alongside other Republicans' attempts to secure nominees' assurances that they will not draw on foreign or international sources in their judgments. Evidence of a new American discourse on international law was seen even earlier in the numerous critical references and direct challenges to Alberto Gonzales's designation of international legal instruments as "quaint" and "obsolete." This position was so heavily criticized (and sometimes even stigmatized) that Gonzales felt compelled to reject it in his opening remarks by declaring that, "Contrary to reports, I consider the Geneva Conventions neither quaint nor obsolete."[79] Despite the fact that the Bush administration asserted they held international human rights standards in high esteem while they made every attempt to circumvent them, some of their statements betray an unstated perception that international law matters. Clearly, the administration felt at least enough of international law's normative force to engage and contend with the regime by packaging and repackaging their policies in international legal terms and justifying their infringements at every step. The more effort and resources they devoted to this end, the more they became entangled in the regime, particularly when confronted with domestic human rights challenges. As Jamil Dakwar of the ACLU's Human Rights Program observed, "All of a sudden the U.S. government or Congress cite international law – even in a bad way. That's an opening to develop mechanisms and oversight."[80]

Beyond this, promising signs of transformed American sensibilities surrounding the notion of human rights also began to emerge. Human rights were increasingly understood as something more than a replica or reiteration of American civil liberties enshrined in the Constitution. There was a nascent sense that the regime serves some purpose, and there was an increased consciousness of the universality or "human" in the human rights concept, as this exchange between CNN anchor Wolf Blitzer and Richard Falkenrath, a former Bush administration aide at a Georgetown Law Center forum also featuring Senator Arlen Spector and Congresswoman Jane Harman, intimates.

Blitzer: Richard, this [detainee rights concerns] is a case where the government tries to balance civil liberties and national security?

Falkenrath [former Deputy Assistant to George W. Bush]: There's a question about whether these individuals have civil liberties in the way that U.S. citizens do.

---

[79] Testimony by Alberto Gonzales, nomination of Alberto Gonzales as U.S. Attorney General before the Senate Judiciary Committee (Jan. 6, 2005).

[80] Telephone interview with Jamil Dakwar, Director, ACLU Human Rights Program, DC (Jul. 10, 2008).

Blitzer: *They are human beings* (with emphasis).

Falkenrath: But Wolf, human rights is different than civil liberties, but here's what I'd like to say –

Blitzer (cutting Falkenrath off): Alright, so let me rephrase; so this is a case where you balance human rights against national security.

Falkenrath: I agree with that. This is just a profoundly difficult problem. Here, I invite everyone to think back into the weeks after 9/11 and project in your mind what the United States would be doing as a result of that attack. We would be launching a global war against terror in which hundreds of thousands of individuals detained all over the world, individuals of many different nationalities, some of whom have current knowledge of current plots to kill other innocent civilians, many of whom will go into action against us at the first opportunity...extremely hard problem for which there was no pre-existing rules, there was no body of international law, there was no world court, there was no prepackaged U.S. statutory regime and the executive branch had to come up with something and there's nothing easier than to throw stones at Guantanamo.

Blitzer: Explain why the Geneva Conventions don't apply.

Falkenrath: You should probably turn to a lawyer for this since I'm a non-lawyer, but this category of combatants does not fit within a category of the Geneva Conventions....[81]

A more formal example was provided in the Senate floor debate on the McCain amendment where Republican senator John Sununu makes the following comment:

Second, I think we are sending an important message to our allies and our adversaries – a message that while the legal standards that are enshrined in the Constitution do not apply to everyone in the world, our commitment to these basic principles of life, liberty, and the pursuit of happiness, our commitment to basic principles of human dignity and human rights do apply and we must find ways to define these standards, to clarify this commitment, even in the area of interrogating enemy combatants and interrogating potential terrorists, suspected terrorists, in the field.[82]

However limited, tentative, and conflicted the move toward a recognition that the human rights paradigm in some way applies to American action, it remains a notable development.

Running parallel to the increased sense that human rights are owed to everyone (even to terrorists and other Muslims) was an increased ability to

---

[81] Georgetown Law, *The War on Terror: Exercise of Civil Defense or Violation of Civil Liberties: A Georgetown Law Forum Discussion Focusing on Military Tribunals and Domestic Wiretapping*, Feb. 16, 2006, http://www.law.georgetown.edu/otp/RecentNewsAndEvents.htm.

[82] Senate floor debate on McCain amendment (Oct. 5, 2005) (speech by John Sununu).

conceive of "American human rights violations" and place the United States alongside other states in contravening human rights norms, in contrast to previous understandings of human rights as simply means for condemning the brutality of far-off dictators and "backward" cultures. In other words, strides were taken in the direction of rejecting American human rights exceptionalism. A column in *The New York Times* recounted the story of the Sudanese al-Jazeera cameraman, Sami al Hajj, who was detained by U.S. authorities first at the Bagram Air Force Base in Afghanistan and later in Guantanamo, allegedly under torture and with little evidence of legitimate charges against him. The column begins, "with the jailing of Mr. Hajj and of four journalists in Iraq, the U.S. ranked No. 6 in the world in the number of journalists it imprisoned last year, just behind Uzbekistan and tied with Burma, according to the Committee to Protect Journalists."[83] Further, in arguing for the provision of due process guarantees to "War on Terror" detainees in his congressional testimony in hearings on the MCA, Rear Admiral John Hutson following the cue of the Supreme Court in its *Hamdan v. Rumsfeld* decision invokes standards of justice of "civilized people" and goes on to detail how American policies fall short of those standards:

However, I believe that successful prosecution entails a full and fair hearing which complies with the dictates of Common Article 3, to the extent that it is a regularly constituted court that comports with the judicial guarantees recognized as indispensable by all civilized peoples. I don't believe that there is any part of that – a regularly constituted court or judicial guarantees recognized as indispensable by civilized peoples – that the United States should or could try to avoid or evade in any way.[84]

The reference to an American need to act in accordance with civilized standards captures an instance of the East/West geography of human rights being turned on its head in the post–September 11th era, albeit an instance with which some members of Congress who attended the session were quick to take exception.

Finally, enlisting Abu Ghraib's vivid images, the campaign was able, in large part, to counter the momentum of policymakers' and a surprising tide of scholars' abstract theoretical indulgences of torture and violations of other international conventions as "necessary evils." As Human Rights Watch's Tom Malinowsky explained, in the first two years following September 11th,

---

[83] Nicholas Kristoff, *Sami's Shame and Ours*, N.Y. Times, Oct. 17, 2006, http://select.nytimes .com/gst/tsc.html?URI=http://select.nytimes.com/2006/10/17/opinion/17kristof.html& OQ=_rQ3D1&OP=3035a631Q2FFv@pFQ2FQ5EEmmQ2FFQ7COOoF)OF). FmaNkNmkF).4ENQ5EQ2Fm5Q27zQ2FUI.

[84] Statement by Rear Admiral John Hutson, United States Navy, Retired, Former Judge Advocate General, U.S. Navy, hearing before the House Armed Services Committee on standards of military commissions and tribunals (Jul. 12, 2006).

he constantly received invitations to debates on the pros and cons of resorting to torture in the War on Terrorism in which "there would be a pro-torture guy" and he would serve as the "anti-torture guy," but that format has largely disappeared in recent years. Still, this could be seen only as a partial or short-lived gain. Although the debate over torture's "necessity" subsided, similar debate over "harsh interrogation techniques" and denials of due process reemerged in 2007 with their championing by a number of Republican presidential candidates.

Taken cumulatively, can these developments be regarded as the beginning of a degree of internalization of international human rights norms? The campaign clearly cultivated an increased awareness of international law by policymakers. As one staffer who came into our interview with a copy of a Congressional Research Service report briefing policymakers on the Convention Against Torture noted, international human rights law had become an issue of extensive debate among legislators and their staffs, whereas before it was rarely considered.[85] Sitting in the Russell Senate building cafeteria, another staffer painted a more vivid picture, "If you asked people in this building what the Convention Against Torture was before, maybe five people would know and they would all be staffers."[86] At various junctures following Abu Ghraib, American congressman, and particularly their staffs, had occasion to actually read, learn about, and contemplate provisions of the Geneva Conventions and the Convention Against Torture. As a result of the process, they were introduced to an alternate legal framework (for many, almost for the first time, even though they were lawyers) as well as to American obligations under that framework. The introduction constituted a necessary (though certainly not sufficient) step toward taking international legal obligations out of the exclusive purview of State Department officials and a foreign policy and diplomacy designation into the realm of domestic implementation.

Despite their universal agreement on the existence of an increased awareness of international human rights norms and instruments among legislators, most campaign participants interviewed in 2006 did not consider themselves to be in the midst of a new American engagement, consciousness, or commitment to human rights. They pointed to the strategic motivations behind the limited policy changes adopted as well as the past and present resistance of administration officials and their congressional allies to human rights–consistent policies and practices. From their vantage point, any attention to international norms was transitory and instrumental. Only one participant, a congressional staffer, hinted at a more profound change by observing

[85] See congressional staffer, *supra* note 20.
[86] See congressional staffer, *supra* note 18.

that it was no longer taken for granted that Americans lead and do not follow on international law. It is the convergence of the two outlooks (of continuity and change) that best describes the moment being captured in the interviews. American policy remained far from strict compliance with international human rights norms; however, modest but significant gains had been made in shrinking the divide between American identity and interest constructions and international norms. The confidence and consensus in the idea that international human rights norms were irrelevant to the American experience had been shaken, but the entrenched notion was still far from displaced in the American imagination.

It was the campaign's ability to lay a foundation for an altered American engagement with human rights propelled by a new international awareness and lexicon that constitutes its greatest achievement. Although concrete evidence of gains in the direction of a more rooted human rights consciousness seemed elusive at the conclusion of the initiatives profiled here, it would materialize later through the changed discourse employed in the debates on the MCA and political dynamics following the 2006 congressional elections in which the Democrats took over the U.S. Congress. In the days leading up to the passage of the MCA, the American media provided unprecedented coverage to the issues of torture, detainee treatment, and the United States' international legal obligations. What was striking within much of the coverage was the centrality and legitimacy accorded to the Geneva Conventions and international human rights norms. The Geneva Conventions increasingly were presented and invoked in a self-standing manner. Although nationalistic and militaristic frames and discourses were not absent; in many instances, they were relegated to the debates' peripheries or, at the very least, they no longer seemed to be human rights advocates' only viable point of entry into mainstream discussions of detainee rights issues.

Following the November 2006 congressional elections, debates surrounding human rights within the "War on Terror" mantra continued to evolve toward legitimation of international norms, although corresponding legislative action was yet to materialize in the New Congress preoccupied with challenging the Iraq War and unveiling Bush administration scandals that held promise of more domestic traction than Muslim and Arab detainees' rights. Nonetheless, Democrats increasingly found themselves in an environment in which it was relatively safe to invoke human rights and international norms more freely and expansively. For instance, in one speech, the new chairman of the Senate Judiciary Committee, Patrick Leahy, ventured to link Guantanamo and Abu Ghraib with the Bush administration's withdrawal from the Rome Statute of the International Criminal Court and went on to criticize not only the U.S. president's decision to not sign on to a pertinent UN treaty prohibiting governments from holding individuals in secret detentions but also the administration's refusal to join an accord banning the use of child soldiers.[87] During the summer of 2008, the House Judiciary Committee held a five-part series of Hearings called "From the Department of Justice to Guantanamo Bay: Administration Lawyers and Administration Interrogations Rules." Challenges to the Justice department's interpretation of international legal obligations were posed throughout the hearings and were particularly prominent in the questioning of leading torture memo author John Yoo.

Given such developments, the biggest achievements of the Gonzales confirmation and McCain amendment initiatives were not to be found in their immediate results; rather, they have been and will continue to be seen in how they set the stage for ensuing human rights struggles in the United States. By 2008, some advocates were more willing to entertain the notion that they were in the midst of a promising transformation. For example, Wendy Patten of the Open Society Institute accepted that human rights advocates were witnessing some overall change in attitudes toward international law in the United States Congress but was quick to note that conservatives hostile to American adherence to the international regime remained a vocal presence.[88]

A New Human Rights Infrastructure

Emerging from of the early formation of the American human rights campaign introduced in this chapter and circumstances both related and coincidental to September 11th were a number of small, but significant, building blocks for an American human rights infrastructure. Namely, American NGOs made important strides toward embracing and promoting the international human rights regime internally. Some of the most prominent U.S.-based INGOs shifted their focus and resources to American human rights practices in unprecedented ways. Although in many instances, the dominant focus started out centered around post–September 11th violations, as time progressed, there were promising signs that these groups are not only expanding but also broadening their focus on domestic human rights violations. Human Rights Watch in particular began positioning its United States program as one of its primary divisions and its U.S. advocacy encompassed investigations into harassment of homosexual teens, prisoners' abuse, women's rights, and labor rights. Although the seeds for the program were sown prior to September 11th, the era's developments helped place the leading INGO's U.S. program front and center in the organization's agenda. Global Rights, which has largely not taken on post–September 11th

---

[87] Senator Patrick Leahy, Address at the Samuel Dash Conference on Human Rights: Constitutional Checks and Balances in the Post-9/11 Era: Revitalizing Congress's Role, Georgetown University Law Center (Feb. 5, 2007).

[88] Interview with Wendy Patten, senior policy analyst, Open Society Institute, in Washington, DC (Jul. 25, 2008).

torture and detainee rights issues, has also developed a substantial U.S. human rights project focusing on racism, poverty, and domestic workers among other issues.

Equally significant are initial steps toward recognizing and contending with the culturally rooted dimensions of American human rights violations. Mirroring the cultural approach a Middle Eastern NGO might take by engaging local television programmers regarding the human rights implications of gender-based stereotypes, roles, and violence depicted in television shows. Human Rights First undertook a major initiative to counter portrayals of torture as an acceptable and effective device by heroes foiling terrorist plots in popular television dramas, a portrayal that the organization claims U.S. soldiers have emulated on more than one occasion. The campaign has encompassed meetings with TV executives and soldiers – both mediated by the organizations' cadre of high-ranking retired military allies. The initiative is promising in that it provides further evidence that American INGOs have committed to approaching American human rights violations in a rooted and multifaceted way and that (whether consciously or unconsciously) they are countering the misguided delineations of the cultural relativism/universalism dichotomy of the East/West human rights geography.

At the same time, the post–September 11th era has also been marked by domestic "civil rights" groups gradually revisiting the international human rights framework and viewing the regime as a viable resource. Perhaps the most striking example of this is to be found in the American Civil Liberties Union's treatment of international human rights in the post–September 11th era. The ACLU had looked into incorporating the human rights framework into its work at various periods throughout its history, but the idea had never materialized in a significant way. As a result, prior to September 11th, the leading American advocacy organization had no in-house human rights experts. Anthony Romero, who had become the organization's executive director one week before September 11th, had joined the ACLU with an interest in some day making human rights more of a priority at the organization. Soon after September 11th, the ACLU developed an International Human Rights Working Group within its "Free and Safe" initiative, and, in 2004, the ACLU launched its Human Rights Program with a staff of three: two attorneys and a legal assistant.

According to the program's director in 2008, Jamil Dakwar, applying international human rights norms and enforcement mechanisms to American action, was the program's primary objective: "We only take up human rights issues focusing on the United States. We will only engage if the U.S. is going to be on the spot," he explained.[89] Four major initiatives formed

---

[89] Telephone interview with Jamil Dakwar, director, ACLU Human Rights Program (Jul. 10, 2008).

the core of the project's efforts: (1) national security; (2) women's rights, namely, trafficking, domestic violence, and detention of girls; (3) immigrant rights such as employer abuses of migrant workers; and (4) racial inequality, encompassing a heavy emphasis on the death penalty and justice system manifestations.

The advocacy methods the program adopted included some of the litigation the ACLU is best known for. It pursued lawsuits against George Tenet and other CIA officials for extraordinary renditions and (along with Human Rights First) Donald Rumsfeld for "War on Terror" torture and abuse policies. The program also took cases in which the United States Supreme Court ruled unfavorably to the Inter-American Court of Human Rights, including one regarding domestic violence victims' right to have restraining orders enforced.[90] Despite these efforts, the crux of the ACLU Human Rights initiative lay beyond litigation. The program began appearing before international human rights treaty bodies; educating other domestic advocacy groups, its constituents, and the public about the relevance and uses of the international framework; facilitating fact-finding visits by UN human rights rapporteurs to the United States; advocating U.S. ratification of additional international human rights instruments such as the Convention on the Elimination of All Forms of Discrimination against Women; and, increasingly, undertaking the type of documentation of abuses and issuance of reports typical of human rights NGOs.

Specific initiatives of the ACLU human rights program shed further light on the shape and scope of the leading domestic advocacy group's entry into the international human rights fray. Although the United States is one of two countries that has not ratified the United Nations Convention on the Rights of the Child, in 2002 it became party to the Optional Protocol to the Convention on the Rights of the Child on the Involvement of Children in Armed Conflict. According to Dakwar, the United States "most likely joined so they could press countries like the Congo on their use of child soldiers."[91] Regardless of its motives in doing so, joining the protocol meant the United States was obligated to appear before the Committee on the Rights of the Child and report on its implementation of the Optional Protocol. The ACLU decided to make full use of the United States' 2008 appearance. In their shadow report to the committee, they presented an investigation and full report on abusive tactics used by the Pentagon in recruiting underage soldiers in the United States. They also took advantage of the American appearance to argue that there was a real need for the United States to ratify the Convention on the Rights of the Child. In making their case, they highlighted three areas in which they contended that children's rights were being violated in

[90] Castle Rock v. Gonzales, 545 U.S. 748 (2005).
[91] See Jamil Dakwar, supra note 89.

the United States: (1) the sentencing of juveniles to life without parole, (2) the allowance of high levels of incarceration of juveniles, and (3) the linkages between the failure of the U.S. education system and juvenile incarceration. Finally they also pressed the United States on post–September 11th detentions of minors beyond American borders, and as a result the United States government revealed that there had been 2,500 minors in U.S. custody after 9/11.[92]

When I asked Dakwar about the ACLU Human Rights Program's biggest accomplishments, he stated that he generally did not speak in terms of "complete victories" but gave another intriguing example of how the program's efforts where making inroads. In 2006, the program learned of racial profiling taking place along the U.S./Mexico border by a local sheriff who did not have the authority for such action. The incident arose around the same time that the ACLU was preparing its shadow report to the UN Human Rights Committee charged with assessing the compliance of states party to the International Covenant on Civil and Political Rights. The ACLU Human Rights Program decided to include the El Paso border incident in the shadow report it was preparing. To further raise awareness, the report was launched publicly in El Paso. Soon thereafter, a local newspaper headline read "El Paso Sheriff Taken to United Nations." In Geneva a Human Rights Committee member questioned the American representative on the incident and the issue was incorporated into the Committee's recommendations to the United States government. The report reached a Texas senate committee hearing and the El Paso Sheriff eventually agreed to suspend the practice.[93]

Although the ACLU Human Rights Program presents perhaps the most dramatic example of American rights-based and social justice groups engaging with the international human rights framework, according to Wendy Patten of the Open Society Institute, as the era progressed many other domestic advocacy groups also began displaying a greater openness to integrating the international human rights framework into their work and it became more and more common to see such groups identify themselves as both civil and human rights organizations.[94] Facilitating American social justice groups' movement toward international human rights was the inauguration of several domestic human rights networks devoted exclusively to the advancement of the human rights regime within the United States. One example was the *Bringing Human Rights Home Initiative* run out of Columbia Law School that in 2007 consisted of a network of 80 lawyers attempting to promote and develop tools for the increased use of international human rights norms in domestic legal processes. A larger effort was to

---

[92] *See* Jamil Dakwar, *supra* note 89.
[93] *See* Jamil Dakwar, *supra* note 89.
[94] *See* Wendy Patten, *supra* note 88.

be found in the US Human Rights Network, composed of over 200 NGOs, grassroots organizations, and institutes invested in social justice or rights-based agendas ranging from countering sexual violence to upholding education rights.

Although the US Human Rights Network was also formed in the post–September 11th era, the coalition's relationship to the era is complex. Much of the impetus for the effort had little to do with September 11th and was merely the progression of domestic social justice movement's attempts to find new avenues for pushing forth their agendas beyond the domestic civil rights litigation framework, which they found to be yielding fewer and fewer tangible results. However, the coalition's creation was not entirely divorced from post–September 11th events either. It drew support from rights groups concerned about the domestic impact of post–September 11th policies (namely, in the immigrant rights and racial profiling fields) and perhaps more significantly it drew momentum from the renewed political and public interest in human rights stemming from "War on Terror" rights debates. Post–September 11th era abuses became an important device for shining the spotlight on domestic rights conditions. For example, in June 2008, the US Human Rights Network introduced an initiative to highlight torture and cruel, inhumane, and degrading treatment within the United States. The project was titled "Beyond Abu Ghraib and Gitmo: Stop Torture in the US" and promotional materials for the campaign put forth the statement "torture does not begin or end outside US borders."[95]

The US Human Rights network's stated mandate was to "support collaborative efforts by human rights groups, develop and disseminate tangible models for the practical application of the human rights framework domestically, and promote capacity building and information sharing among member organizations."[96] Prominently featured on the Network's Web site in 2007 was the question, "Why a US Human Rights Network?" to which the response read as follows:

Underlying all human rights work in the United States is a commitment to challenge the belief that the United States is inherently superior to other countries of the world, and that neither the US government nor the US rights movements have anything to gain from the domestic application of human rights. Network members believe that the US government should no longer be allowed to shield itself from accountability to human rights norms and the US civil, women's, worker, immigrant, LGBTQ, prisoner and other rights movements that stand to benefit, perhaps now more than ever, from an end to US impunity in this regard.[97]

[95] BYOaudio, promotional video, http://www.byoaudio.com/playv/WbQ6tkos (last visited Jul. 27, 2008).
[96] US Human Rights Network, Web site, http://www.ushrnetwork.org/ (last visited May 1, 2007).
[97] Id.

The statement reveals an explicit commitment to challenging American exceptionalism and adherences to East/West dichotomies, and at the same time presents a noticeable contrast with the essential identity–invoking strategy adopted by the antitorture campaign and the INGOs involved with it.

Through such coalitions, American NGOs forged an unprecedented effort to prepare NGO shadow reports to be presented at the United States' appearance before the United Nations' Human Rights Committee and Committee Against Torture bodies charged with the task of evaluating state parties' compliance with corresponding treaty obligations. As Eric Tars of the National Law Center for Poverty and Homelessness (a member of the US Human Rights Network) explained, larger NGOs accustomed to maneuvering within the international regime connected with the grassroots groups who were grappling with issues such as prisoners' rights, economic rights, immigrants' rights, and so on, on the ground but were not necessarily familiar with the international framework. The central organizers of the shadow report process were Global Rights, the US Human Rights Network, the ACLU, Penal Reform International, the American University Washington College of Law Center for Human Rights and Humanitarian Law, and the Bringing Human Rights Home Network. Through e-mails and conference calls, they assembled a group of 142 organizations that would participate in the process. In May 2006, a delegation of twenty advocates attended the Committee Against Torture proceedings, and the following July a delegation of sixty advocates attended the Human Rights Committee proceedings, which Tars pointed out "was certainly a greater interest than had ever been expressed from the United States."[98]

Although the groups with domestic human rights agendas clearly had to share the spotlight with INGO partners focusing on American policies permitting torture and curtailing due process rights in the proclaimed American "War on Terror" (and it was these highly charged issues that attracted the greatest interest in the proceedings, even among members of the UN committee), according to Tars, the domestic groups were able to generate more interest, attention, and coverage of their issues than they had anticipated. More importantly, the process brought a number of small, local, grassroots groups into "the human rights tent."[99] Jamil Dakwar of the ACLU Human Rights Program also spoke of subtle changes in the American government's disposition as civil society groups continued engaging the international processes. According to Dakwar, the United States representatives conceded more in the Convention on the Elimination of all Forms of Racial Discrimination (CERD) proceedings held in 2008 than they had in the earlier CAT

---

[98] Telephone interview with Eric Tars, human rights attorney, National Law Center on Homelessness and Poverty, in Washington DC (Feb. 15, 2007).
[99] Id.

proceedings. "The U.S. was more straightforward in acknowledging failures. They admitted that all migrants should have human rights. It may be a statement with no follow-up, but that is what you start with."[100]

Another major hurdle domestic activists traditionally faced was that the State Department was the only U.S. governmental body engaging with the international framework, and their efforts took place in a virtual vacuum. In other words, except for limited contact to gather information to compile in US reports for UN bodies, the State Department took few steps by way of coordinating or communicating with other agencies within the government regarding how the international rights regime and strategies for its domestic implementation. Following the two initial UN proceedings, the coalition was able to secure an unprecedented meeting:

We asked them to bring together all the different agencies who had participated in giving the information into the US report and we could have an initial conversation and, more importantly, get introduced to the people in each of those agencies, who would at least not look at us like we were totally crazy when we were telling them that they have human rights obligations under these treaties. It was just really getting the contacts that was the most important part. We had a short two-hour conversation. We brought up issues that were sort of highlighting the concluding observations that we found particularly relevant and try to figure out who would be the best people to talk to, to work further. Now we are working on individual meetings with individual agencies. Criminal justice and police brutality oriented groups are meeting with the Civil Rights division of the Department of Justice. The committee recommended the federal government put out federal guidelines on the use of tasers, which is now completely up to the state or even locally based police officers. They recommend the use of the UN minimum standards for prisons... in many ways its things that the federal government wouldn't even object to doing. It's just a matter of actually pushing them to do it and to perceive it as a need and as a problem. This process can really be useful in that aspect because it gives a little bit more legitimacy to the claims of the activists and gives us an opportunity to bring it up and push it at the federal level.[101]

For many of the government bureaucrats involved the meeting was a learning process. As Tars recounts, one of the activists from New Orleans working on Hurricane Katrina–related issues was pushing for Federal Emergency Management Agency (FEMA) to recognize and follow the UN Guiding Principles on Internal Displacement. Having the principles institutionalized would address an array of pertinent subissues. The FEMA representative attending the meeting sat and listened. Then, the activist asked her directly, "are you aware of the UN Guiding Principles" and she said "no."[102] She did, however, also express interest in looking at it, now that she had become aware of the international instrument.

[100] See Jamil Dakwar, supra note 89.
[101] See Eric Tars, supra note 98.
[102] Id.

The situation is illustrative of the lack of any government infrastructure for disseminating or informing government agencies of international
obligation or resources. Such meetings have the potential to provide advocates with avenues to counter the existing structure. As Tars pointed out, the
group was pushing the State Department out of their comfort zone of merely
going through the formalistic motions of reporting to UN bodies. Although
much of the meeting focused on domestic issues apart from the torture and
detainee treatment contests, it can be indirectly linked to September 11th.
Undoubtedly, at some level it materialized as a strategic concession born out
of the need to quell the extensive shaming and criticism of US human rights
commitments in the post–September 11th era.

Another small but potentially promising inroad toward American human
rights institutionalization emerged from the creation of a new Senate Judiciary Subcommittee on Human Rights and the Law. In 2006, with little
fanfare and almost as an afterthought in the end of a speech almost exclusively dedicated to Bush administration rights infringements in the post–
September 11th era, Patrick Leahy, the soon-to-be chairman of the Senate
Judiciary Committee, announced his intention to create a Human Rights
Subcommittee. Neither Leahy nor Dick Durbin, the Illinois senator whom
Leahy has appointed to chair the body, described it as a forum to take up
US human rights violations. Durbin, however, exhibited an inclination to
at least incorporate some scrutiny of US violations by indicating that, in
addition to hearings on the situation of child soldiers in Africa or genocide
in Darfur, the subcommittee was considering hearings on the United States'
frequent post–September 11th resort to the practice of "extraordinary renditions" – the US policy of sending detainees to countries known to have little
qualms with torture for interrogations. On September 21, 2007, as chairman
of the Subcommittee on Human Rights and the Law, Dick Durbin also held
a Capitol Hill briefing on torture and "enhanced interrogation techniques,"
considering a joint report by Human Rights First and Physicians for Human
Rights entitled "Leave No Marks: Enhanced Interrogation Techniques and
the Risk of Criminality."

This limited and tentative opening for considering American human rights
violations committed abroad seemingly holds little promise for expanding
the reach of international human rights norms inside American borders, at
least in the foreseeable future. When I asked Durbin why he thought the
international human rights framework was not being applied to domestic social justice and rights issues, such as American prison conditions, he
seemed confused by the question. Assuming that I was asking simply about
why prisoners' rights were not considered more seriously in America, he
offered his "trashcan theory" – that people want to put what they consider society's trash on the curb and not worry about it. I clarified that I
was not so much interested in American attitudes toward prisoners but the
prospects of applying the international framework domestically. Grasping

the question, the senator shook his head, "No, we should, but we are still far from that."[103] In a similar vein, Leahy revealed that many of his colleagues questioned him about the need to create a human rights subcommittee in the Judiciary Committee (which because of international law's traditional marginalization is viewed as purely a domestic institution) instead of the Foreign Relations Committee where they thought it would be more appropriately placed. Thus, the subcommittee's establishment at once captures the rootedness and persistence of American exceptionalism and power vis-à-vis international human rights norms and presents new possibilities for transcending the same. After all, the United States Senate does now have a new Human Rights and the Law Subcommittee on one of the most influential "domestic" committees within the powerful institution.

There are also a few isolated signs of the institutionalization of human rights within the American media. For example, in fall 2007 *The Washington Post* created and began regularly featuring on its Web site a blog called "Rights Watchers" led by Keneth Roth and Reed Brody of Human Rights Watch. The blog posed a variety of international human rights questions, many of which revolved around American human rights practices – primarily "War on Terror" related but occasionally also inwardly focused. Topics have included, "should administration officials be prosecuted for torture," "are US contractors getting away with murder [in Iraq]," and "US sex offender laws may do more harm than good." A July 28, 2008, post about an International Court of Justice ruling on a Texas capital punishment case was titled "Death Row Dilemma: Is It OK for American States to Ignore International Law?" Interestingly, many of the reader comments to the post make direct references to the American treatment of international law in the post–September 11th era.

Finally, there is a sense of newfound relevance and engagement with international law in American courts and law schools alike. Many of the prominent detainee rights and torture cases that made their way through American courts fused questions of constitutional and international human rights or humanitarian law. American judges and lawyers had to consider questions of executive and commander-in-chief power of the president under the Constitution alongside US treaty obligations under the Geneva Conventions and the Convention Against Torture. The questions presented forced constitutional and international lawyers into unprecedented dialog and collaborations with each other. Consequently, international law that was previously viewed as a separate legal field with limited relevance to core legal issues in the United States increasingly found its place in the center of American legal contests and institutions. As Wendy Patten pointed out, American law schools that had previously treated international law and

---

[103] Interview with Dick Durbin, Chairman, Senate Judiciary Committee Subcommittee on Human Rights and the Law, in Washington, DC (Feb. 27, 2007).

human rights as a boutique, elective, or specialty field of study followed suit.[104] In 2006, Harvard Law School introduced a reform of the required first-year curriculum for its students; one of three new courses of study adopted was international and comparative law.[105]

Each of these areas of American human rights infrastructure development hold significant long-term promise provided they endure and continue to evolve. Perhaps the most important among them has been the new inward focus of American human rights NGOs. As Julie Mertus has noted,

> The impact of the Bush administration on human rights at home has been devastating, but it has served as a wake-up call to many US-based human rights advocates who have previously paid little attention to the abuses at their doorstep. From the largest and most mainstream organizations to the smallest and most radical, human rights organizations are finally moving at least some of their activities closer to home. The US human rights and civil rights movements may have emerged on separate paths, but now they are forging new linkages with one another, and with broader international movements.[106]

Alongside this assessment of the campaign's achievements, including the significant strides taken by the campaign toward overcoming the East/West geography of human rights and the power dynamics inscribed within it, a number of critiques also emerge.

THE PERSISTENCE OF HIERARCHY: A CRITIQUE

In large part, the strategies pursued by the torture campaign accomplished the improbable feat of compelling consequential change within a domestic environment imbued with nationalist sentiment and militarism as foremost analogy for America's global preeminence. Yet despite their various successes on the domestic front, the road traveled also held wider implications – both promising and troubling. Although constructivism recognizes the mobilization of domestic norms and discourses as empirically pivotal to human rights campaigns, the literature has to date not ventured into substantial normative analysis of the frames deployed and their larger implications, beyond specific and immediate human rights objectives. In other words, because it has a tendency to assume the domestic arguments, coalitions, and frames used to further human rights agendas are either normatively neutral or normatively consistent with human rights paradigms (i.e., not power laden) as long as they espouse a pro–human rights end, constructivism offers little direction for more critically assessing or weighing the strategies pursued.

[104] *See* Wendy Patten, *supra* note 88.
[105] Harvard Law School, *Harvard Law School Faculty Unanimously Approves First Year Curricular Reform*, Oct. 6, 2006, http://www.law.harvard.edu/news/2006/10/06_curriculum.php.
[106] Julie Mertus, *Human Rights and Civil Society in a New Age of American Exceptionalism, in* HUMAN RIGHTS IN THE "WAR ON TERROR" (Richard A. Wilson ed., 2005).

Framing and shaming strategies adopted are thus rarely dissected to better understand their effects on global hierarchies. For this reason, I turn to insights from critical human rights theory in laying out two intertwined critiques.

My aim is to approach evaluating the impact of campaign strategies from another angle – one that transcends the here and now. Where appropriate, I also hope to highlight instances of activists' own internalization of the human rights hierarchies challenged in this book. At the same time, I am acutely aware of the innumerable dilemmas, limited choices, and invariable trade-offs with which the campaign was forced to contend. Thus, I attempt to ground and qualify the critique with context and countervailing considerations as much as possible. I find it most fitting to direct the critical assessment toward American human rights NGOs and, to a lesser degree, the media. This is because it is assumed that they have more vested in promoting human rights as an emancipatory enterprise and, as a result, bear a particular responsibility for considering the longer-term and global consequences of their strategies. If they are persuaded, it is up to them to lead campaign partners in adopting a revised approach.

Finally, themes closely related to the two critiques presented here are further developed in Chapter 5, which focuses on the post–September 11th era's lessons for advancing the human rights project. The discussion at hand formulates the critiques most directly stemming from the initiatives presented in this chapter. Its intent is to introduce examples of key dilemmas and tensions brought out during the post–September 11th era to allow the reader to keep the themes in mind as they work their way to the final chapter where they are taken up more broadly.

"This Is about Us, Not about Them," Revisited

The "this is about us, not about them" message of the campaign was not only a frame it could also be considered a rather precise depiction of much of the American debate surrounding torture and detainee rights issues. Those engaged posed questions of how the pictures and policies behind them reflect on American values, their potential for endangering American POWs in the future, how they compromised American interests by fostering further anti-American sentiment, and whether torture is an effective interrogation method. In other words, the concerns raised were limited to the consequences of the administration's policies for Americans and their interests, perpetuating orientalist and dehumanizing portrayals of the Arab or Muslim victims of American human rights violations.

Particularly, when invoked by congressional leaders, the Orientalism implicit in "it's about us, not about them" and similar formulations such as "we have become them" were difficult to miss. As it was constructed, the argument maintained that rights are to be upheld not because detainees are entitled to inherent rights and respect of their dignity but because Americans lay claim to a superior tradition and must not be led astray from it. In other words, many of the voices challenging Bush administration policies appeared to be more preoccupied with the betrayal of Western values than the injustices suffered by detainees. Other tropes designated average American soldiers as the primary victims of the injustice stemming from Bush administration policies. Ultimately an American soldier like Ian Fishback proved to be a more compelling victim than a nameless Iraqi or Afghan who may have been wrongfully detained or subjected to torture and abuse. Often, conservatives who invoked "this is about us, not about them" conflated depictions of detainees whose innocence or guilt had yet to be determined with "a bunch of rouge thug murderers."[107]

Although the disposition of both the media and NGOs was more refined, save a few notable exceptions, they cannot be credited with taking sufficient steps toward countering the discourses that rendered "War on Terror" detainees the faceless and dehumanized Other. It should be noted, however, that as human rights discourses slowly gained in legitimacy and standing, it became "safer" and more commonplace for advocates and the media to reflect victims' voices and stories. For example, a 2006 NPR report featured the voices of several Guantanamo detainees attempting to defend themselves at their Combatant Status Review Tribunals.[108]

Finally, the "this is about us, not about them" formulation and other appeals to a distinct American identity or set of values tied up in rights served as a double-edged sword in one more important respect. Although it was a useful device for linking human rights norms with existing domestic norms, by invoking it so extensively, the campaign was not entirely successful in breaking free from a narrative that placed the United States above other, particularly non-Western, states as a global "human rights leader." The underlying premise of the formulation was that the United States' human rights concerns are limited to the post–September 11th period and foreign detainee issues. The disregard for international norm was exceptional, a mere aberration. Having been led astray from its essential self, the country would be able to redeem the lost identity simply by repudiating the Bush administration's assault. As Human Rights Watch's Tom Malinowsky noted:

The myth that we are perfect at home is a useful myth when it comes to convincing people to do the right thing about Guantanamo or torture in Iraq, because you can say "well, this isn't who we are." Well, actually it is, but that's not helpful.[109]

[107] See Lindsay Graham, *supra* note 30. It is important to note that other actors, including a number of Democratic members of Congress and certainly human rights NGOs, as well as the media, voiced concern for detainees' rights. Further, the adoption of the Orientalist discourse can be a function of meeting political pressures from the dominant discourse or constituents as well as personal beliefs held.

[108] National Public Radio, NPR News, *Tapes Provide First Glimpse of Secret Gitmo Panel*, Nov. 21, 2006, http://www.npr.org/templates/story/story.php?storyId=6514923.

[109] See Tom Malinowsky, *supra* note 4.

In the last sentence, Malinowsky reference was to the occurrence of abuse in American prisons similar to that which occurred in Abu Ghraib, pointing to an important domestic trapping of the message beyond its international implications – by invoking the frame, advocates tend to foreclose avenues through which they could promote the use of the international regime in approaching domestic rights issues, such as conditions of rape and abuse and even cases of torture in domestic prisons. In several interviews, activists, including those representing Human Rights First and Human Rights Watch, indicated that they did not see many openings for using "War on Terror" abuses occurring abroad as back-door routes for approaching human rights violations taking place within the United States. Eric Tars echoed the sentiment in response to a question on the impact of September 11th developments on the efforts of the US Human Rights Network with which he was involved:

The language of human rights was actually being used more, talking about torture, the Geneva Conventions, talking about the Convention Against Torture.... That kind of stuff is actually helpful. The fact that the Geneva Conventions were being mentioned on a regular basis and legislation was being put forward the terms of the treaty. That conversation was useful and I think it has helped the movement. It helped people start to realize that human rights are applicable to the United States, but at the same time, much of the focus has been on abuses abroad and Abu Ghraib, Guantanamo, and there's still certainly not any type of public consensus that the same type of standards that we're trying to apply to Guantanamo or Abu Ghraib, should be applied in domestic prisons. I think there is a general assumption that American prisoners are treated more humanely and if they aren't it's a domestic policy problem and the international standards wouldn't necessarily have anything to do with it. But that's kind of the leap we are trying to make and we've been trying to make. So it's a moving target. It's something we're working on, but we're definitely not there yet.[110]

The "this is about us, not about them" formulation presents a major obstacle for the realization of precisely the leap Tars, his colleagues, and even the INGO advocates invoking the frame aspire to make.

All of these concerns of course stand against the reality that invoking a sense of pride in a dominant identity or promising a return to a lost essential identity are among the few effective avenues available to activists for bringing human rights discourses into settings where opposing norms pervade social and political consciousness. For example, it is common for Middle Eastern human rights or women's rights activists to call for a return to principles of justice and human dignity as the essence of Islam, to contest conservative visions of Islam or Islamic values, or assert that human rights principles are rooted in Islam as a means of furthering their rights objectives. As I will take up in Chapter 4, there are always risks and trappings to such strategies; yet those who adopt it often do so because they see few

---

[110] See Eric Tars, *supra* note 98.

alternatives. Whether the same argument can be made in the present case is debatable. It is difficult to say with any degree of certainty that the campaign would have been able to penetrate American consciousness to the degree that it did had "it's not about them, it's about us" not been so strongly asserted. I will defer the difficult task of balancing these opposing factors until it is more broadly reexamined in Chapter 5.

The Trappings of Entwining Human Rights and Military Agendas

A subsequent critique involves revisiting the campaign's close alliance with high-ranking retired military officials. It is common for human rights activists to invite sympathetic or reform-minded members of governments, political parties, social groups, or religious, civil, or state institutions responsible for rights violations to advocate a human rights position to their respective groups on behalf of human rights forces. Again, this strategy is frequently pursued by Islamic feminists and other women's rights activists in Muslim societies, who enlist the voices and authority of male clerics espousing moderate or modernist interpretations of Islamic jurisprudence to advocate positions that can advance their women's rights agendas. Their reasons for seeking out such interventions are clear. First, the intermediaries approach those committing violations from a considerably greater position of power relative to the rights activists and, second, those with the power to decide whether human rights norms will be upheld are more likely to be persuaded by someone they consider an insider or authoritative leader with shared ideological commitments or aims. In particular, persuading authoritative voices from within military, security, or law enforcement apparatus to endorse human rights practices or positions has been a key objective of innumerable human rights campaigns worldwide because of these institutions' enormous power and propensities to carry out rights abuses. Viewed within these parameters, the American Campaign's turn to high-ranking military leaders willing to publicly advocate a human rights position seems unexceptional, much less objectionable. What better way to move international law from the realm of the "weak" to a position of strength than to have the force of military voices widely accorded legitimacy within prevailing identity politics behind it? Finally, after the McCain and Gonzales initiatives, military allies have proved to be invaluable partners for human rights advocates continued efforts, more so than most of the congressional leaders who took part in the first two initiatives. Human Rights First has enlisted the active participation of their military network in meetings with television producers responsible for glorifying depictions of torture, in producing antitorture training and awareness materials for soldiers, and in initiating dialogs with 2008 presidential candidates on American torture and detainee treatment policies. Moreover, when Barack Obama signed his executive orders to have the Guantanamo Bay detention facility shut down and to reverse much of the Bush administration's torture and detainee treatment policies, it was this group of retired military officials who stood in the background behind him and later advocated the new policies in the media.

Viewed from yet another angle, the generals' act can also be tagged as confronting power. Large numbers of military officials (particularly JAG lawyers) advocating the implementation of Geneva Conventions protections and denouncing gradual introduction of torture and cruel and inhumane treatment into military protocol had been repeatedly overruled, marginalized, and silenced by the Bush administration. Thus, this group of military leaders' highly unlikely and unanticipated defiance of the Bush administration could be interpreted as an act of agency – a challenge to precisely the type of action devoid of agency demanded by the civilian leaders who send them to war and ascribed to them by society once they put on military uniforms. The generals were, after all, traversing a considerable terrain in advocating a human rights position within a dominant culture that constructed them in starkly contrasting terms. Further, figures such as Rear Admiral John Hutson, whose congressional testimony is presented in Chapter 1, were at times highly effective in making the legal and rights-based case for upholding humane standards of detainee treatment.

Despite all of these layers of context, the human rights/military association of the Gonzales confirmation and McCain amendment battles warrants further scrutiny because of the existence of one more key layer of context. The alliance took shape in an era colored by a strong nexus between the domestic hegemony of militarism within American culture, American global military dominance, and profound human suffering resulting from American misadventures with war. Human rights groups sought to challenge specific policies (in part) borne out of this nexus; yet, by invoking the very symbols, metaphors, and institutions of American power and preeminence, they also risked perpetuating it.

Threading together references to the alliance from several field interviews provides a glimpse into the dynamics at play. In explaining why the interventions from the former generals were so persuasive, one congressional staffer informed me, "These are not bleeding heart liberals. These are, by and large, Republican, hawkish, military-mindsets and they are out there saying we've got to have this. That's persuasive to a lot of people."[111] Avi Cover's description of how the collaboration came to fruition was similarly provocative:

So, we, for a long time, were cultivating these individuals and it really began with finding one, just one, and through his network of contacts, we gain some credibility and they can vouch for us and say, "this isn't some crazy fringe group. If you put your name together with them you're not going to be losing your credibility in the

[111] *See* congressional staffer, *supra* note 18.

military." It's a very interesting dance because a lot of these military guys, they work now . . . in the private military industrial complex, so they can't be perceived as some wacko lefty or it would impair their current livelihood.[112]

It is also worth noting that Cover was reflective but not particularly troubled when pointing out that even though his organization arranged for the former military officials' various letters, Human Rights First's name remained largely absent from publicized versions. Finally, Tom Malinowsky's assertion that "particularly with people with a military background, what worked was appealing to their identity, what made them proud of what they were doing" was also revealing.[113]

There are no doubt consequences of U.S.-based human rights INGOs inviting military "hawks" to serve as the public face of their initiatives or permitting the antitorture position to be presented as a matter of military strategy and pride rather than as a human rights imperative (as the absence of Human Rights First's name on the military letters drafted tends to do). It is difficult to invoke pride in what the American military does to persuade leaders to reject torture without also further solidifying or promoting the celebration of militarism constantly infused into American culture and consciousness by political elites, the media, movies, sports events, and so on.[114] Thus, another face of the human rights partnership with the cadre of retired military leaders is one of NGOs not only failing to challenge but also playing a role in furthering domestic constructions and culture legitimating, privileging, or promoting American militarism, albeit in forms compliant with particular provisions of human rights and humanitarian law. Meaning is frequently constituted by symbolism. Aligning with and invoking the status of individuals so closely linked with an institution so synonymous with projections of American power and preeminence at some level conveys at best a failure to challenge and at worst an unspoken acceptance of both the hegemony of militarism within American culture and American military hegemony abroad. The reliance on the military officials seemed to concede that support for war is patriotic and then goes on to clarify that it is not American wars to

---

[112] *See* Avi Cover, *supra* note 10.

[113] *See* Tom Malinowsky, *supra* note 4.

[114] Ken Cunningham, *Permanent War? The Domestic Hegemony of the New American Militarism*, 24:6 NEW POL. SCI. (Dec. 2004). As Ken Cunningham contends, militarism should be understood in structural, material, and cultural terms: "It is a set of practices, policies and institutions and an array of material instruments and artifacts (bombs, tanks, planes, bases, uniforms), and it is a set of attitudes, beliefs and values (i.e. a cultural complex)." He goes on to catalog a number of common notions that accompany militarism:

> . . . uncritical patriotism, simplistic, Manichean thinking (e.g. "good" v. the "evil-doers"), patriarchy, political "Realism," and techno-instrumental thinking (e.g. that difficult, complex social/political problems can be solved by the "correct" application of technology – "more bombs" – and instrumental rationality – improved "cost-benefit analysis," better "deployment of force structure," more efficient utilization of intelligence assets," etc., etc.).

which human rights forces object; rather, it is the use of torture and denial of due process within those wars that are problematic. A move in this direction has on occasion been even more explicitly made. For example, among the honorees at Human Rights First's 2007 annual awards ceremony were the retired military leaders with whom the INGO had closely collaborated on various torture initiatives. A media press release publicizing the awards states:

> The retired generals and admirals, including speakers Gen. Joseph Hoar and Rear Adm. John Hutson, were recognized for their leadership in bringing prisoner treatment back into line with the Geneva Conventions and ensuring that torture is never again a part of U.S. policy. In April 2007, they began meeting individually with presidential candidates to discuss the need for policies that honor the values American servicemembers fight to protect.[115]

The last seven words of the statement concede and perpetuate the very construction advanced by American political elites that the American military's overarching purpose is to further rights and freedom in the world.

Further questions arise surrounding the impact of the coalition on human rights NGOs' own culture, priorities, and advocacy. Only one of the campaign participants interviewed revealed that she had grappled with rights groups' turn to "national security" discourses and symbols, and her concern was largely borne out of discussions undertaken through her work with a coalition of domestic grassroots groups prior to joining Human Rights Watch. The overall absence of noticeable unease and introspection over the potential negative effects of the considerable reliance on military officials during the campaign is significant. As I will discuss in Chapter 5, American human rights and civil rights advocates have come together and mounted an impressive campaign to confront the Bush administration's torture policies; yet relative to this effort, they have been more reserved in challenging the horrors and denial of human dignity resulting from Iraqi civilians' lived experience of war. This is in part attributable to how human rights mandates have traditionally been delineated. Even so, it is fair to ask whether military coalitions of the nature of those forged during the Gonzales and McCain initiatives can have any impact on a human rights INGO's ability to highlight the human toll of American wars, for example, through the need to establish non–"crazy fringe group" credibility to sustain the relationship? Put differently, does the human rights NGO/military coalition run the risk of moving participating human rights groups toward complacency or acceptance of the normalization of American wars?

---

[115] Human Rights First, *HRF Honors Iranian Women's Leader, TV's "Criminal Minds" and Retired Military Leaders at Annual Awards Dinner*, Oct. 16, 2007, http://www .humanrightsfirst.org/media/hrd/2007/alert/375/.

This critique does not challenge American human rights NGOs' decision to elicit the aid of military officials categorically. If, as constructivist analysis would affirm, human rights agendas are well served when advocates cooperate and engage with government officials who currently wield substantially greater power in shaping both human rights policies and waging war, then working closely with military forces should be equally appropriate. Further, as all of the campaign members cited above make clear, bringing in military officials as intermediaries was a very effective and innovative strategy at a time when human rights voices were largely marginalized. Thus, it is not so much the association in and of itself but the nature and boundaries of the relationship that presents the most pressing need for re-examination. The critique is invariably tied up with a question regarding the degree to which American human rights NGOs should become entangled in the spirit, symbolism, and dominant rationales for American militarism.

CONCLUSION

In the post–September 11th era, a full-scale American human rights campaign focused exclusively on American human rights practices took shape. The mobilization and collaboration among American human rights NGOs, the media, and select congressional leaders on a domestic human rights front was unprecedented in recent times. Though it did not achieve its immediate legislative and policy goals, the American human rights campaign canvassed played a critical role in bringing human rights norms and international law into American political consciousness and discourses. The understanding of international human rights norms in the American imagination as intended largely for others was in many ways unsettled. This evolution in discourse and consciousness gave way to the development of a limited American human rights infrastructure with the potential to continue countering American exceptionalism in the human rights field even after the dust from Bush administration "War on Terror" human rights practices has settled. Still, despite its formidable gains, in several key respects, the campaign continued to reinforce American power and exceptionalism vis-à-vis human rights, demonstrating an imperative for human rights advocates to more critically reassess key elements of the strategies they pursued.

THREE

The Middle Eastern Gaze on American Human Rights Commitments

Five years after September 11th, vast quantities of ink and analysis had been devoted to Western-based efforts to either uncover or challenge American exercises of power in the Middle East. Yet the other side of the equation – the various forms of Middle Eastern resistance to the era's Abu Ghraibs and Guantanamos on the one hand and deployments of human rights and democracy rhetoric as pretext for military interventions in the region on the other – has largely gone unnoticed. Despite being at times entangled in local governments' or opposition forces' more self-serving rebukes of American policies, currents within Middle Eastern civil society endeavored to pose a variety of challenges to the United States' contradictory human rights course in the post–September 11th era. As a result, for the first time in their recent history, Americans were conscious of an intense returned Middle Eastern gaze in the human rights field. Through its focus on the Middle Eastern answer to American human rights transgressions and appropriations, this chapter provides a glimpse into yet another dimension of the reconfiguring of global human rights' geography that has been onging since September 11th – the addition of mobilizations, challenges, and critiques directed from the Middle East to the United States to the preexisting West to East traffic.

MIDDLE EASTERN INITIATIVES CHALLENGING AMERICAN HUMAN RIGHTS VIOLATIONS

Prior to September 11th, American and Middle Eastern human rights exchanges generally followed a set itinerary closely adhering to broad precepts and assumptions of the East/West geography of human rights. American-based INGOs investigated human rights conditions and allegations of violations in Middle Eastern countries, sometimes through collaborations with local Middle Eastern NGOs. Seminars, lectures, and conferences on particular human rights conditions in a Middle Eastern context were held at American universities, NGOs, and policy forums, occasionally featuring victims' ghastly accounts of the injustices they endured. From time to time, protests were organized in front of Middle Eastern embassies and consulates in Western countries to highlight particularly egregious human rights violations. American INGOs issued reports and put out statements condemning the violations outlined, demanding that the Middle Eastern state in question comply with its international legal obligations and recommending that United States compel compliance through various diplomatic and/or economic pressures. U.S.-based NGOs attempted to stir American public opinion to prompt American citizens to take up the particular human rights concerns with government representatives and insist that the American government act in accordance with the human rights INGOs' recommendations. The American human rights groups themselves spearheaded lobbying efforts to the same ends – American interventions or condemnations of the human rights violations taking place. Middle Eastern human rights issues also received varying levels of coverage or investigation in American media. In the rare cases that the political space existed for it, Middle Eastern media covered the reports issued by Western INGOs regarding Middle Eastern rights violations. Middle Eastern government officials in turn took up defending their practices and reiterating their sincere commitment to upholding human rights.

Throughout the process, the human rights violations being detailed were often explicitly or implicitly linked to Middle Eastern culture, whereas American culture was viewed as neutral, even nonexistent, based on a construal of culture as rooted exclusively in ancient customs and traditions and divorced from modernity. The Middle Eastern commitments to cultural and religious relativism and the American commitment to rational universalism in application of human rights were assumed. As a result, the interactions were highly imbued with power dynamics surrounding who had the authority to wage human rights criticisms of whom, who was answerable to whom, and whose practices were open to scrutiny. Accordingly, Middle Eastern human rights forces generally only looked inward toward domestic human rights conditions and, although they did pose critiques of American appropriations and alliances with repressive regimes in the region, they never took on organized initiatives or mobilizations directed at American human rights practices. As critical scholars have noted, the flow of assessments, organizing, evaluation, and judgment went in one direction.

In the post–September 11th era, this swarm of activity that had become the staple of contemporary human rights activism also began to take shape in the reverse direction. Although there remained a considerable discrepancy in scale, Middle Eastern human rights advocates, media, and governments took up the issue of American human rights violations, rendering human rights a primary site of struggle during the era and the ensuing human rights engagements an unprecedented two-way encounter.

Civil Society Mobilizations

In January 2007, the fifth anniversary of Guantanamo was met with a coordinated round of global protests. In Yemen, a human rights advocate and academic I was interviewing handed me a flyer for a press conference coordinated by two of the country's leading human rights NGOs, the National Organization for Defending Rights and Freedoms (HOOD) and the Human Rights Training and Information Center, to be held the next day, January 18th. After the interview, I called Khaled Alanesi, my contact at HOOD, to ask if I could attend. "You are welcome," he replied. Several NGO leaders, a recently released Guantanamo detainee named Mohammad Ahmed al-Asadi, the mother of a detainee still at Guantanamo, and the father of a detainee released from Guantanamo but being held by Yemeni authorities delivered passionate speeches, weaving together condemnations of American policies, emotional appeals, and invocations of human rights and international law. The family members held up large framed photos of their sons. HOOD passed out a flyer containing information about the prison, the number of detainees it held, and mobilizations against the prison's operation. A representative of another NGO, the Democracy School, passed out a color flyer. On one side of the flyer were displayed various pictures suggesting detainee abuse at the facility. On the other side were two depictions of the Statute of Liberty; one was accompanied with an American flag displayed plainly and the words *Freedom of Expression* and the other accompanied by an American flag over which the electric wires of a prison fence were transposed and the words *freedom to torture*. After the statements, scores of reporters posed questions and conducted interviews. The commemoration was only the most recent attempt by Yemeni civil society to challenge American human rights violations following September 11th. HOOD and other Yemeni human rights organizations had in the past held numerous press conferences, protests, and vigils, sometimes in front of the U.S. embassy. A July 2006 protest in Sana'a had drawn over one thousand participants.

In April 2004, Sana'a had hosted the first of four international conferences devoted to detentions and abuse taking place at Guantanamo Bay. The conference was organized by Amnesty International and HOOD. This time, American and other Western human rights lawyers and activists traveled to the Middle East to convene and discuss strategies for mobilization against American (not Middle Eastern) human rights infractions with Middle Eastern counterparts and Guantanamo detainees' families. Of the five themes on the conference agenda, two pertained to affirming/upholding the universality of human rights, with the clear implication that American human rights practices were rooted in relativism and exceptionalism. The conference's keynote speaker was the Yemeni human rights minister, Amat Al-Alim Al-Soswa, who condemned American practices using opaque but nonetheless unmistakable shaming devices:

Progress and civilization must not be measured only by scientific, technological, and military progress. They must be measured by the human conscience, the degree of disapproval of human rights violations, and by what we can do to bring human sufferings to an end.[1]

The outcome of the initial conference was the "Sana'a Appeal" issued by Amnesty International and the creation of a Yemeni committee directed by leading Yemeni human rights activists with a sole objective of investigating U.S. abuses in Guantanamo and Abu Ghraib. The second conference along the same theme was again held in Sana'a, a third was held in Bahrain, and the final one was held in England. The conferences received coverage in local Yemeni media. Beyond the fact of the coverage itself, the familiar human rights devices and lexicon employed both by the media and human rights activists they cited were noteworthy. One publication reported:

Human rights activists in Yemen condemned the USA's military trial in Guantanamo Bay of two Yemenis. The trial of four prisoners, also including a Sudanese, and an Australian, started on Tuesday and is being widely criticized throughout Yemen for not meeting the minimum standards of a fair trial.

"How can we expect the trial of Guantanamo prisoners to be legal if evidence is not shown and defendants are not given the opportunity to hire lawyers?" asked Khalid Al-Anisi of the National Organization for Defending Rights & Freedoms (HOOD) in Sana'a. "We have been working closely with international human rights organizations throughout the world to come up with a solid statement denouncing such actions done in the name of justice. What justice is this?"[2]

What is remarkable about the article is its unequivocal assertion of a Yemeni voice and authority to assess American Guantanamo policies and their correspondence with "minimum standards of a fair trial." It is the Yemeni human rights lawyer who authoritatively condemns the actions of the United States and expresses outrage over American human rights transgressions. Another Yemeni media account of the series of conferences is equally revealing:

In liaison with Amnesty International, the Sana'a committee for the defense of Guantanamo detainees is to organize a conference in London in December. Senior lawyers and human rights activists will take part to discuss detainee conditions in Guantanamo prison. Chairman of the committee, lawyer Mohammed Naji Allaw, told

---

[1] Amnesty International, press release, *End Human Rights Scandal in Guantanamo and Other Places*, Apr. 11, 2004, http://web.amnesty.org/library/Index/ENGPOL300172004? open&of=ENG-USA.

[2] *Guantanamo Trial of 2 Yemenis Unfair*, YEMEN TIMES, Aug. 24, 2005, http://www .yementimes.com/article.shtml?i=767&p=front&a=2.

26 Sept.net that the conference would hear testimonies of released detainees. A photographic exhibition will also be held to portray the suffering of the detainees, he said.[3]

The piece signals an approach that humanizes and privileges the detainees and their stories, somewhat in contrast to the course taken by civil society actors spearheading the American campaign domestically.

On various occasions, other Middle Eastern human rights organizations similarly committed their efforts toward challenging American human rights practices. For example, following the suicide of three Guantanamo Bay detainees in June 2006, the Arab Organization for Human Rights called for the immediate closure of the facility, condemned the United States Department of Defense's rejection of an independent probe into the incident, criticized American officials' comments that the suicides were a publicity stunt, and called for bringing to justice those responsible for abuses at Guantanamo and other American detention facilities.[4] The Bahrain Center for Human Rights staged several public protests and vigils in Manama (which included activists dressing in orange jumpsuits and wearing handcuffs), provided free screenings to a documentary on Guantanamo, monitored and publicly commented on judicial developments in U.S. courts, traveled to New York to meet with American lawyers representing Bahraini detainees, and called on international organizations and Bahraini authorities to urgently pursue diplomatic efforts to free the detainees.

In addition to reporting on local NGOs' activities, Middle Eastern media often took up the issue of American human rights practices on their own. Opinion pieces would evaluate American actions through an international law rubric:

The issue is whether the fighters should be treated in line with the requirements of the Third Geneva Convention. That Convention is an example of the humanitarian values that the US is fighting to uphold. So it was shocking to learn that the US Defense Department had decided to ignore it by classifying the captives not as prisoners of war, but as "unlawful combatants." This arbitrary decision has the effect of depriving the prisoners of their rights.

But how can the US reach this conclusion, when Article 4Ai of the Convention includes among POWs: "Members of the armed forces of a Party to the conflict, as well as members of militias or volunteer corps forming part of such armed forces"? This seems to cover both the Taliban and Al Qaeda.[5]

[3] *Sana'a Committee for Defense of Guantanamo Detainees to Hold Meet in UK in Dec.*, YEMEN OBSERVER, Jul. 30, 2005.

[4] *Arab Rights Body Calls for Immediate Closure of Guantanamo Bay Detention Center*, MENA, Jun. 15, 2006.

[5] *The Problem of the Taliban Prisioners*, DOHA GULF TIMES, Jan. 17, 2002.

They also published scathing editorials employing the same shaming techniques used in Western editorials condemning Middle Eastern human rights violations, with titles such as "Contempt for Law," "Torture Camps," "Outsourcing of Torture," and "Indictment."

Middle Eastern newspapers not only told the personal stories of the detainees and their families but also ran stories on American Supreme Court decisions and legislative developments affecting detainees' rights, such as passage of the Military Commissions Act. The Saudi *Arab News* put forth this sober assessment of the United States Supreme Court's decision in *Hamdan v. Rumsfeld*, which was considered a relative human rights victory among many observers in the United States because of its recognition of the applicability of the Geneva Conventions to the United States in Guantanamo cases:

> The ruling is not about the treatment of the 450 or so detainees at Guantanamo, 80 of them Saudis. It does nothing to bring their release any closer or ensure the camp's closure. The ruling is simply about the powers of the president. President Bush can therefore quite easily obtain the appropriate authority. All he has to do is ask Congress to change the law. . . . Far more important is the Supreme Court's decision, as part of its ruling, that the Geneva Conventions apply to the detainees. . . . It could even end up with the camp being forced to close – although if it does, it will be because it has become an embarrassment for Washington, not because it would be considered illegal in any future Supreme Court ruling. If anything, Thursday's ruling implies that Guantanamo is legal under US law; it effectively said that the detainees can be held, as prisoners of war, for as long as the war on terror continues but that they have rights. Clearly if they are to be held, they have to be held somewhere.[6]

Finally, Middle Eastern media occasionally visited and reported on Guantanamo. The London-based pan-Arab *Al-Sharq al Awsat* ran an eight-part series on various aspects of the prison. From time to time Middle Eastern media would also ask American officials to justify their policies to Middle Eastern audience in interviews. For example, *Al-Sharq al-Awsat* featured an interview with John Bellinger, legal advisor to former Secretary of State Rice, in which he is forced to justify the U.S. Guantanamo policy.[7] Although the article headlines with Bellinger's "challenge" for critics to propose alternatives to Guantanamo, at one point, the article states, "Bellinger, however, admitted that there is no set timeframe for the closure of the detention center as there are tens of detainees who will not get the chance to be tried,"[8] in effect highlighting the American official's admission of the contingency of American human rights guarantees and commitments.

---

[6] *Ruling on Gitmo*, Arab News, Jul. 1, 2006.
[7] *Rice's Legal Adviser Says the States That Criticize Guantanamo Must Present an Alternative Instead of Making Hollow Statements*, Al Sharq Al Awsat, Nov. 7, 2006.
[8] *Id.*

On rare occasions, Middle Eastern initiatives against American violations made it through to mainstream media in the United States. On May 23, 2006, a story aired on American National Public Radio that profiled efforts by Bahraini MPs and human rights activists to protest the United States' detention of three Bahraini nationals in Guantanamo. The story featured a gathering at the house of MP Sheikh Mohammad Khaled, at the conclusion of which the group decided to form a committee designed to lobby the Bahraini government to press its American ally to release the remaining Bahraini detainees it holds at Guantanamo. The story featured a clip by human rights activist Nabeel Rajab stating, "It's a humanitarian issue. It's not a terrorism issue. It's a violation of human rights committed by the United States government."[9]

A trace of Middle Eastern activism against American human rights practices even reached the United States Supreme Court. Among the numerous *amici curiae* (friend of the court briefs) submitted to the U.S. Supreme Court in the landmark *Hamdan v. Rumsfeld* case, was one submitted on behalf of HOOD. It began with an introduction of the organization:

With the advent of the "War on Terror," HOOD became involved in protecting the rights of more than 100 Yemeni citizens held at the United States Naval Base at Guantanamo Bay and sponsored international conferences, in association with Amnesty International and other international human rights groups to focus attention on the Guantanamo detainees' treatment by the United States. In particular, the organization believes that Petitioner's continued detention and trial by a military commission present pivotal questions about the rule of law in the United States.[10]

Although from there the brief, drafted by American lawyers, is predominately centered around constructions of the United States' role as a global human rights leader and frames American policies as posing an obstacle to the realization of human rights and democratization in the Middle East (rather than as independently objectionable), the opening statement signals a limited shake-up of the traditional rules surrounding who has the voice and legitimacy to evaluate who in front of a leading American institution. What was perhaps more groundbreaking was the fact that American lawyers taking the seminal case to the Supreme Court felt the need to invoke the voice of Yemeni human rights actors (even it was painted as falling strictly within the confines of the East/West geography) to strengthen their case.

[9] All Things Considered, *Leaving Guantanamo: Bahrainis Protest Prison* (National Public Radio Broadcast May 23, 2006), http://www.npr.org/templates/story/story.php?storyId=5426095.
[10] Hamdan v. Rumsfeld, 126 U.S. S.Ct. 2749 (2006). Brief of Yemeni National Organization for Defending Rights and Freedom (HOOD) as Amicus Curiae Supporting Petitioner; HOOD's English-language Web site can be accessed at http://www.hoodonline.org/index.php?lng=english&.

Another key institution in which a Middle Eastern gaze was reflected was the United States House of Representatives. Although within the dozens of congressional hearings on Guantanamo, Abu Ghraib, and U.S. torture policies testimony was taken exclusively from American policymakers, military officials, and human rights advocates while the voices of former detainees and victims were conspicuously missing, there was one late, yet notable, exception. Maher Arar, the Syrian-Canadian man who had been detained by U.S. authorities as he switched flights in New York's JFK airport and then sent to Syria to endure thirteen months of torture, was a primary witness at a joint hearing on the topic of extraordinary renditions held by the International Relations Committee's Subcommittee on International Organizations, Human Rights, and Oversight and the Judiciary Committee's Subcommittee on the Constitution, Civil Rights, and Civil Liberties.

Although Arar is a Canadian citizen who had not been to Syria since he had been a teenager, his beard, accent, and religious commitment ensured that he would be viewed as belonging more to the East than to the West. Certainly the U.S. government's decision to deport him to Syria rather than Canada despite his pleas for the latter action spoke to such an outlook. Arar's appearance at the hearing was via video feed because he remained on a U.S. government no-fly list. He began his testimony by countering his dehumanization, declaring his victimhood, and pointing to the immorality of the American practice that had turned his life upside down. "Let me be clear – I am not a terrorist. I am not a member of al-Qaeda or any other terrorist group. I am a father, a husband, and an engineer. I am also a victim of the immoral practice of extraordinary rendition."[11] Continuing to mirror testimonials of human rights violations that American lawmakers were accustomed to hearing in relation to non-Western countries' practices, Arar went on to detail the denials of due process by the United States government and months of incessant torture by Syrian officials to whom the United States had released him. Throughout the testimony and questioning that followed, Arar was articulate and compelling, repeatedly pointing to the immorality, injustice, and double standards of the treatment he had endured. Additional pieces of his testimony will be taken up in the discussion in Chapter 5 of the post–September 11th era's lessons for advancing the human rights project.

Arab Governments Pressuring the United States

In much the same manner that human rights groups traditionally exerted pressure on the United States government to press human rights issues with

---

[11] Rendition to Torture: The Case of Maher Arar, Testimony before House Subcomm. on International Organizations, Human Rights, and Oversight and House Subcom. on the Constitution, Civil Rights, and Civil Liberties, 110th Cong. 1 (2007). (Oct. 18, 2007), http://judiciary.house.gov/hearings/hear_101807.html.

Middle Eastern officials, in the post–September 11th era, some Middle Eastern activists lobbied their governments to bring up the plight of Guantanamo detainees in their high-level sittings with American counterparts. Although it is almost impossible to know what really transpires behind closed doors no matter which direction the human rights rebukes are slated to go, the pressure from domestic actors often compelled Middle Eastern governments to at least publicly demand accountability from or pronounce challenges to the United States with respect to its detention policies. For example, Jordan requested the United States provide it with the charges against its citizens held at Guantanamo[12] and in March 2007, the upper house of the Bahraini Parliament urged the United States to either give the remaining Bahraini detainees a fair trial or repatriate them.[13] On numerous occasions, Yemeni officials made similar calls for either the provision of due process or the release of Yemen's over one hundred Guantanamo detainees. Despite its many public pronouncements and criticisms, the American and Yemeni advocates working on the cases were convinced that the Yemeni government was not doing all that it could to secure the release of its detainees. HOOD placed a letter from American lawyers to this effect on its Web site and an ad hoc volunteer group of American lawyers later traveled to Yemen to meet with Yemeni officials and persuade them to take up the issue with American counterparts more aggressively. The perception and/or reality that Middle Eastern governments are more apt to act on the urging of Americans rather than local attorneys is testament of how the East/West geography continued to operate even within episodes notable for its unsettling on that of their own.

In some instances, it was clear that Middle Eastern governments' references to Guantanamo and Abu Ghraib were as instrumental and politically motivated as the American government's incessant referencing of Saddam Hussein's "torture and rape chambers" had been in the early days of the Iraqi invasion. As I argue in Chapter 4, highlighting American violations were no doubt a convenient means of diverting attention from local human rights failings and discrediting the entire human rights enterprise. Still there were countless MPs and even officials (usually with lower levels of influence) within Middle Eastern governments who (also) challenged American policies out of a sense of conviction and disdain for the contradictions inherent in the path on which the Bush administration had embarked. For example, a few months prior to her resignation, Yemeni Human Rights Minister Alsoswa, speaking at a panel on Guantanamo at the Middle Eastern Studies Association annual meeting, laid out a critical picture of the ways in which American pressure in the counterterrorism arena served as a real barrier

[12] *Jordan Asks US to Provide Charges Made against Detainees in Guantanamo* Al Dastur, August 30, 2004, at 1. c
[13] Bahrain Center for Human Rights, Gulf News, *US Urged to Repatriate Bahraini Prisoners*, Mar. 21, 2007, http://www.bahrainrights.org/en/node/1108.

to Yemen's provision of certain human rights guarantees. Further, even if many Middle Eastern government officials had given in to the notion of a harsh *realpolitik* power-infused world order, a part of them still felt the indignity of Abu Ghraib and Guantanamo also directed at them as Muslims or Arabs and was accordingly moved to challenge it at some level on moral grounds. Determining to what extent a Middle Eastern government official's condemnation of American human rights failings was instrumental and to what extent it was borne out of personal sense of conviction was a complicated, if not impossible, undertaking.

Parting with East/West Scripts

Middle Eastern media and public discourse was replete with explicit challenges to underlying assumptions of the East/West geography – though often entangled in inflammatory or otherwise problematic assertions. This statement in a *Jordan Times* op-ed by a former Jordanian government official following Abu Ghraib was typical:

They should never assume the high moral ground of coming to civilize us and teach us how to behave, how to reform, how to promote human rights, how to promote the status of women, how to fight corruption, how to improve education and how to respect the law. Yes, we need all of that, but not from them. We do not want our women to follow the example of that woman torturer who was ecstatic about the pain and humiliation she was inflicting in torture sessions on Iraqi male prisoners. We do not want to learn their inhumanity, their lies, their cruelty, their injustice, their lawlessness, their corruption, their extremist ideologies, their conspiracies, their racism, their contempt and selfishness, their double standards, the terror in their society and their schools, and the evil that is driving them to destroy our world. If that is what they have to offer, God bless our backwardness and save us from that so-called "freedom."[14]

Despite its clear patriarchal undertones signaled by the fear that "our women" will follow Lynndie England's example, the critique not only encompassed a clear rejection of the American authority to pass judgment on Middle Eastern human rights practices, it also linked its indictment of American human rights violations to American culture. What distinguishes such a statement from countless others with similar formulations issued prior to September 11th is the fact that although it eschews American human rights practices and prescriptions, it does not eschew the entire human rights project. Although I will discuss the significance of the new posture for the local legitimacy of human rights in the Middle East in Chapter 4, its significance relative to the politics and hierarchies embedded in global human rights dynamics are equally noteworthy. At some level, it suggests a view of

[14] Hasan Abu Nimah, *Not from Them*, JORDAN TIMES, May 5, 2004.

human rights whose terms are no longer set exclusively by the United States or the West but is potentially serious and introspective nonetheless.

A similar altered consciousness can also be detected among many of the region's human rights advocates, though typically in a more refined form. Jamal Abdullah al Shami, the director of Yemen's Democracy School, maintained that before 9/11, human rights groups largely adopted the West's human rights values, whereas now they increasingly challenge them.[15] Numerous others also indicated they had moved beyond the East/West binary in the post–September 11th era. "We have to get rid of this view that [the US] is a pure democracy, it has no weakness. Democracy is also a process . . . there is no formula where there is no human rights violations . . . no, at the end it's human nature," offered Amal Basha of Yemen's Sisters' Forum for Human Rights.[16] Another telling indicator of Middle Eastern activists' emergent trend was for Middle Eastern advocates to extend their gaze beyond their own borders and into Western territory. In the interviews conducted, I encountered repeated references to discrimination against Muslims and Arabs in the United States and Europe. As Basha notes,

Now we are engaged in a movement where we need those Western countries to protect the human rights of the minorities. Not to view every Muslim in the West as a potential terrorist. And this is what has been happening. You are a terrorist by (the way you) look. We are looking at the West and see they are losing this tolerance vis-à-vis the different minorities. And this is what we try to remind those Western countries.[17]

Finally, Middle Eastern activists were involved in campaigns that pressed their governments to resist American pressure to sign Bilateral Immunity Agreements, exempting Americans citizens and employees accused of international crimes in their countries from being subject to the jurisdiction of the International Criminal Court. The topic, treated as aiding American strong-arm tactics in the way of skirting accountability under international law, became a campaign taken up widely by human rights advocates and was debated in the media as well as legislatures in several Middle Eastern countries, including both Jordan and Yemen. In Egypt, the Cairo Institute for Human Rights sent a letter to the Arab League urging its secretary-general to add the issue of Arab states signing bilateral agreements with the United States on the agenda of an upcoming Arab summit. "The stance of Arab states must not be limited to meaningless verbal condemnation [of human

[15] Interview with Jamal Abdullah al-Shami, chairman of the Democracy School, in Sana'a, Yemen (Jan. 23, 2007).
[16] Interview with Amal Basha, Yemeni Women's Rights Activist, in Sana'a, Yemen (Jan. 22, 2007).
[17] Id.

rights violations] in light of the immoral bilateral agreements some of these governments signed which protect war criminals, giving them free reign to commit their crimes," the letter stated.[18]

The Kuwaiti Experience

Perhaps one of the most fascinating examples of the way in which the East/West geography of human rights was turned on its head in the post–September 11th era was to be found in Kuwait. There were twelve Kuwaiti nationals detained at Guantanamo Bay following September 11th. Kuwaiti activists aided by their government led an impressive campaign to have these detainees either freed or granted basic due process rights. Once some of the detainees were released from Guantanamo, it was the Kuwaiti judicial system, not an American one that provided them a fair trial.

A Kuwaiti Human Rights Campaign in the United States

In 2002, Khalid al-Odah, the father of Guantanamo detainee Fawzi al-Odah, founded the Kuwait Families Committee. Al-Odah was a retired Kuwaiti lieutenant colonel who had spent considerable time training in the United States. As a result, he spoke near perfect English and had some grasp of American sensibilities. The Families Committee charged itself with the exclusive task of advancing the rights of Kuwait's Guantanamo detainees. As al-Odah described it, the group adopted a four-pronged strategy: (1) litigation, (2) collaboration with local and international human rights NGOs, (3) a comprehensive media effort both in Kuwait and in the United States, and (4) the pursuit of diplomatic channels.[19]

The Kuwait Families Committee hired experienced attorneys from prominent American law firms to represent them in litigating the detainees' cases in the United States. As a result, two challenges to Fawzi al-Odah's detention in Guantanamo Bay were heard in the United States Supreme Court, each time serving as a part of what were hailed as landmark decisions: *Rasul v. Bush*, *Al Odah v. United States* in 2004, and *Boumediene v. Bush*, which was consolidated with *Al Odah v. United States* in 2008. Both decisions upheld Guantanamo detainees' rights to challenge their detention in U.S. courts.

The Families Committee realized early, however, that litigation alone would not be enough to affect the policy changes they sought. As al-Odah explained, "At the beginning we were swimming against the current. It was very difficult for us to explain ourselves." Thus (apparently on the advice of another American attorney) the group decided to also hire Levick

---

[18] Al-Ahram Weekly Online, Amira Howeidi, *One Law for US*, May 13–19, 2004, http://weekly.ahram.org.eg/2004/690/fr2.htm.

[19] Telephone interview with Khaled al-Odah, founder, Kuwait Families' Committee (Jul. 17, 2008).

Communications, an American public relations firm that styles itself as specializing in high-stakes and crisis situations. In an article in a public relations publication, Richard Levick, the president of Levick Communications, described the adoption of a two-tiered public relations strategy – one track aimed at putting "a human face on the then invisible detainees in Guantanamo" and the other at "helping Americans understand how the issues faced by the detainees affect all Americans."[20] These two objectives were largely pursued through "media outreach." Dozens of op-eds by al-Odah and lawyers Tom Wilner and David Cynamon were published in American newspapers and the American attorneys held numerous press conferences and media events and participated in television interviews and debates. According to Levick, on several occasions, American judges working on detainee cases openly cited articles resulting from the team's media efforts in their rulings.[21] Another firm was hired to design a Web site (www.kuwaitifreedom.org) in which sympathetic pictures of the detainees and their families as well as Guantanamo-related news and op-eds were featured. Finally, some members of the Families Committee's American team lobbied members of Congress on detainee rights policies. Generally either reminding Americans of their values tied up in rights and rule of law or submitting that Guantanamo policies would give rise to radicalism and thus threaten their security, the arguments being forged in these efforts were clearly framed and formulated to resonate with an American audience. In contrast to the "it's not about them, it's about us" tune of the campaign presented in Chapter 2, here the message largely formulated and delivered by American attorneys and public relations specialists seemed to oscillate (sometimes awkwardly) between "it's about us" and "it's about them."

In Kuwait, al-Odah and the Families Committee pursued local and regional human rights activism. They attended the international conferences on Guantanamo described earlier in the chapter, organized protests in London and Kuwait City, and waged a domestic media campaign designed to ratchet up pressure for the Kuwaiti government to take action. Al-Odah described the groups' media efforts in Kuwait as very successful, stating that the issue received wide coverage in Kuwaiti newspapers, TV, and radio. "If you ask anyone on the street what is Guantanamo, they will know. They will tell you that it is a human rights issue. They will know how many Kuwaitis have been released and how many still remain. They will know about the legal process for the Kuwaitis once they came home."[22] The Families

---

[20] Richard Levick, *PR Perspectives: A Long-Term Struggle . . . How a Media Campaign Helped Turn the Guantanamo Tide*, Dec. 2005, http://www.workinpr.com/industry/research/2005_12_prperspective.asp (last visited Aug. 10, 2008).

[21] *Id.*

[22] *See* Khaled al-Odah, *supra* note 19.

Committee also joined forces with other Kuwaiti rights activists to place the Guantanamo issue center stage in a visit by George Bush in January 2008. Kuwaiti civil society members, particularly women, had been invited to participate in forums and press conferences with the U.S. president. As part of a coordinated effort, in each of those events, Kuwaiti advocates raised the Guantanamo issue.

The final strategy pursued by the Kuwait Families Committee was to prompt their government to place diplomatic pressure on the United States. According to Tom Wilner, the Kuwaiti government's commitment changed over time. As he explained it, initially, the United States' security forces assured the Kuwaitis that the detainees were real threats, but as time passed, the Kuwaiti ambassador to Washington began to suspect that that was not the case. Soon, the Kuwaiti emir, foreign minister, and ambassador took the lead on the diplomatic front and were, in fact, quite effective.[23] Khalid al-Odah offered a similar assessment of the Kuwaiti government's role. He stated that the Kuwaiti government was very cautious at first, but "we managed to persuade them to stand beside us."[24] Al-Odah believed that by the time of the 2004 decision in *Rasul v. Bush* and *Al Odah v. United States*, the group's cause had the Kuwaiti government's full support.[25] In the end the Kuwaiti government paid millions of dollars to fund the Families Committees' American legal representation and public relations services. "Without them, we could not have done it," al-Odah offered.[26]

The Kuwait Families Committee's work in the United States also spurred a limited conservative backlash. With a large portrait in an ornate frame hanging on the wall behind him in his office just blocks away from Capitol Hill, Tom Wilner skimmed through e-mail after e-mail accusing him of "hating America" and "representing the enemy." However, the most systematic challenge to the Kuwaiti initiative came from Debra Burlingame, the sister of Charles Burlingame III (the pilot of one of the airplanes highjacked on September 11th) and an outspoken member of "9/11 Families for a Safe and Strong America." Burlingame published numerous articles in *The Wall Street Journal* and other (namely, conservative) American publications and testified before Congress on the Kuwaiti initiative. She argued that the American law firm initially hired by the Families Committee took on the Kuwaiti case because of long-standing financial connections and interests in the Middle East:

The firm's Abu Dhabi office states that it has pioneered the concept of "Shariah-compliant" financing. In Kuwait, the firm has represented the government on a

---

[23] Interview with Tom Wilner, Kuwait Families' Committee attorney, in Washington, DC (Jun. 27, 2008).

[24] *See* Khaled al-Odah, *supra* note 19.

[25] *Id.*

[26] *Id.*

wide variety of matters involving billions of dollars worth of assets. So the party underwriting the litigation on behalf of the Kuwaiti 12 – from which all of the detainees have benefited – is one of Shearman & Sterling's most lucrative OPEC accounts.[27]

She further attempted to publicly unveil the Levick PR strategy of showing detainees' human face, calling it a "false narrative" and "propaganda."[28] In her efforts, the entire Kuwaiti initiative in the United States is portrayed as a foreign government funding work that is against American interests at a time of war in the name of human rights.

The Kuwaiti initiative presents a number of intriguing parallels with foreign human rights promotion initiative, generally undertaken by the United States and other Western countries in the Middle East. A Kuwaiti human rights group was given millions of dollars by the Kuwaiti government to fund local actors' human rights campaign in the United States. Although the funding was not directly provided to an American human rights NGO, much of the funding did go to lawyers for the purpose of spearheading human rights litigation and promotion, often in close collaboration with human rights lawyers and American NGOs like the Center for Constitutional Rights. Further, hiring a PR firm is clearly more a habit of wealthy Persian Gulf states than human rights campaigns pursuing particular agendas in the United States. However, it is interesting to note that ultimately the PR firm's strategies of (1) framing the issues in ways that resonated with domestic audiences to humanize human rights victims and (2) consciousness-raising among the public and policymakers through communicative processes are identical to those typically used by human rights forces. Similarly, the protests, media coverage, and public outcry inside Kuwait, the shaming of U.S. officials based in or traveling to Kuwait, and the attempts to press the Kuwaiti government to place diplomatic pressure on a close foreign ally mirror key elements of past Western human rights campaigns directed toward Middle Eastern states and other Eastern locales.

Perhaps what is more fascinating than the parallels between the Kuwaiti initiate and Western human rights promotion efforts in the Middle East and elsewhere are the parallels between the conservative American response to the human rights initiative and traditional responses by conservatives in the Middle East toward American human rights promotion projects. The local advocates receiving foreign funding are discredited as betraying national interests and promoting foreign interests and even religious-cultural

---

[27] Debra Burlingame, *Gitmo's Guerilla Lawyers: How an Unscrupulous Legal and PR Campaign Changed the Way the World Looks at Guantanamo*, WALL ST. J., Mar. 8, 2007 http://www.opinionjournal.com/editorial/feature.html?id=110009758 (last visited Aug. 1, 2008).

[28] *Id.*

values, as Burlingame's reference to Shearman & Sterling's work in Shariah-compliant financing is meant to do.

Upholding Detainees' Rights in Kuwaiti Courts

Khalid al-Odah saw the Kuwait Families Committee's efforts as geared toward ensuring "the Kuwaiti detainees have their day in court, but a neutral court, not something like the Military Commissions, which were unacceptable."[29] After years in detention without due process, several of Kuwait's Guantanamo detainees did finally receive a fair trial and their day in court. Their day in court, however, was to be provided by a Kuwaiti judicial process, not an American one.

In 2005 and 2006, a total of seven Kuwaiti nationals were released from Guantanamo (five in 2005 and two in 2006). Part of the understanding between the Kuwaiti and American governments facilitating the release was that they would be prosecuted in Kuwait. In public trials held before criminal, not security courts (which had been abolished in Kuwait in 1995 to wide Western acclaim), the men faced charges of engaging in activities that would harm Kuwait's political position by joining al Qaeda, committing hostile acts against a foreign country (the United States) in a manner that harms Kuwaiti political interests, and collecting donations for an illegal organization.

Generally, the United States had little to offer by way of evidence other than brief investigative summaries largely based on interrogations conducted by American troops in Pakistan, Afghanistan, or Guantanamo. Kuwaiti defense attorneys asked the court to find the American investigative summaries inadmissible as evidence because the defendants had falsely confessed to stop their torture at the hands of American authorities – torture they argued had included beatings with chains, electric shock, and sodomy.[30] To make their case, the defense also admitted a UN Human Rights Commission report on Guantanamo that detailed instances of physical and psychological torture carried out by American authorities.[31] At the same time a provision of Kuwaiti law banning the use of confessions obtained under duress was also invoked.[32] The Kuwaiti courts accepted the defense arguments and the American submissions were not admitted into evidence. According to the *Washington Post*, the Kuwaiti judges found the U.S. information unreliable,

[29] See Khaled al-Odah, *supra* note 19.
[30] Jurist Legal News and Research, Tatyana Margolin, *Released Guantanamo Kuwaitis Maintain Innocence, Oppose Use of US Evidence*, Feb. 7, 2005, http://jurist.law.pitt.edu/paperchase/2005/02/kuwaiti-detainees-say-they-made-false.php. *See also* Moamen al Masri, *Lawyers Bid to Exclude Gitmo Transcripts*, ARAB TIMES, Apr. 10, 2006, http://www.cageprisoners.com/articles.php?id=13330.
[31] See Khaled al-Odah, *supra* note 19; Rajiv Chandrasekaran. *A 'Ticking Time Bomb' Goes Off*, Washington Post, February 23, 2009 at A01, http://www.washingtonpost.com/wp-dyn/content/article/2009/02/22/AR2009022202384.html.
[32] See Khaled al-Odah, *supra* note 19.

writing, "these reports are not serious and are not worth consideration," and "we do not feel comfortable trusting them."[33] All of the detainees were acquitted of the charges by the Kuwaiti courts. The prosecutor appealed, but the Kuwaiti Supreme Court ultimately upheld the lower court decision, agreeing that there was not enough evidence to convict the former Guantanamo detainees.[34]

The Kuwaiti prosecutions (as well as number of other trials of released Guantanamo detainees in other Middle Eastern countries) added yet another dimension to the reconfiguration of the East/West geography that the human rights era had produced. Instead of American courts considering foreign human rights violations and granting victims rights denied to them abroad, it was a Middle Eastern court that was considering American human rights violations and granting victims their due process rights denied by the United States. At the conclusion of the second set of trials, Khaled al-Odah was widely interviewed. His statement regarding the fate of the four Kuwaiti detainees remaining in Guantanamo is revealing: "We call on the United States to either give our four sons a fair trial in America or any other place in the world, or to hand them to Kuwait so that they can be . . . given their legal right to defend themselves."[35]

AMERICANS TEACHING/LEARNING HUMAN RIGHTS IN THE MIDDLE EAST

Middle Easterners felt an immense sense of indignation and injustice in witnessing the United States' not only violating such core international human rights norms as the prohibitions on torture and provisions of due process, and not only blatantly co-opting human rights discourses to further policies wrecking havoc in the region, but also pursuing both courses simultaneously. As a result, in virtually every step American officials took to teach and preach human rights, they encountered a Middle Eastern lesson on the same topic. The challenge to usually low-level and (when they ventured beyond designated safe audiences) higher-level American officials came in the course of American human right promotion initiatives, American attempts to bolster its image in the Middle East, or the frequent convergence of the two.

Perhaps the first to be confronted with the Middle Eastern rebuke of U.S. government policies have been American embassy officials in Middle Eastern countries. Amal Basha recounted one such encounter. Basha

---

[33] *See* Rajiv Chandrasekaran, *supra* note 31.

[34] Jurist Legal News and Research, Holly Manges Jones, *Kuwait High Court Upholds Acquittals of Former Guantanamo Detainees*, Jan. 22, 2006, http://jurist.law.pitt.edu/paperchase/2006/07/kuwait-high-court-upholds-acquittals.php.

[35] Associated Press, *Kuwaiti Court Acquits 2 Former Guantanamo Bay Prisoners of Joining al-Qaida in Afghanistan*, INT'L. HERALD TRIBUNE, Mar. 4, 2007, http://www.cageprisoners.com/articles.php?id=19262.

is a confident woman and seasoned activist. She had received a bachelor's degree in political science from Cairo and a master's degree in international development from the University of Suffolk in England. She worked briefly in the Yemeni Ministry of Industry, in the United Nations Development Programme (UNDP) for nine years, and UNICEF in the run-up to the Beijing Conference on Women's Rights before she decided to start her own NGO dedicated to women's rights and status issues. Although in her mid-forties, she wears trendy clothes and an equally trendy shoulder-length hairstyle, and a spirited Arabic dance song serves as the ring tone for one of her two cell phones. The day of our interview she wore a colorful scarf around her shoulders while her head was bare. This alone distinguishes her from 99 percent of the women one encounters publicly in Sana'a, who are fully covered in black. Despite the fact that her outward appearance sets her apart in this way, her personality and grasp of Yemeni social dynamics and sensibility seems to allow her to connect with people throughout the socioreligious spectrum and across generations. I observed this at a gathering of young women at her house several days after our interview.

Dodging accidents waiting to happen left and right in Sana'a's anything-goes traffic as she drove us from a Girl's Leadership Conference where civil society members were gathered to her office, Basha recounted an exchange with U.S. embassy representatives who had come to observe a regional forum they had funded through the Middle East Partnership Initiative (MEPI):

In the opening session of the democracy forum, we invited the representatives of the US Embassy. We invited three people, including the deputy head of mission and he came and he was one of the speakers in the opening session. And then I made a critical speech about democracy – because we had three people who did not come because of security reasons. . . . I had to also talk about what is happening in Iraq. I said look, we are really fond of democracy, but you plant democracy with people, not with tanks, like the Americans are promoting, and he did not like it. I said, those countries who are promoting democracy should set themselves as examples in respecting human rights. And I talked about the double standard. And he said, "this is a women's [issues] event. If we want to talk about foreign policy we should have another conference." He was separating our course and the political issues.[36]

In Basha's account, she not only refuses to turn a blind eye to American human rights abuses but also challenges the American officials' (and government's) propensity to treat human rights conditions as emanating exclusively from internal and domestic sources, divorced from American interventions such as the Iraq War.

When I paid a visit to the Democracy School, its director Jamal Abdullah al-Shami, a middle-aged man who sports Western professional attire and a secular demeanor, described a similar encounter between U.S. embassy officials who had come out to observe American democracy-promotion

[36] *See* Amal Basha, *supra* note 16.

efforts in action and a number of thirteen- and fourteen-year-old participants of the NGO's "Children's Parliament" initiative, another MEPI-funded project. As he chronicled it, one young participant asked, "if the United States always defends human rights, then why is it one of only three states that has refused to ratify the United Nation Convention on the Rights of the Child?" The embassy official responded by describing the complexity of congressional approval and the barriers posed by federal/state divisions. According to al-Shami, the children were not convinced, replying, "When you started the war in Iraq, the Congress immediately agreed. Why did they?"[37] The Democracy School pursued the conversation. A couple of days after my departure from Yemen, they had arranged for a meeting between a group of these youth and U.S. embassy representatives to discuss U.S. foreign policy. In this fashion, what an American politician sitting in Washington may view as a clear means to demonstrate America's goodwill and good intentions (i.e., through inaugurations of American-funded democratization initiatives featuring Middle Eastern women and children) also turns into an occasion for the Middle Eastern participants to confront the American "observers."

Finally, American embassy officials in Yemen were charged with presenting and leading discussions of the U.S. State Department's Country Reports on Human Rights Practices. Sa'ad al Gadsi of the Women's Forum for Research and Training told me that when the U.S. embassy convened a meeting to discuss its 2005 report on Yemen with local civil society members, it was the American representatives whose governments' human rights practices and credentials were interrogated by the Yemeni audience, even human rights activists who largely agreed with the American assessment of Yemen's human rights failings.[38] When the topic came up in conversations at the U.S. embassy, it was abundantly clear that officials involved had found the meeting trying. A commentary on the State Department reports in the Egyptian daily, *Al-Akhbar* captures the tone of the Middle Eastern challenge:

The report included every place on earth, with the exception of the American prisons and what is happening inside the United States itself. The Bush administration, which had the guts to issue this report, itself is involved in inhuman crimes against the defenseless detainees in Iraq, Afghanistan, and Guantanamo. It issues laws that shackle the civil freedoms of its citizens. It also approves weapons shipments to regimes that have a black human rights record.[39]

Occasionally, higher-ranking officials visiting the Middle East received the same treatment on venturing to public forums or meetings with

---

[37] *See* Jamal Abdullah al-Shami, *supra* note 15.
[38] Interview with Sa'ad Gedsi, director, the Women's Forum for Research and Training, in Sana'a, Yemen (Jan. 12, 2007).
[39] Ayman Ju'ma, *Human Rights*, AL AKHBAR CAIRO, Apr. 5, 2005.

journalists or human rights advocates. In an article entitled "Miss Popularity: Karen Hughes Learns That Winning Muslim Hearts and Minds Requires Changing US Foreign Policy," the *Houston Chronicle* describes the Bush confidant charged with improving the United States' image in her first visit to the Middle East. The piece reports, "In Egypt, opponents of the Mubarak regime criticized the administration for preaching democracy while supporting autocracies such as those in Egypt and Saudi Arabia. In Saudi Arabia, female students informed Hughes that they were happy not voting or driving and did not envy the American way of life," and "in Turkey, female political activists voiced opposition to Bush's decision to invade Iraq."[40] The piece concludes, "If Hughes learned anything on her trip, it is that few Muslims view the United States as a true champion of peace, freedom and democracy, or an objective broker between Israelis and Palestinians." In an *Arab News* article, Khaled Batarfi elaborates on a similar encounter with other high-ranking State Department officials:

I asked two US officials the same question on two different occasions and received the same response. They were Liz Cheney (Dick Cheney's daughter), assistant secretary of state for Middle and Near East, and Lorne W. Craner, assistant secretary of state for human rights, democracy and labor. Both were supposed to explain why America's human rights record today is so poor; how the American conscience tolerated Guantanamo and Abu Ghraib; why the leader of the free world sends prisoners to dictatorships for torture; why the U.S. kidnaps suspects, ships them to secret prisons in bases around the world, even without the knowledge of host countries. Without flinching, the two top officials started by pointing to Arab police states and human rights records. They were basically saying: "You are in no position to criticize us on such issues because you fared worse!" Lorne Craner went further to compare the American justice system with that of the worst Arab and Muslim countries in his defense of his administration's treatment of Muslim and Arab prisoners. He also compared citizen rights in America to ours. The argument goes like this: "Before you point a finger at our systems take a minute to examine yours! We are still way ahead of you. Learn and follow. Once you are our equals, then you may be qualified to discuss our shortcomings!"

"So now you are comparing your superpower, world-leader nation with our Third World countries?" I answered in disbelief. "If so, who are you to preach to us? If we now refer to the same value system, then please come down from your high moral ground and stop showing us the way."[41]

Human Rights advocates I interviewed in both Yemen and Jordan also indicated that from time to time they received visits from American congressional or State Department delegations. Shaher Bak the commissioner general of

---

[40] *Miss Popularity*, HOUSTON CHRONICLE, Oct. 5, 2005, http://www.chron.com/cs/CDA/ ssistory.mpl/editorial/3384161.

[41] Khaled Batarfi, *Wrong Comparison, America!* JEDDA ARAB NEWS, Mar. 11, 2007.

Jordan's National Center for Human Rights said that when such delegations visited, it was his duty to explain the circumstance of human rights in Jordan and tell them that "what they are doing is wrong," and it is not helping local rights promotion efforts.[42] Khaled Alanesi and Mohammad Naji Allaw of HOOD indicated that on similar occasions, they frequently embarked on critical discussions of American foreign policy and even human rights conditions in the United States.[43]

The flip side of the interaction between Middle Eastern civil society representatives taking shape in the Middle East were similar exchanges emerging from the State Department hosting Middle Eastern civil society members in the United States through its International Visitors Program, primarily for them to experience American democracy and human rights first hand. Khaled al-Hamdi was a young Yemeni journalist who took part in the program immediately after the 2004 presidential elections. His trip was organized around the theme of the American electoral process at work and the journalists attending were encouraged to write articles about the process once they returned home. As Hamdi recounted, during the program, it was often the Middle Eastern participants who criticized the American media, particularly its coverage of the war in Iraq.[44] In essence, the Middle Eastern journalists challenged American formulations of what constitutes press freedom and independence in relation to the corporatization of American media. Jamal Abdullah al-Shami of the Democracy School also brought up his International Visitors Program trip in our interview. On several occasions during the visit, he had sought permission to see Sheik Mohammed Ali Hassan al-Moayad, a Yemeni man convicted in New York courts of conspiring and attempting to lend support to al Qaeda and supporting Hamas; both circumstances surrounding the trial and a seventy-five-year prison sentence were widely viewed in Yemen as miscarriages of justice. Al-Shami's request of access to the prisoner was denied due to the sensitivity of the case. However, the fact does not detract from the significance of the dynamic – a Middle Eastern human rights activist visiting the United States, ostensibly to learn about American human rights conventions seeks to see a prisoner, with the clear implication that he is skeptical of the vetting of American justice and wishes to investigate further on his own, not unlike U.S.-based human rights advocates' agendas in visits to Middle Eastern sites.

Finally, in Afghanistan and Iraq, scores of American bureaucrats and advocates of the human rights and rule of law initiatives funded by the United States government set out to introduce American legal models and promote the implementation of international human rights instruments and

---

[42] Interview with Shaher Bak, Commissioner General of Jordan's National Center for Human Rights, in Amman, Jordan (Jun. 28, 2006).

[43] See Amira Howeidi, *supra* note 18.

[44] Interview with Khaled al-Hamdi, Yemeni journalist, in Sana'a, Yemen (Jan. 13, 2007).

standards. In July 2005, about five hundred Justice Department employees and contractors were stationed in Iraq,[45] with much of their work devoted to developing Iraqi legal and judicial institutions. Sometimes members of the military were assigned to such rule of law initiatives. In their efforts to incorporate international legal norms within Middle Eastern legal institutions, Americans involved would themselves sometimes gain increased familiarity and consciousness of the international legal framework. For example, Major Sean Watts, who taught at the U.S. Army's Judge Advocate General School, stated that he saw U.S. military law increasingly moving in the direction of human rights law. He explained his prediction by noting that he himself first encountered the UN Convention for the Elimination of All Forms of Discrimination against Women (CEDAW) in Afghanistan when he was charged with working with local Afghan officials on the convention.[46]

All of these encounters stood for the proposition that within virtually every programmed, scheduled, or budgeted occasion devised by American government officials or (and, to lesser extent, nonprofits) to "teach" human rights principles and build human rights structures in the Middle East, the Americans involved would face some sort of lesson, critique, or impassioned rejoinder.

THE FUNDING CONUNDRUM

United States development aid and humanitarian assistance programs have long been viewed as the soft side of American power and considered useful instruments for taking the edge off of U.S. foreign policy by promoting the United States' image as a global leader in the spread of human welfare, rights, and freedom. In the post–September 11th era, the American government again sought to infuse earnestness, benevolence, and elements of consistency into its Middle East foreign policy by funding various human rights and democratization initiatives. The Web page introducing the United States Agency for International Development's (USAID's) *Branding Guidelines* candidly lays out the strategy:

Since 9/11, America's foreign assistance programs have been more fully integrated into the United States' National Security Strategy. This elevation to the so-called "third-D" (development being added to diplomacy and defense) increased the need for U.S. foreign assistance activities to be more fully identified in the host country as being provided "from the American People." We have been identified as "America's

---

[45] Dan Eggen, *Attorney General Makes Quick Trip to Iraqi Capital,* WASHINGTON POST, Jul. 4, 2005, at A01.

[46] Presentation by and conversation with Major Sean Watts at 1st Annual Samuel Dash Conference on Human Rights, Georgetown Law Center (Apr. 10, 2006).

good-news story" and have been tasked to make our efforts more visible and better known in the countries where we work.[47]

Perhaps even more than Americans, Middle Eastern populations and civil society actors alike are attuned to the instrumental dimensions of American funding of various human rights and democratization initiatives in the region. This has often meant that Middle Eastern advocates have pursued avenues to either resist or subvert American attempts to co-opt them through funding. They have pursued this course primarily in one of two ways: by refusing U.S. government funding or taking the funding but continuing to challenge and interrogate American human rights practices and policies at every opportunity.

The first response to American attempts to legitimate Middle Eastern interventions through its financing of local human rights NGOs – that of simply rejecting the funding – was most predominant in Jordan. As far as I could observe, the Jordanian Society for Human Rights was clearly starving for funds. The office was scantily furnished with plastic lawn-style chairs and a few desks. On the afternoon I visited, there were no staff other than the director and Ibrahim al-Sane' informed me that the fax machine did not work. Yet he was emphatic in his refusal to accept American government funds. He said that he had received an offer of funding from Freedom House, but he knew that the American organization and its funding was tied to the U.S. State Department and there was no way he could accept such funding strictly as a matter of principle. The director of a more visibly thriving Jordanian human rights NGO also indicated that, as a matter of policy, the NGO did not accept money that could be traced back to the American government. At some level, she saw the decision as one of maintaining credibility domestically but also articulated it as a conflict of interest:

Last year we were working on lobbying and we established a coalition to support the International Criminal Court, while the US is against it. . . . we were working against them and they worked against us by signing a (bilateral) agreement. So imagine the conflict of interest between us and the States.[48]

She explained that the NGO sometimes did cooperate with American NGOs. Just one week earlier they had signed an agreement with the American Bar Association's Rule of Law initiative to receive American law school interns. Yet, as a matter of policy, they refused all funding from American-based NGOs: "We declare to the public that we don't accept US money and we have to be credible on the issue."[49] Francis Abuzayd, the director of

---

[47] U.S. Agency for International Development, *USAID Branding*, http://www.usaid.gov/branding/.
[48] Interview with Jordanian human rights advocate, in Amman, Jordan (Jun. 4, 2006).
[49] *Id.*

Freedom House's Amman office, revealed that approximately 50 percent of the Jordanian organizations they wished to fund refused their aid.[50]

The second approach that was predominate in Yemen encompassed a willingness to accept U.S. funding of rights projects but to resist American hegemony as they encountered it. NGO leaders who accepted American government funds had no illusions about the fact that the money offered to them served an intended purpose of painting a positive veneer on objectionable and unjust American policies intimately linked to the region's human rights conditions – that in a sense the American government intended to enlist them in a public relations and image-boosting campaign. This consciousness was perhaps most evident in my interview of Mohammad Naji Allaw of HOOD:

We know that human rights are colonial rules. They want people to think that the West is civilized, while it is not. The West has maintained some civilization in comparison with developing countries. So they want to justify their use of force by saying they are taking those developing countries out of the jungles and the dark ages and get those monkeys according to Darwinism.... Today there is an American colonialism. American colonialism would justify its use of force to their own populations by saying they are developing these countries. So they have different NGOs working around the world gathering intelligence.... And the horrible thing is, they have been educating their people that they are the ideal and those people are just a bunch of savages.[51]

Although generally the tone adopted was somewhat more diplomatic and less inclined toward conspiratorial explanations, most of the Middle Eastern activists accepting American funding shared the underlying premise of Allaw's statement. This disposition meant that activists were constantly occupied by a concern with maintaining their independence (both perceived and real) and either countering or co-opting American attempts to co-opt and instrumentalized them. Accordingly they were apt to publicly and privately challenge American equations whenever an occasion arose. Each indicated that they accepted the funds as long as there were "no conditions" attached by the Americans. Amal Basha of the Sisters Forum for Human Rights took up the funding issue extensively in her interview:

Until last year we were boycotting any funding from the State Department. The SAF door has been knocked on several times by USAID: "Why aren't you asking for funding? Why aren't you submitting proposals?" They came with guidelines for proposal writing and said, "Just write whatever you want and we are ready." We had a lot of debate and discussion.... We had a political stance. I mean the [United] States is an occupying state.

[50] Interview with Franscis Abuzayd, Amman office director, Freedom House, in Amman, Jordan (Jun. 6, 2006).
[51] Interview with Mohammad Naji Allaw, Coordinator, HOOD in Sana'a, Yemen (Jan. 15, 2007).

...

And then we had an internal discussion and we said, "Well every donor has its own political objectives. We have to be careful. We have to cooperate with any funding agency that will serve our interests. What is our interest if we work with a MEPI initiative. Promoting democracy is also a priority for us. You cannot defend human rights in an oppressive system, in an oppressive regime. If your voice is not heard, how can you defend your rights?" And then we had a discussion and said, "Ok, this is our program, 1, 2, 3, 4...." Because every country is influenced by the others, we said we need to have a regional program so that we can gain support and influence in each country. So we proposed to make a democracy forum for women for the whole region. So then they come to us and said, "Libya, Sudan, and Syria should not be part of this." And I said, "Hey look, this is the type of impositions or conditions that we don't really like. This is *our* program and this is what we want to do. If you don't want it, we don't want MEPI." I said, "How come you want to promote democracy and leave holes? We are cooperating with democratic forces... how do you want us to exclude them? I mean, you are on the political level between states, I understand. But for us, we are a human rights movement, a women's group, we are feminists. We need to be all together." And I said, "that's fine; we don't want to apply for MEPI." And, you know, the lady, she was very nice. She said, "I completely agree with your argument, but it is not us, it is not MEPI. It is the Congress that made the conditions that these countries should be excluded from any assistance." But she said, "you can invite these people, you can engage them in your activities... I would encourage you to look for another funding, parallel funding and bring these people."[52]

As Basha's narrative intimates, many activists who decided to accept American funds did so based on a premise that they could at once further their own human rights agendas and push back against the operation of American power on sensing its edge. Cooperation and criticism stood shoulder to shoulder. "All of these human rights and civil society organizations, we cooperate but at the same time we have a critical stance on the US policies."[53] Thus an unintended result of American funding of and cooperation with Middle Eastern NGOs was increased occasion for the type of argumentation, persuasion, and critique profiled in the previous section.

HOOD presents another fascinating case study. As noted, although the NGO covers a variety of domestic civil and political rights cases, it has been unique in its active pursuit of Guantanamo cases and U.S. "War on Terror" policies in Yemen. The directors explain that the reason they can pursue such cases is that they do not have to rely on outside funding. The NGO sprang from and is closely affiliated with Yemen's largest law firm (of twenty-three lawyers) and it claims to fund Guantanamo and related initiatives independent of foreign funding: "You might ask why is HOOD the only organization talking about those cases and why we are strong is because we fund ourselves. We don't need the Americans or the West or Europe to fund us. So we take some of our own money as lawyers and

[52] *See* Amal Basha, *supra* note 16.
[53] *Id.*

spend it on human rights cases."[54] Despite their determination to pursue
and independently fund their own human rights agendas as well as the fact
that Alanesi and, more poignantly, Allaw offer a scathing critique of the
United States government, they welcomed funding from U.S. government
sources, provided it was not accompanied by any conditions and it was
"transparent."[55] "It is good that there is some money spent on freedom and
rights and not all the money is spent on violence and force," Alanesi adds
with unmistakable sarcasm. The duo seem to adopt a view that prompting
American funding of substantive human rights efforts by an NGO that
does not hesitate to challenge American human rights violations is itself
a subversive act. A week after my interview with the HOOD directors,
a U.S. embassy official told me that HOOD had applied for and would
likely receive a MEPI grant to review the Yemeni Judicial Authority Law.
Although he had no intention of funding "a Guantanamo Defense Fund,"
he was willing to consider funding HOOD's domestically focused projects
because the HOOD lawyers were the most respected in the country. "It's
like al Jazeera. We don't always like the way they do things, but we are
glad that there is at least one NGO in this country that will stand up to the
government and say 'you are wrong. You have egg all over your face.'"[56]

In Jordan, one of the few civil society organizations I came across that did
accept some U.S. funding was a community-based radio station. Amannet
accepted MEPI funding through Freedom House for programs focusing on
women's rights issues. The station also broadcast parliamentary sessions
live and covered the news with a focus on investigative reporting, placing
reporters in highly populated places like refugee camps and poorer areas
like East Amman: "We try to get away from the government and elite, even
the civil society organization, because these people are after the media to say
we are very active and we do this and that."[57] As a very sharp and articulate
young reporter, Sawsan Zaideh explained the station preferred to focus on
water shortages or unemployment and corruption at the level of municipal
government. Their reporter specializing in human rights issues had famously
taken on undercover stories on conditions in Iraqi and Palestinian refugee
camps. Another project attempted to capture the oral history of Palestinian
refugees.

I took up the question of funding with Zaideh extensively. She explained
that to maintain their independence, Ammannet tried to attract small donations from a variety of donors for each program. Her program on the
media was sponsored by a Danish NGO. Zaideh told me that taking MEPI

[54] *See* Mohammad Naji Allaw, *supra* note 51.
[55] *Id.*
[56] Interview with U.S. embassy official (I), in Sana'a, Yemen (Jan. 23, 2007).
[57] Interview with Sawsan Zaideh, journalist for Ammannet Radio, in Amman, Jordan (Jun.
     28, 2006).

funding for the women's issues program had not been a subject of contention because of the station's commitment to maintaining its independence:

> What we believe here, we don't mind to have money from the US government, but it is conditioned not to have any kind of interference, any kind of trying to impose agenda on us. Because we believe that there are a number of projects funded by the US government and they have political agendas, in our case, we are open to everyone, but you can't interfere, you can't impose.[58]

She argued that Jordanians could differentiate between NGOs that took on Western priorities and groups that dealt with "what matters to people." Nonetheless, she admitted that the station had little motivation to prominently display the MEPI logo on their Web site, as per the U.S. government's "branding" requirements for receiving the funding:

> Freedom House is funded by MEPI which is US government. What we did on the homepage of the program – I call it manipulation to be honest – but it's like you justify your manipulation by your good intentions. So we keep the logo small, but we acknowledge Freedom House because they are doing a very good job in Jordan. But MEPI, it is known by people that it is governmental. . . . It is politicized and it is linked to the Bush administration, not any American administration. That's why people are sensitive to MEPI in particular. People here are clever.[59]

Middle Eastern NGOs' repeated reference to maintaining independence (actual and perceived) is rooted both in a broader and more long-standing concern that by accepting Western funding developing world NGOs become beholden to Western priorities, protocols, and approaches and in concerns particular to the Middle Eastern context, given the contemporary posture and role of the United States in the region. There can be little doubt that at some level Western priorities and prescriptions will overshadow local ones; however, I was surprised to find that most of the Middle Eastern activists I interviewed did not identify this as a pressing problem. Although Zaideh referred to the disconnect between Jordanians' human rights priorities and foreign donors' zeal to focus on issues such as honor killings, she had only praise to offer Freedom House for its deference to Ammannet's own priorities and direction. Zaideh's account matched that of Francis Abuzeyd, the Director of Freedom House's Amman office, who had in an earlier interview displayed an acute awareness of the widespread skepticism and legitimacy deficits with which the nonprofit organization, created and funded by the United States government and, at various junctures, affiliated with such inflammatory figures as Donald Rumsfeld and Paul Wolfowitz, operated. Accordingly, she placed considerable emphasis on Freedom House's policy of going out of its way to allow local partners' to establish priorities and develop projects around those priorities.

[58] *Id.*
[59] *Id.*

Overall, the Ammannet example paints a fascinating picture. To appear consistent with the human rights and democratization rhetoric it has tapped into, particularly elements that espouse tolerance for criticism and diverging views, the United States government ends up funding an organization whose work in substance bears little of the United States' imprint. Although there are few overt criticisms of U.S. policies on the air, the programming largely diverges from any kind of American script on rights issues, including its treatment of women's rights. The station instead often highlights Palestinian and Iraqi refugees' rights and suffering and its understanding of human rights is firmly centered around economic and social rights in stark contrast to the American conception of human rights. Again Zaideh's comments are instructive:

What's supposed to be the basic needs [*sic*] is supposed to be part of human rights, the education, the accommodation – all these things. After the American double standard, people started to mix these things. Because they started to feel that their daily needs, their basic needs is something different from human rights. Human rights just means you are allowed to say whatever you want to media. This is the way even that they are promoting human rights and democracy – not having prisons, freedom of expression, that women are completely free, but not your food, clothes, education, accommodation. You know what I mean because the Americans are not talking about these things. They are talking about just like limited parts and this is I believe the double standard because at the same time they are calling for free speech, they are collaborating with the government which is the main problem for the people in providing them with their basic needs. For example, America, the US administration is pushing governments for more free speech, but they are not pushing governments to be more accountable or to provide people their basic needs, to change their economic policies, for example. Even when I think deeply about it, there is a real contradiction between human rights and the capitalist system. They don't coexist.[60]

The fundamental challenge mirrors, for example, HOOD's pursuance of Guantanamo detention cases, or the tenor of the Democracy School's Children's Parliament distribution of flyers alleging American human rights abuses at Guantanamo Bay, while simultaneously accepting American funding. Although it is likely that most Middle Eastern NGOs making use of American funding have little choice but to decry American human rights practices and "double standards" to maintain their domestic legitimacy, the activism and discourses employed by the NGOs profiled clearly went beyond obligatory or strategic denunciations, making it very difficult to singularly categorize them as passive instruments of U.S. foreign policy. No doubt that at some level they do serve an instrumental function. However, aware that the United States needs them to sell the compassionate and benevolent hegemon image as much as they need funding, many Middle Eastern

[60] *Id.*

NGOs accepting American funds are able to negotiate considerable latitude in pursuing their agendas, with the threat of simply rejecting U.S. funding as leverage. As a result, American government funders become increasingly resigned to the "no conditions" parameters (even if in practice they are more relative than absolute). Through the process, the United States loses more and more control over which human rights agendas, messages, and voices its funding strengthens.

ASSESSING THE IMPACT OF THE MIDDLE EASTERN RESPONSE

Mirroring the outcome of American and Middle Eastern human rights trajectories charted in Chapters 2 and 4, the Middle Eastern response to the American human rights posture following September 11th was at once groundbreaking and deficient. Perhaps one its most basic achievements was its affirmation of the proposition that despite its unparalleled material power and relentless efforts to reproduce the "America as human rights guardian" narrative through various public relations campaigns, funding initiatives, and other efforts to win "hearts and minds," the United States was simply unable to shape the Middle Eastern perception of its policies, actions, and intentions in the post–September 11th era. *The Washington Post's* Phillip Kennicott provided a powerful commentary to this effect in the days following the publication of the Abu Ghraib photos:

On the streets of Cairo, men pore over a newspaper. An icon appears on the front page: a hooded man, in a rug-like poncho, standing with his arms out like Christ, wires attached to the hands. He is faceless. This is now the image of the war. In this country, perhaps it will have some competition from the statue of Saddam Hussein being toppled. Everywhere else, everywhere America is hated (and that's a very large part of this globe), the hooded, wired, faceless man of Abu Ghraib is this war's new mascot. The American leaders' response is a mixture of public disgust, and a good deal of resentment that they have, through these images, lost control of the ultimate image of the war.[61]

American human rights violations and the ever-present accusation of "double-standards" was placed centrally in the consciousness of the Middle Eastern actors, even among those accepting American funds for their human rights initiatives. Thus, at the most fundamental level, the Middle Eastern challenge to the United States is one that simply rejects American deployments of power through productions of knowledge in accordance with long-standing subjectivities roughly paralleling the core assumptions of the human rights paradigm's East/West geography.

[61] Phillip Kennicott, *A Wretched New Picture of America: Photos from Iraq Show We Are Our Worst Enemy*, WASHINGTON POST, May 5, 2004, at C01.

In addition, the forms of resistance profiled in this chapter all shared a common element of holding power to account – again, often employing the emancipatory underpinnings of the human rights framework. Through mobilizations against American human rights violations, through constant assertions of the contradictions between American human rights and free-dom rhetoric and American alliances with some of the region's repressive regimes, and even through putting American funding to use in furtherance of their human rights agendas, Middle Eastern actors attempted to transform oblique American appropriations into more tangible human rights advances.

However, if each of the forms of resistance presented in this chapter are examined more closely, gains can be only be described as mixed. The human rights mobilizations directed from the Middle East to the United States laid out at the beginning of the chapter were significant due to their modest inroads toward diversifying and expanding the flow of global human rights traffic. Ironically, these efforts were limited in scope and, consequently, impact as a result of inadequate funding. Beyond the United States gov-ernment whose refusal to fund such human rights campaigns was to be expected, other international and Western funders seemed to encourage Middle Eastern NGO initiatives that looked inward. It was more difficult for them to envision Middle Eastern NGOs undertaking serious initiatives that expanded their focus beyond local contexts. Challenging the United States' transgression would be considered a task best left to the big Western-based actors. As a result, because funding was not readily available for such efforts, only a handful of Middle Eastern human rights groups devoted sub-stantial time and effort to the projects challenging American human rights violations. Coordination of the disparate efforts taking shape was also seri-ously deficient and to the extent it did take shape, it too often sprang out of efforts instituted in New York or London. Local efforts were often ad hoc and scattered. As a result, there was no concrete infrastructure for East-to-West human rights activities put in place despite the era's groundbreaking rise in disparate efforts to that end. One sign of this was that the Yemeni NGO committee developed to pursue American abuses in Guantanamo and Abu Ghraib seemed to have dissipated or become effectively inactive by the time of my visit in January 2007. These circumstances shed consider-able light on the connections between global sources of funding and the prospects of developing world NGOs' capacity to meaningfully challenge the East/West human rights geography.

Despite their undeniable limits, the mobilizations that did take shape can set an important precedent and potentially paved the way for expanded efforts focusing on Western human rights transgressions in the future. This is because though they were limited, the steps taken by NGOs such as HOOD pushed the notion of Middle Eastern actors monitoring and mobilizing against American human rights violations (beyond rhetorical denunciations) past a conceptual and psychological threshold, moving from the realm of the unimaginable to the realm of the possible, fitting and appropriate in the minds of many Middle Eastern civil society actors and Western audiences alike.

Assessing the impact of the innumerable Middle Eastern critiques posed in the countless personal exchanges and interactions among American government officials, journalists, advocates, soldiers, and citizens and the same Middle Eastern actor in the post–September 11th era is equally complex. The idea that the teacher/pupil dynamic in which American previously placed so much faith had gone into disarray was frequently evoked in editorials and commentaries. Thomas Friedman captured what many Americans saw as "the new warped reality" in a column in *The New York Times* entitled "Leading by (Bad) Example."[62] In the piece, he described a delegation of Iraqi judges and journalists abruptly leaving the United States, "cutting short its visit to study the workings of American democracy." The delegation is appalled by witnessing George W. Bush link his Supreme Court nomination of Harriet Miers to her religious credentials, hearing that soldiers participating in a televised question-and-answer session with the American president were coached on what to say, a practice used by their own authoritarian leaders, and seeing George Bush defend "his right" to authorize torture, with one delegate declaring, "We are going home now because I don't want our delegation corrupted by all this American right-to-torture talk." Freidman concludes by admitting that the story he detailed is a "fake news story" but is sorry that "it is so true." Friedman's commentary stood as one of many American acknowledgments of the Middle Eastern gaze, as well as the now-blurred line between global teacher and pupils in matters accorded the human rights and democracy caption, a line many Americans, including the author, longed to be reinstituted.

At some level, Americans government officials charged with executing and defending American post–September 11th human rights policies also displayed consciousness of the Middle Eastern challenge and its validity. The 2006 State Department Human Rights Country Report begins by noting, "We recognize that we are writing this report at a time when our own record and response to terrorist actions taken against us have been questioned."[63] In denying American interference with the Yemeni government's decisions to keep Yemeni citizens released from Guantanamo in detention locally, one U.S. embassy official mumbled, "Frankly, they are getting fairer treatment here than they were in our hands." Another embassy official offered, "Guantanamo has done a lot of damage to public opinion about the United

---

[62] Thomas Freidman, *Leading by Bad Example*, N.Y. TIMES, Oct, 18, 2005, http://select
.nytimes.com/2005/10/19/opinion/19friedman.html?_r=1.

[63] "Introduction" 2006 Country Reports on Human Rights Practices, available at http://www
.state.gov/g/drl/rls/hrrpt/2006/.

States in Yemen. There's no question about that and I think anybody would recognize that. It's the kind of thing that makes us look just like the regimes we are criticizing."[64]

Yet, as was commonplace among American officials spanning the ranks, just as soon as he had conceded the parallel, he proceeded to qualify it:

What I try to point out to people, however, is that we are not just like the other regimes. First of all these detainees are not dead. Second, they do have access to the ICRC. There is some argument going on within the US legal community about what happens to them and what rights they should have under the Constitution . . . that would not be allowed to happen within a lot of other countries. People should give us slack and allow us to work within it. That said, they are free to criticize us and they should feel free to do so.[65]

Elsewhere when I asked directly about the critiques of American human rights policies he encounters, he stated:

A lot of them are almost nonsensical. That is why I start out each of my talks with a quick sketch of American civics. I explain that this is how the American government is structured and this is how decisions are made. It's not a conspiracy theory. It's not three guys in a backroom somewhere. Congress really does have power. The supreme court really does have power. A lot of times I introduce the topics myself. . . . I'll bring up the subject of Guantanamo, for example, and say you didn't like it. A lot of people in America didn't like it. They challenged it. They went to the Supreme Court and the Supreme Court said the president's policy for detainees is wrong. This policy is now dead and the administration and the Congress had to come up with something else. Now, you may not agree with that either. A lot of people in the states may not agree with it but there is a system for us to make these changes. And a lot of times I get big smiles and people come and say, "I kind of wish it was like that here." And that's the point I'm trying to make – that we are not perfect but there is a system there and it's not just the whims of the few that drive what our country does. We make decisions based on what we consider to be our national interest.[66]

First, as in Khaled Batarfi account of his exchange with senior State Department officials, U.S. officials remained firmly committed to their espoused position within global human rights hierarchies. The sentiment as Batarfi described was indeed one of "Before you point a finger at our systems take a minute to examine yours! We are still way ahead of you. Learn and follow. Once you are our equals, then you may be qualified to discuss our shortcomings!"[67] Within the formulation, Middle Eastern critics (even if they are journalists or human rights activists) were discredited through association with their oppressive regimes (and most likely, in an unstated fashion, to their oppressive cultures). Their ability to put forth serious human

[64] See U.S. embassy official, *supra* note 56.
[65] See U.S. embassy official, *supra* note 56.
[66] See U.S. embassy official, *supra* note 56.
[67] Khaled Batarfi, *Wrong Comparison, America!*, JEDDA ARAB NEWS, Mar. 11, 2007.

rights challenges was accordingly confined to the realm of human rights violations emanating from discrete internal sources. Second, there was a sense that allowing Middle Eastern critique of American practices was an exercise, lesson, or demonstration of American-style tolerance and mastery of democratic precepts. The type of assumption of a higher moral authority and "leader of the free world" designation never wavered. Thus, once appointed Attorney General Alberto Gonzales still made repeated trips to Iraq to observe U.S. Justice Department efforts to develop the Iraqi legal system and even met with the Iraqi Ministers of Interior and Human Rights (again, as an overseer), despite his key role in setting the legal groundwork for the era's various cases of torture and abuse in American-ruled prisons.

In the final analysis, although U.S. officials were conscious of the Middle Eastern indictment of their policies, most were rarely moved or persuaded by it. Concessions materializing arose primarily out of a concern over damage to American interests caused by Middle Eastern "perceptions" of United States policies. El Obaid El Obaid, was a young Canadian-Sudanese legal scholar who had moved from Montreal to Sana'a to head up the UNDP's Yemen human rights initiative. He faulted the substance and essence of the Middle Eastern critique:

First of all, they (US officials) don't get a good dose of critique, but they are comfortable when they get the conspiracy theories and when they get the sweeping indictments... the problem I am having here is there is hardly any sophisticated critique. There's hardly any critique that actually bugs the Americans. So that critique comes from Westerners or somebody who is a foreigner... but from the locals, it's either conspiracy theories, or its red carpets, some people who make critiques but at the same time, they are quite eager to please.[68]

El Obaid is correct in noting that the prevalent infusion of conspiracy theories and sweeping indictments woven into many Middle Eastern challenges to American policies provide American officials with an easy way to dismiss Middle Eastern critiques altogether; this is clearly displayed in the U.S. embassy official quoted above's labeling of the critiques he encounters as "almost nonsensical." However, my field research does not support El Obaid's broader position that a solid and forceful Middle Eastern critique never took shape. Middle Eastern voices consistently highlighted the litany of contradictions marking the American position vis-à-vis human rights in the post–September 11th era: the tremendous gaps between practice and rhetoric, the gaping holes in American conceptions of rights, and the various ways its power and interests usurped the normative motivations asserted. Although they were not articulated in the same legalistic terms

---

[68] Interview with El Obaid El Obaid, UNDP, Chief Technical Advisor, UNDP Human Rights Project in Yemen in Sana'a, Yemen (Jan. 24, 2007).

many Western-based challenges took, the moral and rational grounding of the Middle Eastern argument was firm.

I would contend that the limited impact of the Middle Eastern critique can in large part be attributed to the continued operation of power relations, facilitated by the hierarchies embedded in prevailing human rights discourses. An article by Thomas Risse, one of the few constructivist scholars whose work considers the effects of international power relations on processes of argumentation and communication, illuminates further. Using Habermas's critical theory of communication, Risse finds that actors can theoretically engage in a "logic of argumentation" or truth-seeking to pass judgment on or justify applications of international norms.[69] Even when arguments are strategic, a consequentialist logic prevails, and actors embark on the process without any openness to being persuaded; movement toward the "logic of argumentation" is still possible, as these actors must formulate ever more sophisticated responses to challenges and justifications for the positions they maintain. Following Habermas, as ideal preconditions for rational argumentation Risse cites actors recognizing each other as equals and each side's equal access to a public discourse for those participating. Although conceding that these ideal preconditions are rarely in existence, he maintains that power relations need not impact the boundaries and content of argumentation absolutely. He points to evidence from psychology to contend that "biased or self-interested communicators are far less persuasive than those who are perceived to be neutral or motivated by moral values."[70] So those who wish to limit their discourse to strategic rhetoric will quickly learn that others will not be willing to buy it and will thus eventually be forced in the direction of engaging in more meaningful forms of argumentation. Risse proposes that the real issue is not whether "power relations are absent in a discourse, but to what extent they can explain the argumentative outcome."[71] To answer the latter question, Risse offers several criteria. In Risse's view, if these conditions are generally favorable, even absent an ideal speech situation, truth-seeking can take place to varying degrees. The first criteria Risse lists is "Whether conditions of nonhierarchy are maintained

[69] Thomas Risse, 'Let's Argue!': Communicative Action in World Politics, 54:1 INT'L ORG. 9–10. (2000). In responding to the validity claims in each others' assertions, parties are forced into an exercise of argumentation that facilitates persuasion and diminished the impact of interference from power relations and social hierarchies between the parties: "Where argumentative rationality prevails, actors do not seek to maximize or to satisfy their given interests and preferences, but to challenge and to justify the validity claims inherent in them – and they are prepared to change their view of the world or even their interests in light of the better argument." The three primary types of validity claims Risse identifies are those that concern the truth of assertions made, those that focus on the moral rightness of the norm's underlying arguments, and those that concern the truthfulness and authenticity of the speaker.
[70] Id. at 17.
[71] Id. at 18.

such that actors reframe from making use of their rank or status in order to make arguments."[72]

Applying Risse's theoretical insights, it can be argued that although the imbalance of power did not absolutely bar Middle Eastern critiques of the United States from having an impact, the processes of argumentation and shaming that *did* take shape remained considerably limited by American government officials' persistent adherence to an entrenched hierarchy according them a superior status in matters relating to human rights. There are several reasons for this, including reasons rooted in the ideology and even psychology of Bush administration officials. However, it cannot be denied that one of the biggest determinants of the American posture was its facilitation by the enduring terms and tenets of the East/West human rights geography. One side simply enjoyed greater access to the discourse around which the debate was centered. Thus, in a circular fashion, the impact of the Middle Eastern critique being waged was abated by the very power-laden normative formulations it sought to challenge.

The final Middle Eastern challenge profiled – that of civil society NGOs' treatment of American funding fared only slightly better. In refusing to accept American money, Middle Eastern NGOs took a near certain path toward preventing their co-option and disrupting American strategies designed to spread "America's good news story." It was clear from the field research conducted that as a result of the high incidence of NGOs refusing their sponsorship, American funders became sensitized to local NGOs' constant threat to simply pull out and were (at least to some extent) forced to be more accommodating in who they funded and under what terms. Further, in the case of those NGOs that did accept American funding, the collaboration could easily turn into a kind of mutual co-option, in which the human rights group used American money for projects with objectives coinciding that American goals and/or rhetoric but left other resources (at the very least, time and effort) aside for projects that challenged American human rights policies and prescriptions.

Still, despite the many elements of resistance and subversion present, at its roots, the fact that large segments of the Middle Eastern human rights NGO sector accepted and were in fact dependent on American funding remained problematic and limited the impact of whatever challenge was being posed. As long as Middle Eastern NGOs were accepting funds from the United States government, American officials could either come to believe or frame the fact as an endorsement of their espoused role as global human rights invigilator, teacher, and guardian. After all, what could fit better into the narrative of the traditional East/West hierarchy of human rights than the United States' financial sponsorship of Middle Eastern NGOs? The essence

---

[72] *Id.* at 19.

of the type of dynamic involved comes through in comments made by State Department official Gretchen Birkle in presenting the 2004 State Department Human Rights Country Reports. When questioned about Abu Ghraib, she poses the rhetorical question:

As a result of that [Abu Ghraib], would it be better if we just turned inward and stopped working with other governments and other NGOs on the human rights situation? I think the answer to that is no. We have received much information and much encouragement from folks in the field, many in your countries, who are encouraging us to continue our work. And I think that really addresses how we felt about writing these reports.[73]

In the same fashion, that NGOs embrace of American-funded initiatives can easily be interpreted by U.S. officials as an indicator that the United States' leadership (even in its post-September 11th constitution) is wanted and needed. As Chapters 4 and 5 discuss, the question of whether and what form of American leadership and interventions are effective and needed is a complex and multifaceted one. However, the fact remains that such funding combined with the operation of power dynamics discussed above also reinforces and permits American officials to slip comfortably into traditional mentorship roles. These dynamics and the ensuing casual treatment of Middle Eastern challenges came out in my discussion with one of the U.S. embassy officials interviewed in Yemen:

There is a genuine civil society movement in the Arab world, where men and women are forming organizations and lobbying for liberalizing their regimes and we are working with those forces. We are not imposing anything. Its not one sided; it's a two-way thing. Sometimes these groups and the governments we work with do point to Abu Ghraib and say this is inconsistent; you do this and then you come here to talk to us about. . . . I had this personally in Morocco a few years back when the bombing of Afghanistan took place. We were in the process of spending some democracy money with some civil society groups and I had a four-hour session over an *iftar* (meal to break the daily fast during the month of Ramadan). They had decided not to take our money to protest our policies in the Middle East and Afghanistan. I had a long discussion with them and said let's deal with the issues that you are specialized in and that are mutual interests and where we don't disagree. We are talking about human rights in Morocco. We are talking about women's rights, democracy-building, all of which we agree on and we have some money to help you do what you want to do. So if you don't like what we are doing in Afghanistan or Palestine, criticize us on that but work with us on what you agree with. Don't boycott us on things that are of benefit to you . . . if a civil society group feels strongly about the Palestinian issue, I ask them, "Do any one of you specialize on the Palestine issue?" No; no one had Palestine in their name. "Have any of you done the research on the different peace plans proposed – any specific views on the roadmap? No. So

---

[73] U.S. Department of State, press conference held by Gretchen Birkle, senior coordinator, Democracy, Human Rights and Labor, Bureau of Democracy Human Rights and Labor, Washington, DC (Feb. 28, 2005), *available at* http://fpc.state.gov/fpc/42855.htm.

why are you cramming this into our discussion of civil society and democracy? The reasons what is happening in Palestine is happening have nothing to do with them probably? And if you want to send a letter of protest to the American government, send a letter of protest."[74]

When it comes to their work within domestic contexts, Middle Eastern NGOs and civil society are depicted as formidable agents of change and their critiques are rhetorically welcomed. However, the official's response to the critiques pertaining to American policies is imbued with trivialization of both the charges and the groups posing the critiques. The interaction is clearly structured by the U.S. official's position as patron, although the NGOs' threat to refuse funding remains a powerful response.

CONCLUSION

Developments following September 11th gave rise to several forms of resistance and challenge directed at American policies by Middle Eastern civil society actors. These efforts were significant primarily for the way they altered the landscape and flow of global human rights engagements and the important precedents they set for movement in that direction in the future. In relation to global power dynamics, more than anything the dynamics detailed in this chapter speak to the misguidedness of zero-sum conceptions of the operation of power during the era. Neither the American exercises of power nor the Middle Eastern attempts to circumvent it through the human rights medium prevailed in any absolute terms. Instead, human rights remained a site of struggle in the encounter between the two contexts, firmly positioned between hegemony and emancipation.

---

[74] Interview with U.S. embassy official (II), in Sana'a, Yemen (Jan. 23, 2007).

FOUR

American Imprints and the Middle East's New Human Rights Landscape

In the post–September 11 era, the Middle East stood at the center of American experiments with both the violation and promotion of international human rights norms. This chapter traces how the Middle East's human rights landscape was transformed through the chain of events set in motion by these American experiments. The chapter begins by considering the contradictory effects of American post–September 11th human rights transgressions – the new prism through which the international legal system came to be filtered in the Middle East – on human rights consciousness in the region. The chapter then turns its attention to the American reform agenda, its co-opting by Middle Eastern governments, and its tentative openings for moving the Middle Eastern human rights project forward. The final section highlights transformations emerging from the confluence of both American abuses and promotion initiatives within the realm of religious/secular dynamics in the Middle East's human rights field. By assembling a string of empirical snapshots reflecting Middle Eastern voices and experiences during the era, the chapter draws a picture of the period as characterized by considerable engagement, flux, and transformation – at some junctures regressive or illusory, at others tangible and far-reaching – amid the backdrop of its successive human rights failings.

HUMAN RIGHTS THROUGH THE PRISM OF AMERICAN VIOLATIONS

An immense sense of disillusionment and false promise has pervaded the Middle Eastern encounter with human rights in the post–September 11th era. If prior to September 11th, the Palestinian condition had made it difficult for Middle Easterners to place faith in the international human rights regime's promise, after September 11th, the war and occupation of Iraq, Guantanamo Bay accounts, Abu Ghraib images, and CIA black sites, all with their inescapable racial and anti-Muslim undertones, moved human rights even farther away from Middle Easterners' lived experience of justice and dignity.

Of the cases of abuse and torture at the hands of the American government uncovered, Abu Ghraib in particular was etched in Middle Easterners' consciousness. It served at once as proof and analogy of Iraqi (and by extension Middle Eastern) subjugation, disempowerment, and suffering. Ismail Daud, an Iraqi activist working in Amman, described the episode as simultaneously providing a window into the Iraqi experience of denials of dignity and casting a dark shadow over the human rights ideal:

First of all, what happened in Abu Ghraib, it may be strange for you, but for Iraqis themselves, we were aware about these actions. They are living it. The random shooting and killing civilians is usual thing in daily life in Iraq. So it was not strange. It was strong because it's documented in pictures.... These kinds of actions are the main reasons why people don't trust human rights anymore, speaking about human rights. It was the truth, but nothing new for Iraqis. They realize from the beginning there were thousands of Iraqis detained and they tell you stories that are very bad. But Abu Ghraib was the document. Not the only document, but the published document, because we also document stories of violations from the beginning, but it has not been widely published like the Abu Ghraib story ... it reflects badly on the idea of human rights in Iraq.[1]

For Middle Easterners who widely identified with and in fact lived the Abu Ghraib scandal through its elaborate media coverage, the episode's use of dogs, sexual violence, and humiliation targeting Middle Eastern cultural and religious sensibilities told of the international power asymmetries and hierarchies at play. An Egyptian professor quoted in *Al-Ahram* asked: "I wonder if the pictures are deliberate: a message to the Arabs that summarizes an opinion: This is what we think of you, this is what you deserve."[2] An editorial in the Doha Gulf times argued, "The torture in Abu Ghraib is symptomatic of a wider disease. A subconscious belief that all Arabs and Muslims are evil terrorists who deserve what they get. In armies, ignorance, racism, and brutality go hand in hand."[3]

After Abu Ghraib, Guantanamo shaped post–September 11th Middle Eastern consciousness surrounding notions of human rights and justice. In contrast to Abu Ghraib, Guantanamo's presence was a constant in the post–September 11th period, enduring year after year. It was also official policy for which the American government made no apologies. As such it served as an incessant and unequivocal reminder of the gaping discrepancy between the standards of justice applied to Arab and Muslims and those Americans

---

[1] Interview with Ismail Daud, Iraqi human rights activist, working with the Italian NGO Un Ponte Per, in Amman, Jordan (Jun. 26, 2006).
[2] Al-Ahram Weekly Online, Amira Howeidy, *One Law for US*, May 13–19, 2004, http://weekly.ahram.org.eg/2004/690/fr2.htm.
[3] Editorial, *Brutality a Symptom of Ingrained Racism*, DOHA GULF TIMES, May 1, 2004.

claimed for themselves. To many in the Middle East, the fact that detainees were taken to Guantanamo so that they could be treated "in a way that would not be allowed in US Soil"[4] demonstrated the hierarchy and discrimination embedded in American's practice of human rights. The fact that international norms could be thwarted with so few repercussions again spoke to the operation of international power asymmetries. In a statement put out following the suicide of three detainees, the often fiery Arab Lawyers Union captured the Arab view of the operation of power versus justice reflected in Guantanamo's presence: "All measures of justice are brushed aside in relations governed by the law of power rather than the power of law."[5]

Perhaps even more than the prominent cases of torture and abuse that took the global spotlight, the Middle Eastern disillusionment with human rights resulted from witnessing the day-to-day horrors of a war conducted in violation of international law and then witnessing the immense violence and human suffering it produced being largely written off as collateral damage and considered to be within the bounds of humanitarian law. That there was neither a substantial mobilization nor identifiable legal recourse to challenge much of the human toll on Iraqis made the human rights project seem like an abstraction plagued by a gulf between theory and practice. Where international human rights and humanitarian organizations did intervene, their focus on particular American military practices in conducting the war, rather than the unjust cause of the conflict, seemed out of place to most in the Middle East. This was because so much of Iraqis suffering stemmed not from direct American actions but the violent civil war and chaos the American intervention had spurred.

At the same time, placed against the backdrop of the immense violence and insecurity filling Iraqis' lives, American human rights promotion projects in Iraq appeared grossly out of touch and disconnected from the country's unfolding human tragedy. An Arab activist working on an Iraqi human rights project in Amman describes the widely felt sense of disconnect among Iraqis:

If I am an Iraqi living in Iraq and I can't guarantee that I leave my house in the morning or my kids go to school in the morning, I can't be sure we will make it to the house at the end of the day, why would I care about human rights? So you can't really sell human rights to people. . . . The harsh reality makes it a luxury. We can't talk to people about human rights when they cannot eat. I mean you advocate that for people to believe their lives will improve, but when they only see violation of their own rights it becomes very difficult to target them.[6]

---

[4] *Contempt for Law*, ARAB NEWS, Feb. 17, 2006.

[5] GlobalResearch.ca, *ALU calls for Immediate Closure of Guantanamo Detention after the Suicide of Three Arab Detainees*, Jun. 27, 2006, http://www.globalresearch.ca/index.php?context=va&aid=2709.

[6] Interview with Arab human rights activist, in Amman, Jordan (Jun. 4, 2006).

Even Middle Eastern activists observing the phenomenon from a distance were perplexed by American prescriptions. "I mean look at the victims. All of these people are dying, are cut up and blown up ... do you think they are going to support democracy, while they lost everything?" Amal Basha of the Yemen-based Sister Forum for Human Rights put forth.[7]

When rights were instituted in the Iraqi context, they appeared even more misplaced by the fact that they could not be meaningfully exercised. For example, as Daud went on to explain, after the American invasion, in contrast to other populations in the region, Iraqis' freedom of expression was officially recognized; yet, it remained absent in practice. "In Iraq you have access to information. You have hundreds of newspapers. You can speak about anything – legally, I'm saying. In reality, if you speak, the militias will kill you."[8] Similarly, Iraqi author and activist Haifa Zangana notes that in the same way that the legal provisions of gender equality in personal status law were largely rendered meaningless by life under a brutal dictatorship, American attempts to champion women's rights were rendered meaningless by the fact that women's lives were "marked by violent turmoil" and "lack of security and fear of kidnappings [made] them prisoners in their own homes, effectively preventing them from participating in public life."[9]

Piecing these developments together, the picture Middle Easterners observed was one of power facilitating the United States' license to violate international human rights and humanitarian laws with little sanction or accountability while at the same time enabling the appropriation of the human rights and freedom mantra to paint a veneer of morality to American policies. Accordingly, Middle Easterners who followed and to a large extent experienced the Iraqi tragedy as their own had trouble envisioning how the international human rights regime served to protect their dignity or positively impacted their lives in any tangible way. To the contrary, because they appeared to contravene what critical international law scholar Amy Bartholomew has called "the most elementary principle of legal justice: that internally legitimate law must be universalistic and symmetrical, displaying equal recognition, equal applicability and impartiality,"[10] American post–September 11th human rights policies further detracted from the already tenuous legitimacy of the international human rights order in Middle Eastern eyes. The human rights ideal of upholding universal human dignity

---

[7] Interview with Amal Basha, director, Sisters Forum for Human Rights, in Sana'a, Yemen (Jan. 22, 2007).

[8] *See* Ismail Daud, *supra* note 1.

[9] Haifa Zangana, *The Three Cyclops of Empire-Building: Targeting the Fabric of Iraqi Society*, *in* EMPIRE'S LAW, THE AMERICAN IMPERIAL PROJECT AND THE WAR TO REMAKE THE WORLD 254–255 (Amy Bartholomew ed., 2006).

[10] Amy Bartholomew aptly uses the term in her work on human rights following September 11th, *supra* note 9, at 175–176.

was instead increasingly understood as a hollow, elusive, and out-of-reach promise intimately linked to global power politics. "Let's speak about the foreign policy of the United States; it gives a very bad impression to people about human rights. They see it is a political weapon," the Iraqi activist Ismail Daud concluded.[11] During the course of my field research in Jordan and Yemen, his formulation was put forth in one form or another in virtually every interaction I had, from formal interviews to casual conversations with taxi drivers.

As a result of these dynamics, American human rights policies moved aspirations of international justice to the fore of popular Middle Eastern consciousness. Although the United States poured millions of dollars into domestic rule of law initiatives in the region, an equally (if not more) acute Middle Eastern yearning was for the international rule of law, signaling the incongruence between American grand schemes for spreading freedom internally and Middle Eastern aspirations for international justice and equality, within each side's calls for human rights and human dignity. Journalist Anthony Shahid highlights the discrepancy between the emphasis on freedom versus justice in his book *Night Draws Near: Iraq People in the Shadow of America's War*:

Time and again, I am struck by how seldom I hear the word *hurriya*, "freedom" in conversations about politics in the Arab world. It does appear but often in translations or in self-conscious comparisons to the West, where the word is omnipresent. Much more common among Arabs is the word *adil*, "justice," a concept that frames attitudes from Israel to Iraq. For those who always feel they are on the losing end, the idea of justice may assume supreme importance.[12]

Again, the sense of being "on the losing end" Shadid describes is almost always formed in reference to international power dynamics.

If this popular pulse for international justice is largely missed by Americans who understood rights and freedom in primarily domestic terms (beyond their own borders) and who stand in a position of power globally, it has not been missed by Middle Eastern leaders. As in the past, in the post–September 11th era, local ruling elites were often all too happy to exploit this popular disillusionment with human rights and even reinforce the associations between notions of human rights and American cultural and political hegemony. In other words, they sought to manipulate their populations' moral indignation over imperialist experiences past and present to forge their own political agendas ahead. State-controlled newspapers ran headlines such as "International Human Rights Watchdogs: US

[11] *See* Ismail Daud, *supra* note 1.
[12] Anthony Shadid, Night Draws Near: Iraqi People in the Shadow of America's War 15 (2005).

Gravest Threat to Human Rights."[13] In effect they willingly adopted American appropriations of human rights and allowed a blurring of the lines between the instrumental dimensions of American human rights discourses and the concept itself to escape being held accountable by human rights standards. The tactic did, however, have its limits, particularly after September 11th, when governments faced both American pressure and public backlash toward their own close ties with the American government. In Sana'a, the National Organization for Defending Rights and Freedoms's (HOOD) Khaled Alanesi described the complex and contradictory government policy that emerged from these dynamics:

You ask about criticizing the U.S. This was allowed in the past. The government was happy we criticized the U.S. So they taught us to criticize the U.S. so we don't criticize them. So it's not a new thing to criticize the U.S. We have always been told to do so. To criticize imperialism and the West and what they do against us and that the West is conspiring against us. They draw them as the enemy of our culture or our religion. After 9/11, we are more limited in our ability to criticize the U.S.[14]

Still, as the era progressed and Iraq rapidly moved toward chaos and reports of American human rights violations accumulated, Middle Eastern leaders found more and more avenues for discrediting the human right project. First, they portrayed American abuses as testament to human right being little more than an idealistic dream borne out of naiveté and divorced from the true Machiavellian ways of the world. Second, they argued that civil society and internal calls for human rights only equipped the United States with a pretext to intervene and by extension that rejecting human rights was a means of resisting foreign domination and upholding political and cultural autonomy. Finally, they adopted the American slogan that Iraq would serve as the model for democracy and human rights in the region. In an attempt to associate the human rights and democratization project with the chaos and instability gripping Iraq, Middle Eastern autocrats repeatedly posed the rhetorical question, "Is this the democracy and human rights you want?"

In the same vein, although they took every opportunity to showcase human rights nongovernmental organizations (NGOs) to foreign and international audiences, Middle Eastern governments simultaneously pursued strategies to delegitimize civil society forces.[15] As Khaled Alanesi and Mohammad Najji Allaw of HOOD explained, the Yemeni government went to great lengths to discredit them by presenting them as foreign agents domestically and terrorist sympathizers to the Americans and International

[13] *International Human Rights Watchdogs: US Gravest Threat to Human Rights*, Akbar a Yom, June 16, 2007.
[14] Interview with Khaled Alanesi, executive director, HOOD, in Sana'a, Yemen (Jan. 15, 2007).
[15] *See* Amal Basha, *supra* note 7.

Organizations.[16] In this way, American human rights abuses in the post–
September 11th era forced rights advocates in the region to maneuver a
treacherous terrain. On the one hand, they had to disassociate their own calls
for human rights from widely resented American policies and the warped
conception of human rights they evoked. On the other hand, they had to
counter local leaders' propensity to both exploit the War on Terrorism band-
wagon to justify further repression and exploit American double standards
to discredit and delegitimize them and their work:

We have been caught in a quagmire. Yes, we are supporting the fight for democracy
and the point of promotion of democracy. At the same time we have been associated
with the Americans. "And what about Abu Ghraib and Guantanamo and torture?
And we are the agents of the Americans with its good and bad things." I mean, yes,
we are with the Americans for democracy, but we are against the Americans for this
conduct.[17]

"It's a situation that discourages us from promoting democracy loudly,"
Basha lamented sitting on the couch in her Sana'a office.[18] Yet despite their
dismay, Middle Eastern human rights activists (working outside of the Iraqi
context) were conscious that there was another side to the Middle Eastern
encounter with human rights in the post–September 11th era.

American Abuses and Human Right Idea's New Legitimacy in the Middle East

At the same time that post–September 11th developments provided Arabs
and Muslims renewed reason to approach human rights with skepticism,
they had also spurred a new engagement and connection with the human
rights idea. Just as it had in the United States, Abu Ghraib served as a
pivotal moment for human rights engagement and consciousness in the
Middle East. In line with prevailing anti-imperialist, nationalist, and Islamist
discourses, American human rights abuses at Abu Ghraib were interpreted as
ultimate proof of human rights being nothing more than a tool of American
geopolitical ambition. However, because the torture and abuse depicted
was widely seen as directed toward the Arab or Muslim man and not any
particular individual, many in the Middle East felt the effects of the violation
and a profound sense of disempowerment on a very personal level. The
Abu Ghraib pictures allowed Arabs and Muslims to empathize and identify
with the torture victims in a way that they ordinarily would not when
considering torture taking place at home. In other words, human rights
violations committed by their own leaders were further removed than those
that were witnessed in the Abu Ghraib photos. In their search for a response,

[16] See Khaled Alanesi, *supra* note 14.
[17] See Amal Basha, *supra* note 7.
[18] See Amal Basha, *supra* note 7.

Middle Easterners turned to and invoked the moral authority and sanction of universalist human rights discourses more directly. The Arab advocate working on Iraqi human rights promotion from Amman recounted these dynamics:

It probably brought home the concept of human rights more strongly than anything else. People started debating human rights issues in talking about Abu Ghraib.... What is your right to be treated like a human being in dignity? It brings it closer to home. Ok, why have we been treated that way...? First, that the double standards are there, but at the same time there were some things that were done in Abu Ghraib that nobody has ever heard of before. It makes people feel more like victims. Why were we victimized by the Americans? It reinforces this whole feeling that Americans are targeting Arabs and Muslims. If you are an outsider, you feel sorry for the people in orange jumpsuits. But if you are in the country itself that has been really effected by it, not only by this, but so many other things, it will make you much more aware of what your rights are and how to fight for them.[19]

An account in *al-Sharq al-Awsat* in the wake of Abu Ghraib similarly argued that the American abuses spurred a significant popular engagement with human rights:

Since the Abu Ghraib prison crime was exposed, the biggest discussion group in the Arab world has been human rights, and this is a fine thing. The subject of human rights, freedom, and the state of the prison has taken over every conversation (in the Arab world), after many years when the Arabs talked little about the value of the individual and the severity of the torture and killing. The Arabs became accustomed to not dwelling on things that do not concern them.[20]

Gauging public sentiment, political leaders and associated media also took to enlisting human rights to condemn American violations at Abu Ghraib and Guantanamo. For example, Egyptian President Hosni Mubarak called the abuse "abhorrent and sickening, and against all human values and human rights confirmed and defended by the international community,"[21] and the Kuwaiti cabinet called the actions "against norms, international law, and human rights."[22] Bringing in preexisting frustrations over Guantanamo, *Al-Ahram*, Egypt's prominent state-controlled daily, wrote, "Those detained in Guantanamo Bay have no rights at all.... Human Rights groups are outraged by America's systemic violation of international law," and then went

---

[19] *See* Arab human rights activist, *supra* note 6.
[20] Ahmad al-Rab'i. Al-Sharq Al-Awsat, May 10, 2004, cited and translated by Middle East Media and Research Institute (MEMRI), available at http://memri.org/bin/articles.cgi?Page=subjects&Area=middleeast&ID=SP71804. (MEMRI is a partisan nonprofit organization that often provides selective, but nonetheless useful, translations of Middle Eastern Media.)
[21] Al Quds Al Arabi, May 14, 2004.
[22] Al-Sharq Al-Awsat, May 9, 2004.

on to quote a local human rights activist, stating, "International humanitarian law and the international system – the UN – are under attack by the United States."[23] Firm endorsements of previously demonized human rights international nongovernmental organizations (INGOs) ensued: "Amnesty International has hit all the right chords in response to the suicides, qualifying the incident as the 'tragic results of years of arbitrary and indefinite detention' and called the prison 'an indictment' of the Bush administration's deteriorating human rights record."[24] Finally, commentaries often articulated the rationale behind and logic of human rights safeguards in describing the injustices they saw taking shape:

These deaths reflect the desperation for a basic human need – a need for justice, a need to have someone hear what these incarcerated people have to say, then be duly punished if a crime has been committed or be set free. Three of the detainees are now gone without ever having seen a court or enjoyed a system of justice that is held so dearly by their captors.[25]

As reports of human rights violations from Guantanamo, Bagram, CIA black sites, and Haditha accumulated following Abu Ghraib, international norms recognizing sovereign equality, rejecting racial or religious hierarchies, and prohibiting torture and abuse reflected and gave expression to current Middle Eastern aspirations of justice. More than religious or cultural relativist justifications to evade international human rights norms generally ascribed to them, many Middle Easterners sought the universal application of human rights norms as a means of countering international abuses of power. This increased emphasis on human rights is supported by international legal scholars Jutta Brunnee and Stephen J. Toope's argument that "Rules are persuasive and legal systems are perceived as legitimate when they are rooted in 'thick' acceptance by the citizenry, an acceptance 'vitalized by an appreciation of the reasons why these rules are necessary."[26]

Beyond a renewed appreciation for the normative regime, Middle Easterners' who were caught between domestic authoritarianism and American hegemony often looked to international laws, institutions, and processes as their last recourse for achieving justice. This was captured in the words of Mohammad Al-Deraji, an Iraqi biologist-turned-human rights activist. Simultaneously working from his laptop, handling consecutive calls through a cell phone headset, and giving journalists' interviews in Amman, Deraji's demeanor was marked by tremendous urgency. When we sat down to speak, he articulated the view that Iraq needed international investigators, international committees, and a transitional justice process that addressed both

---

[23] *See* Al-Ahram Weekly Online, *supra* note 2.

[24] *Indictment*, Arab News, Jun. 12, 2006.

[25] *Indictment* Arab News, Jun. 12, 2006.

[26] Jutta Brunnee and Stephan Toope, *International Law and Constructivism: Elements of an Interactional Theory of International Law*, 39 COLUM. J. TRANSNAT'L L. 19 (2000).

THE MIDDLE EAST'S NEW HUMAN RIGHTS LANDSCAPE

human rights violations committed during Saddam Hussein's rule and violations committed following the American occupation.[27]

Even when advocates were confronted with continued skepticism about human rights norms' legitimacy rooted in their audiences' associations of human rights with American appropriations and violations, post–September 11th developments provided opportunities for persuasion and consciousness-raising. Although in the American context, human rights advocates resorted to framing international human rights norms as quintessentially American to promote compliance with the international framework, Middle Eastern advocates endeavored to disassociate the regime from the United States and its policies while continuing to argue for the human rights norms' universality and rootedness in Middle Eastern and Muslim traditions. Nizam Assaf of the Amman Center for Human Rights Studies put forth the following comment:

We say this is not a French product. This is not USA product. This is international, universal. In Quran [it is] written like this. Jean-Jacques Rousseau says this. Ibn Khaldoun says this. They say, "Americans, they want human rights by tanks." We say, "No, this is [an] exception. This is wrong. Don't deal with this. Human rights, they are yours. You must participate."[28]

For some human rights advocates, the argument is not only strategic but also borne out of conviction. One Jordanian activist was emphatic in his contention that Arabs have their own conception of human rights that was rooted in Islam and has endured for fifteen centuries. He then urged that the notion that human rights is what the United States knows, be abandoned. Although rights advocates and Islamic reformist have posited similar arguments revolving around human rights' applicability, authenticity, and universality long before September 11th, this line of argument carried little sway as large sectors of the region's population had bought into American appropriations of human rights, often reinforced by their governments and Islamist oppositions alike and widely identified human rights as essentially Western. American policies directly affecting Arabs and Muslims after September 11th, however, rendered arguments for the regime's relevance to the Middle Eastern experience and legitimacy outside of American politics considerably more persuasive. The director of a prominent Jordanian human rights NGO recounted that when her audiences questioned the legitimacy of the human rights paradigm based on American post–September 11th policies, she would reiterate that the United States is not a member of most human rights conventions and that it is the only state that has not

---

[27] Interview with Mohammad Al-Deraji, Iraqi human rights activist, in Amman, Jordan (Jun. 2, 2007).
[28] Interview with Nezam Assaf, director, Amman Center for Human Rights Studies, in Amman, Jordan (May 29, 2006).

ratified the UN Convention on the Rights of the Child. Then she found that the audience would become more comfortable engaging with the international regime. American noncompliance transformed perceptions of the international human rights regime as primarily an instrument of American power to being a legitimate tool for challenging power and injustice (both American and Middle Eastern).

These developments provide a glimpse into an important emerging trend and shift in subjectivity in the region. Whereas previously dominant anti-imperialist discourses provided limited space or legitimacy to human rights, as the September 11th era progressed, increasingly human rights were invoked and understood as essentially emancipatory. Khaled Alanesi of HOOD made this point with great confidence in our interview:

Regardless of the understanding of human rights as a Western concept, each day people are more and more convinced that they have rights. . . . There is no doubt that the people have been convinced by the idea of human rights and it is not like before where they understood human rights as a Western concept which would take them away from their customs and religion. So now they are not seeing it as a challenge to their religion and customs, but what people doubt is how serious the United States and the government are about human rights.[29]

Sitting in a large newly acquired office with empty walls and unoccupied space, save his desk and a table for visitors, Robin Perry, the American Bar Association Rule of Law Initiative's young resident coordinator in Yemen, observes the phenomenon, somewhat in amazement:

I was in Jordan for a couple of months, and, you know, the irony of it is that the US champion of human rights – or, supposedly, because of its human rights violations in Abu Ghraib and Guantanamo and so on, has actually ignited some sort of interest in human rights in the Middle East, which is really ironic. HOOD is always in the paper because of the Guantanamo issue and various other issues. It has activated this big engagement. It has also tapped into the broader Middle East political debate about [authoritarianism].[30]

Even Khalid al-Odah of the Kuwait Families Committee whose son had been had been detained in Guantanamo without trial for seven years and counting, noted that "One of the good things that came out of 9/11" was that it gave rise to human rights initiatives in the region and "really gave people the sense of the need for human rights."[31]

[29] *See* Khaled Alanesi, *supra* note 14.
[30] Interview with Robin Perry, ABA resident advisor in Yemen, in Sana'a, Yemen (Jan. 25, 2007).
[31] Telephone interview with Khaled al-Odah, founder, Kuwait Families' Committee (Jul. 17, 2008).

The new interest in, engagement with, sense of relevance – even imperative of human rights – in the post–September 11th era in turn provided advocates with new space and opportunities to pursue their agendas. As the post–September 11th era progressed, it became increasingly difficult to encounter the cultural relativist, values-based, or economic development as foremost priority line of rejections of the human rights paradigm that were previously the subject of tremendous debate.

Bringing International Norms into the Domestic Realm through the Back Door

Even as Middle Eastern activists resented the post–September 11th era's new litany of pressures coming down on them from multiple directions, they did not hesitate to also exploit the new possibilities emerging from its paradoxes. First, through their condemnations of American violations, they bolstered their credibility as autonomous and indigenous actors and the legitimacy of the human rights paradigm by painting it as equally applicable to American and Middle Eastern violations. In this way they preempted accusations of foreign instrumentalization. Standing on this firmer ground, they circumspectly tapped into the passion and indignation generated by widely resented American abuses in the region. Again, although most Middle Eastern regimes provided activists with limited space to launch direct and forceful attacks on domestic human rights violations, as a populist gesture and means of diverting blame, they generally did allow for (and often encouraged) criticism of the West and the United States. In a manner resembling domestic activists' attempts to draw parallels to "America's Abu Ghraib" (i.e., abuses in domestic prisons), Middle Eastern activists endeavored to channel the focus from American violations back to local human rights conditions by highlighting their parallels. Thus, after posing their critique of American policies leading to Abu Ghraib, a few voices called for Arabs to acknowledge their own hypocrisy and double standard in waging their criticisms of American practices while systemic torture and human rights violations were abound at the hands of their own leaders. One commentator in *al-Sharq al-Awsat* writes:

A crime is not a crime unless it is committed by foreigners. Torture is carried out by the Arabs with the consent of the Arab press, which is always silent about it. When someone tries to bring this up, he is accused of damaging the Arabs' good name and of acting for the Zionist camp.[32]

In an article entitled "Abu Ghraib Holds Mirror to Arabs," *The Christian Science Monitor* reported that "beneath the official condemnation and occasional anti-American protests is an awareness that torture takes place

[32] Ahmad al-Rab'i. See *supra* note 20.

across the Arab world almost every day, and that it's difficult to condemn the actions of the United States without taking a hard look at what happens closer to home."[33]

In Jordan and Yemen, I encountered this mirror effect on numerous occasions. El Obaid El Obaid, of the United Nations Development Programme (UNDP) human rights initiative in Yemen, observed,

A lot of people are realizing this is a two-way street.... Criticizing the American Abu Ghraib brings back Arab or Muslim Abu Ghraib practices, one. Two, criticizing the West for limiting certain freedoms, especially freedom of expression, speech, and thought, has become also a bit morally bankrupt because realizing it from the other side creates an awful lot of problems as well.[34]

Manar Rishwani, a young columnist at one of Jordan's most influential reform-oriented newspapers, *al-Ghad*, outlined the argument for introspection he regularly makes in his columns:

Is it the time to talk about human rights? OK, I agree no one can say it's not important... but some people are trying to convince us it's not the time now, you are giving the United States the pretext to occupy other countries or at least to make a real influence over its regime.... If I am talking about myself, I disagree with them completely. They are who is responsible for giving the United States the real pretext to invade other countries.[35]

Rishwani calls on Arabs to move beyond citing Orientalism and instead ask "why does the Orientalist still survive?" He contends that it is easy for Americans to co-opt images of Arabs or Muslims as not valuing human rights and democracy because the images are rooted in some truth and considerable contemporary history. Although he was critical of the United States for taking advantage of this, he argued that Arabs must take responsibility for and confront such "weaknesses" as a means of preventing foreign powers' exploitation as well as achieving progress and dignity domestically:[36]

I live half century in the world and I am a victim, only a victim. And I think it's my fault as Arab and Muslim. You will hear many things about United States. You will hear many things about Abu Ghraib, about Afghanistan, about supporting dictatorship in the region. That's true, but how to stop this circle and start again? How to get out of it?

. . .

Ok, after September 11th until Iraq invasion, things were going ahead, but after Iraq invasion, after civil war, after Abu Ghraib, governments are trying to use this picture

---

[33] Dan Murphy, *Abu Ghraib Holds Mirror to Arabs*, CHRISTIAN SCIENCE MONITOR, Jun. 4, 2004, http://www.csmonitor.com/2004/0604/p06s01-wome.html.

[34] Interview with El Obaid El Obaid, UNDP, Chief Technical Advisor, UNDP Human Rights Project, in Yemen (Jan. 24, 2007).

[35] Interview with Manar Rishwani, columnist for Al Ghad, in Amman, Jordan (Jun. 6, 2006).

[36] *See* Manar Rishwani, *supra* note 35.

and images and say, Ok, this is the alternative. This is not accepted. This is not my choice between this brutal dictatorship and occupation. It's between humanity or not, whether its by United States, by national governments, etc. It's not different to be tortured by national or by an American.[37]

Rishwani's call for simultaneously holding American and Middle Eastern governments accountable through norms rooted in "humanity" keeps the focus on local regimes' repression while at the same time maintains legitimacy through its indictment of American actions.

Although the voices that point to the Middle East's own double standards are actually the voices of rights advocates who had been pushing for human rights all along, as with the American case, the mere fact that rights advocates were given the space to posit such an internal critique is indicative of a normative shift of at least some significance. The new space has occasionally also translated into limited human rights inroads. According to Shaher Bak of Jordan's National Human Rights Center, Abu Ghraib presented Jordanian human rights advocates with an opportunity to increase public awareness and governmental responsiveness to prisoners' rights issues, securing greater access and oversight privileges to some Jordanian prisons:[38]

Yes it [Abu Ghraib] opened a debate and it opened the doors for our people to start visiting these areas and every year we have one or two rounds of trips. We go inside. We inspect everything.... We visit those who are called "from illegal organizations" and normal people and we listen to them and we prepare a report and go to the Minister of Interior and we give him this report and we deliver a copy to the director of security and...after our first report came out, everyone from the parliament to the unions' liberty committee started and said they would like to go and see the jails.

...And now there is the beginning of real consideration that people inside should not be exposed to torture.... Now they start talking about...improving their conditions, improving their situation.... It's moving slowly, but it's improving. Officers in charge, they know these people have rights. They have to be treated with dignity. I don't say everything has changed. No, I don't say that – absolutely not. I don't say that they stopped completely but they started to care. They started to train officers.... So there is a change. How long it's going to take I really don't know.[39]

The slow movement Bak described is illustrative of how Middle Eastern governments can be trapped by their own appropriations. Having fanned the flames of outrage against American ambitions and exercises of power in the region to detract attention from their own abuses, they feel compelled to offer concessions when advocates successfully highlight the uncanny

---

[37] See Manar Rishwani, *supra* note 35.

[38] Interview with Shaher Bak, Commissioner General of Jordan's National Center for Human Rights, in Amman, Jordan (Jun. 28, 2006).

[39] See Shaher Bak, *supra* note 38.

resemblances and connections between their governments' repression and despised post–September 11th policies of the American hegemon. It is fascinating to note that both American and Middle Eastern human rights advocates resorted to the same strategy of indicting their governments' human rights abuses through parallels to the abhorred attributes of the "other."

In cases where censorship precludes drawing direct linkages between American and Middle Eastern actions, there is an indirect subversive dimension to some of the coverage/condemnations of American violations, even among state-owned or state-affiliated publications. By describing American violations, journalists are often posing indirect indictments of Middle Eastern governments either collaborating or engaging in identical practices. Two commentaries in the Saudi-based *Arab News* have this effect. The first comes from an article entitled "Outsourcing Torture" that condemns American "extraordinary rendition" practices:

Now comes no less serious evidence that US spies have been kidnapping terrorist suspects and handing them over to governments where beatings and torture are a regular part of the treatment of detainees, against whom no guilty verdict has yet been delivered by the courts. Investigations are under way in three European states – Sweden, Germany and Italy – into the abduction of suspected international terrorists, who were then flown, often in US aircraft, to third countries for interrogation in order to wring confessions from these individuals.[40]

It is of course known to the reader that the "governments where beatings and torture are a regular part of the treatment of detainees" and to whom torture is outsourced by Americans in the post-September 11th era are Arab countries. Implicit in the condemnation of the American practice is the Middle Eastern collaboration. Taking on the issue also provides an opportunity to condemn torture and detention without due process under the protection offered by the ambiguity of whether the challenge is to the United States, local rulers, or both. Another article in the same publication addresses

. . . questioning around the world, both by the US and a number of foreign governments. Many of these were arrested in Afghanistan and flown to Guantanamo Bay where they were treated like caged animals, even though many later turned out to be innocent. Likewise, governments from Indonesia, the Philippines, France, Spain and Kenya, have all arrested hundreds of suspects and subjected them to long periods of imprisonment, often holding them incommunicado, before trying and convicting them.[41]

Again, in the list of countries involved, the names of Middle Eastern countries involved, including Saudi Arabia, are conspicuously absent.

---

[40] Editorial, *Outsourcing Torture*, ARAB NEWS, May 21, 2005.
[41] Editorial, *In Retrospect*, ARAB NEWS, Apr. 24, 2006.

AMERICAN HUMAN RIGHT PROMOTION

The post–September 11th era's corollary to new American experiments with human rights violations of the likes of Abu Ghraib and Guantanamo was the American grand scheme for human rights and democracy promotion in the region. To this end, the United States moved toward applying new levels of pressure on Middle Eastern allies to institute political reforms and allocated considerable funds to Middle Eastern human rights and democratization initiatives. The impetus for the undertaking lied in several converging factors. First, the appearance of progress on the human rights and "spread of freedom" front was clearly essential to how the Bush administration sold its costly Middle Eastern military and political interventions both at home and abroad. Second, once it had chosen to enlist the moral authority and positive normative associations of the human rights framework, American leaders felt compelled to reconcile at least the most glaring contradictions between their policy and rhetoric. As constructivists note, endorsing a norm creates an impetus for consistent behavior,[42] particularly given the melding of the norm with American identity constructions. This is because actors adopt such identities not solely for material ends but also because they want to be able to think well of themselves and be well thought of by others.[43] Although many members of the Bush administration astoundingly saw little contradiction in their championing of human rights and their stance on torture, due process rights for "War on Terror" detainees, or the Iraq war, they did display greater awareness of and preoccupation with the contradictions emanating from the reform agenda they officially embraced and their continued political, military, and economic ties with some of the region's most brutal regimes. This consciousness is reflected in George W. Bush's 2003 National Endowment for Democracy Speech, where he stated, "Sixty years of Western nations excusing and accommodating the lack of freedom in the Middle East did nothing to make us safe – because in the long run, stability cannot be purchased at the expense of liberty," and went on to declare that the United States will adopt a new strategy in the region.[44] Third, influential neoconservative voices within the administration were ideologically committed to both pursuing America's moral mission in the world and safeguarding American interests through political (and economic) liberalization in the Middle East.

[42] Thomas Risse and Katheryn Sikkink, *The Socialization of International Human Rights Norms into Domestic Practices: Introduction, in* THE POWER OF HUMAN RIGHTS 7 (Thomas Risse, Stephen Ropp, and Kathryn Sikkink eds., 1999).

[43] See Risse & Sikkink, *supra* note 42, at 8. *See also* Martha Finnmore and Kathryn Sikkink, *International Norm Dynamics and Political Change*, 52 INT'L ORG. 887 (1998).

[44] The White House, *President Bush Discusses Freedom in Iraq and Middle East: Remarks by the President at the 20th Anniversary of the National Endowment for Democracy*, Nov. 6, 2003, http://www.whitehouse.gov/news/releases/2003/11/20031106-2.html.

After an initial bout of alarm and insecurity over the prospects of Americans posing meaningful challenges to their repressive means of sustaining power, Middle Eastern leaders increasingly came to read the American stance as tentative and reactionary, not substantial – a policy whose course would run out. As the former Yemeni minister and current chairman of the Human Rights, Liberties and Civic Organizations Committee in Yemen's Shura Council, Mohamad al-Tayeb, noted, some Middle Eastern governments began "betting on the American failure in Iraq."[45] On the American side, once the idealism and momentum of the American grand scheme had waned as a result of the unrelenting bad news flowing out of Iraq, the reform agenda increasingly took on the air of a face-saving and damage control operation. As a result, the pressure to reform was often accompanied by a sense among those at the top in the United States and in the Middle East that appearances could stand in for substance if necessary. American pressure was also marked by significant ebbs and flows, with increasingly more ebb than flow as the era progressed, the Iraqi centerpiece project fell apart, and Islamists gained ground through the very democratic processes promoted by the American government. These dynamics allowed Middle Eastern regimes to mitigate the potential impact of American pressure in two primary ways: by co-opting the reform process and enlisting the counterterrorism mantra as a pretext to limit rights and liberties.

Co-opting Reform

To maintain their vital ties with the United States (and in cases like Yemen's, to prevent American military intervention akin to those carried out in Afghanistan and Iraq), many of the Middle East's authoritarian regimes selected the route of professing their renewed commitment to improving their countries' human rights conditions. Human rights were accordingly placed both centrally and widely within official government agendas, but concessions were to be limited to those viewed as safely under the ruling elite's control. Middle Eastern governments' co-opting of human rights took many forms. First, leaders took up and incorporated (usually very general) human rights discourses. A quote from a 2004 speech by Yemen's president, Abdullah Saleh, prominently displayed on the homepage of the Yemeni embassy in Washington, typifies the trend, "Human rights are tightly connected to democracy and the state of law and order. Therefore, we should remove anything that contradict [sic] them and stand against all forms of discrimination, oppression and exploitation for the human being and his rights."[46] Nizam Assaf, director of the Amman Center for Human Rights

---

[45] Interview with Mohamad al-Tayeb, chairman of the Human Rights, Liberties and Civic Organizations Committee in Yemen's Shura Council and former Yemeni minister, in Sana'a, Yemen (Jan. 21, 2007).

[46] Embassy of the Republic of Yemen, Washington, DC, http://www.yemenembassy.org/ (last visited Jul. 6, 2007).

Studies, satirized the human rights vogue among the Middle East's autocrats. "If you listen to the speeches of the King, he can say it better than me, really, and when I am reading I benefit from this."[47]

Second, designed to at once quell foreign criticism and intercept funds that might otherwise go to civil society forces with more drastic and immediate blueprints for change, Middle Eastern governments began conspicuously placing domestic human rights institutions within various ministries, agencies, and departments. Just a few of the governmental or quasigovernmental human rights bodies I encountered in Jordan included the Human Rights Section of the Prime Minister's office (staffed by a person who had moved to a new position in Egypt), a human rights complaints division within the prison system, a Public Freedoms Committee in the Parliament, and a National Center for Human Rights; moreover there were rumors that the Interior Ministry was creating a human rights division, a move that was formally announced the following October. Third, state institutions would sometimes take part in human rights initiatives with NGOs (usually in areas of human rights posing the least political costs such as women's, children's, or disabled persons' rights) to further demonstrate their intent to promote human rights. For example, Mizan, a human rights and legal aid NGO, cooperated with the Jordanian government in juvenile justice and women-at-risk programs. The group also implemented a media campaign including TV spots about constitutional rights in cooperation with the Jordanian Ministry of Political Development. Further, a number of "NGOs" headed by ruling government elites or their families sprang up in the same spirit of creating the appearance of a vibrant civil society but at the same time drying up independent NGOs' funds from Western sources. Finally, symbolic gestures were made with Western sensitivities in mind in the politically safer realm of women's rights. Since Yemen's Ministry of Human Rights was created, all three ministers appointed have been women, something the directors of Yemen's prominent human rights NGO, HOOD, portrayed as a ploy to deceive Western audiences, who they viewed as easily awed by the presence of a woman representing the Yemeni government at international fora.[48]

---

[47] See Nezam Assaf, *supra* note 28.

[48] See Khaled Alanesi, *supra* note 14. It is interesting to note that the two did not seem to see any benefit to having a woman serve as human rights minister. In criticizing the Yemeni Ministry of Human Rights Allaw extents the monkey analogy in the following manner:

"So what is the job of the Ministry – to say that everything is ok and to attend international conferences to defend Yemen. The presence of a woman by itself in an international conference – a bunch of monkeys having a woman come to Geneva and talk about human rights . . ."

Although at some level he is making a statement that is hard to deny – that Middle Eastern governments appoint a woman to such a position in large part according to calculations of Western perceptions, the statement also provide a glimpse into the duo's own patriarchal biases.

A major effect of the co-opting taking place was an optical illusion of activity and progress surrounding human rights, but the actual impact was to remain minimal, given the resources and purported effort committed. Nizam Assaf, the middle-aged head of the Amman Center for Human Rights Studies with a doctorate in international relations and a knack for a comedic satire, sketched a caricature of Middle Eastern governments' arguments to Western actors that further facilitated this process:

The regimes, they are adopting their policies and their faces according to these changes, only to tell the Western countries and the USA that "we appreciate human rights and we want to change our situation . . . but we are facing difficulties. First of all we have financial difficulties. Second, we have technical difficulties. We don't know how to arrange free elections. Please help us. Our officers need more training. . . ." They are playing with this. It looks like they really want to learn to be democratic. I think that this is a joke. You need five or ten years to learn and realize how to organize free elections or to have observers or to have independent judiciary. . . . Our regimes are lying to the international community and the United States is also lying to our regimes. Both of them, they know each other and both of them they are lying in their relations.[49]

With a sigh, he concluded, "The victims are the people."[50]

Threats from Terrorists and Other Muslims

A few minutes after sitting down to speak with Ibrahim al-Sane, the soft-spoken president of the Jordanian Society for Human Rights, a formidable middle-aged man barged into al-Sane's cramped office. Al-Sane introduced him as an experienced Jordanian rights activist. After a quick apology, our visitor proceeded to frantically fill al-Sane in on a new crisis. That day, two local newspapers had published unofficial draft versions of a new Jordanian terrorism law. The activist was appalled by the proposed legislation. There was no clear definition of terrorism provided, yet there were provisions for legal sanctions against individuals who visited suspected terrorists, suspects could be detained without a court order for extended periods, and judicial recourse came only in the form of state security courts composed of two army judges and one civilian judge issuing decisions through majority votes. After I briefly introduced myself and my research, the activist elaborated on the source of his frustration. As he saw it, in the past few years the Jordanian government had been facing increased pressure from domestic NGOs, foreign NGOs, and even the quasigovernmental National Center for Human Rights, which had put out a highly critical 2005 annual report. Thus, the government was looking for legal means to reign in civil society and instill fear in its population. Fighting terrorism à la the American example

[49] *See* Nezam Assaf, *supra* note 28.
[50] *See* Nezam Assaf, *supra* note 28.

provided the perfect cover. He considered the new draft legislation practically a copy of the American Patriot Act. After detailing the many ways in which American bad faith and double standards in the human rights field posed obstacles to the advancement of human rights in the region, he concluded by saying that the best service the United States could offer to efforts for promoting human rights in the Arab world was to not say anything about human rights at all. On his departure, al-Sane detailed the workings and challenges of the society. Our conversation ended with al-Sane shaking his head, "On the new draft terrorism law, we will now start organizing against it along with other human rights NGOs."[51] After considerable objections from domestic and international human rights advocates and a two-day parliamentary debate in which the Islamic Action Front, Jordan's leading Islamist opposition party, voiced concerns about the legislation's potential assault on liberties, the law passed the Lower House on August 26, 2006, and was enacted soon thereafter. There were no public American objections to the legislation.

The era's signature "War on Terror" offset the potential impact of American pressure on Middle Eastern governments to observe human rights, and, in some instances, produced pressure on local governments to actively violate international human rights norms through pressure to keep particular suspects detained and through soliciting "interrogation assistance" in rendition cases. Middle Eastern governments in turn made full use of the sanction to tighten their grips on power (although, as discussed in Chapter 3, there were also instances in which they challenged the American approach to September 11th). This was particularly true in the case of the Yemeni government, which repeatedly implied that the arrests and detentions it undertook after September 11th followed American requests and that the government had no choice but to oblige to escape the fate of Afghanistan or Iraq.[52]

Even supposing they were inclined to do so, American officials had already largely foreclosed their ability to credibly question detention policies and legislation falling in the "counterterrorism" category. This is clearly reflected in Alberto Gonzales's response to a question regarding whether he had brought up questions of detainee mistreatment by Iraqi forces with the Iraqi Interior Minister in a meeting on his third trip to Baghdad in August 2007:

Our country gets criticized about that, too. Scrutiny about, say, the issue of Guantanamo and what we're doing there. And so I spoke about the importance of just making sure that as people are detained here in this country that they're dealt with humanely, that they're treated fairly. These are very, very difficult issues. They're

---

[51] Interview with Ibrahim al-Sane, director, Jordanian Society for Human Rights, in Amman, Jordan (Jun. 1, 2006).

[52] *See* Khaled Alanesi, *supra* note 14.

issues that we wrestle with in our own country. And we have tremendous resources and a tremendous history in these kinds of issues. And yet they're issues that we still struggle with today. So the fact that these are issues that Iraqi officials are struggling with is not surprising at all.[53]

The lack of American will or legitimacy on the topic meant that human rights advocates were, for all intents and purposes, on their own when it came to confronting Middle Eastern states' policies slated as security or counterterrorism measures.

At the same time, Middle Eastern leaders tapped into Americans' fluid, blurred, and overlapping conception of categories of terrorists, Islamists, and other Muslims. As Nizam Assaf explained, Middle Eastern regimes often sent Americans a clear message: "we are modern, we are your friends. There are enemies within our societies. Our people are enemies for you and we are your friends. So, please keep me in my position."[54] More specifically:

They use the Action front and most of the Muslim Brotherhood parties as a scarecrow.... We are Muslim countries. If we give real democracy to them, they will take all the seats in the parliament. We will have another Algeria. We will have chaos. So we want to control democracy.[55]

Mohammad Naji Allaw of HOOD spoke of a similar dynamic in Yemen:

So the government uses this notion of people violating the law to justify its own violations of the law. It doesn't want people to really get used to the idea of the rule of law. So the government does not want people to proceed peacefully because that would restrict government action. So they can say because we are a developing country and we have tribes and uncivilized people, we must break the law.[56]

In this way Middle Eastern leaders produced and mirrored precisely the Orientalist representations of the region's Arab and Muslim populations as irrational, violent, volatile, and premodern, which are integral to the American image of the region. In justifying their human rights abuses, they similarly parroted the underlying rational of American post–September 11th detainee treatment policies – that some parts of the population are backward, uncivilized, and brutal, defying or lying beyond the human rights regime's guarantees; thus they are not entitled to human rights or full protection of the law. Given the Bush administration's undeniable adherence

---

[53] Babak Dehghanpisheh, *Baghdad Mission*, Newsweek, August 11, 2007, http://www.msnbc .msn.com/id/20228140/site/newsweek.

[54] *See* Nezam Assaf, *supra* note 28.

[55] *See* Nezam Assaf, *supra* note 28.

[56] Interview with Mohammad Naji Allaw, coordinator, HOOD, in Sana'a, Yemen (Jan. 15, 2007).

to the formulation, it was a stance Americans were hardly in a position to challenge.

The Fruits of Co-option

Despite posing significant barriers, Middle Eastern governments' attempts to circumvent the reform process set in motion by the United States were neither entirely successful nor cost-free. Emerging from the crevices of the post–September 11th terrain plagued by American and Middle Eastern appropriations of human rights have been a number of unprecedented openings for meaningful human rights progress. The openings have come primarily in the form of greater (though still indeterminate) space for activism, new governmental human rights institutions, and increased overall resources for civil society forces pursuing human rights agendas and activism. As constructivist scholarship predicts, the more governments who violate human rights norms succumb to international and domestic demands to demonstrate a genuine and consistent commitment to upholding international human rights norms, the more one strategic concession can spur another and human rights norms can become institutionalized or even internalized through normative effects within political and social structures. Thus, although Middle Eastern governments' elaborate efforts to co-opt human rights reforms and discourses are frequently meant to reign in human rights progress, their efforts often fail due to the trappings inherent in the undertaking.

Tentative Space

Almost all of the Middle Eastern human rights activists interviewed indicated that they now had greater space for vocalizing human rights claims and criticisms. For those Middle Eastern states that officially signed on to the American reform agenda, it was clear that cracking down on local rights advocates amid the increased global scrutiny attracted by post–September 11th developments would not bode well. In many instances, this meant that although the red lines drawn around human rights activism throughout the Middle East would not disappear, the boundaries in place could frequently be pushed to new limits. As Nizam Assaf noted, human rights forces were "using this moment to have their impact":

They are declaring, "We want human rights, we are pressuring the regimes. . . ." This is good for us because we feel that a little bit we are on the safe side. The regimes will not come to pressure us. A little bit, we are not sure, but. . . . We know that our regimes are in a moment in which they want to prove for the U.S. that we are your only friends. Another alternative will be anti-American. So they are obliged to be in a position of not attacking us or in a position where they will open little corridors for us in which we can move.[57]

57 *See* Nezam Assaf, *supra* note 28.

By the time Assaf had made this statement it was already apparent that at least at the level of speech and discourse, he was operating within an expanded domain, having begun our interview with a passionate indictment of Arab regimes:

We are in a region, the Arab countries, we have one-man states. This means every-thing and every human being and every animal, all belong to this one man – you call it president, king, emir, whatever. There is no real democratic atmosphere. No real freedom. No real human rights, with the exception of citizen rights . . . to have a house, to get married. But you go to the political rights, you cannot feel that you have citizens in these countries. You have only serfs. There is no real participation, there is no real transparency. There are no free people. We have free serfs who can move and sleep.[58]

Throughout the discussion, Assaf never once relinquished his critical and indignant tone.

Another indicator of Middle Eastern governments conceding expanded political space lay in the realm of press freedom. New media legislation passed in 2006 meant that newspapers no longer required government approval prior to publication, although it remained widely understood that journalists should contact government officials and include the government's perspective in every human rights story and that direct criticism of the royal family was off limits. Despite his overall cynicism about the state of human rights in Jordan, Ibrahim al-Sane of the Jordanian Society for Human Rights conceded that in light of the new legislation Jordan now had a relatively good press law ("If it was a ten, it is a five now"). The expanded space meant increased coverage of human rights issues ranging from reports of legisla-tion designed to curtail political and civil rights, government detentions and human rights advocates' objections to them, and even accusations of torture or other rights abuses being alleged by INGOs and UN officials, within the pages of major national publications. Two of Jordan's most popular newspa-pers, *al-Ghad* and *al-Ra'y*, had journalists specializing primarily in coverage or investigations of local human rights issues. In January 2007, *al-Ghad* and *al-Ra'y* published an add containing the message: "We want to know! We want to speak! We want to write! Since the Press and Publication and the Right to Access Information Law is one of the pillars of freedom and democ-racy, we call on you to show solidarity with us to pass laws that guarantee the right to access information and prevent apprehension, imprisonment, and heavy fines and do not expand the incrimination of journalists." The add was sponsored by the National Center for Human Rights, the Center for Defending Freedom of Journalists, Abu-Mahjub Creative Productions, thirteen Jordanian newspapers, and Ammannet, the community-based radio

[58] *See* Nezam Assaf, *supra* note 28.

station. Such developments positioned the local media as a key emerging pillar of a human rights infrastructure in Jordan. Although Jordan and Yemen are perhaps ahead of most other Middle Eastern contexts, a trend toward increased room for veiled criticism and increasingly more direct human rights challenges can be seen throughout the region though with great diversity in degree.

The expansion of the boundaries around speech cannot of course be attributed to American pressure alone. Numerous other factors have worked alongside or in conjunction with "the American project to spread freedom" in the region. Prominent among them is the rise in influence of Arab cable news channels, most notably al-Jazeera, which has undoubtedly spurred complex human rights engagements in the post–September 11th era. Although a thorough analysis of how Arab satellite news outlets have transformed the region's human rights discourses is beyond the scope of this study, within the fieldwork conducted, it was difficult to miss the widespread impact of the region's satellite news phenomenon. For example, in Yemen, I encountered a television with a cable news channel (usually al-Jazeera) running in the background in the offices of the foreign minister, a women's rights NGO, and both low- and high-ranking foreign service employees in the American embassy. Reviews of al-Jazeera were mixed, with some citing it as a negative force that politicized and sensationalized human rights issues and others viewing it as an important medium for raising human rights consciousness and posing human rights challenges to Arab regimes. Nizam Assaf stood with the latter group:

There is progress, mostly after September eleventh but also before that, especially with the satellite TVs. There is a very huge step forward in freedom of speech. I think with the issues with which they are dealing...the women's rights, political rights. And some TVs like al-Jazeera...little by little they are dealing with issues relating to the leaders. They are coming to the red and sometimes they cross.[59]

In terms of engaging human rights issues and discourses the new medium stood in stark contrast to the state-run news outlets, which were previously the only source of news for large majorities in the region. Although al-Jazeera was launched before September 11th, it took off in the post–September 11th era and in many ways, its prominence was closely linked to its various challenges to both American and local rulers' abuses of power following September 11th.

Despite the rise in opportunity for posing increasingly bold human rights challenges fostered by Middle Eastern governments' need to respond to mounting foreign and particularly American pressure, advocates continued to operate in the dark with only a rough sense of what level of activism

[59] *See* Nezam Assaf, *supra* note 28.

was safe and what would render them detained within the new uncharted landscape. Just as quickly as the lines of permissible human rights claims had been redrawn to provide increase space, they could be redrawn for achieving the opposite, generally with little warning other than more bad news from Iraq. Still, in those contexts where the government had openly professed its commitment to human rights norms, advocates became equipped with yet another (though admittedly blunt and unreliable) tool with which to fight back when targeted: leaders' own words affirming human rights commitments. "Sometimes we get quotes from [the King's] speeches and throw it in their faces when we get harassed. It's a kind of support for us."[60]

Particularly in Jordan, activists also frequently expressed frustration that the increased discursive space had not translated into substantial legal and political reforms. On more than one occasion, I encountered the statement: "Democracy in Jordan means talking about democracy."[61] Nizam Assaf similarly offered a bleak prognosis:

The influence of such transformation in dealing with the issues, in speaking about the issues, making dialogue, awareness, training, conferences... this is good. But if you want to see the influence, does it reflect on the nature of the regimes. I can say no.[62]

Local advocates' skepticism can hardly be considered unfounded. Even the limited gains made in freedom of expression, were perpetually threatened. In the year following my visit to Jordan, the government attempted to rein in press freedoms through several new pieces of legislation, including a new press and publications law that would impose prison sentences for journalists committing "press offenses" and the so-called Access to Information Law that enabled government officials to withhold information relating to national security, public health, and personal freedoms and granted officials thirty days to provide journalists information in sanctioned categories.[63]

Despite this considerable gap between the new space for approaching human rights and the achievement of tangible human rights gains, the new discursive space should not be easily dismissed. All of the discourses, engagements, and consciousness-raising surrounding human rights and its appropriateness or legitimacy within Middle Eastern social contexts lays an important foundation for the social acceptance of international human rights norms, increasing the prospects for movement in the direction of the framework once further openings emerge. The Yemeni MP, Mohammad al-Tayeb, observed that so much of what followed September 11th, particularly

[60] Interview with Sameer Jarrah, chairman of UNIHRD, in Amman, Jordan (Jun. 29, 2006).
[61] Interview with Jordanian human rights activist, in Amman, Jordan (Jun. 1, 2006).
[62] See Nezam Assaf, supra note 28.
[63] Mohammad Ben Hussein, Journalists Say Access to Information Law Hinders Press Freedoms, JORDAN TIMES, Jun. 24, 2007.

Middle Easterners' access to freer media has opened up Middle Easterners' eyes to the world. In the same vein, the new space and discourses have opened up Middle Easterners' eyes to human rights conditions in their own countries. "Even if this openness doesn't last with the same vigor, it will be hard to make people go back to the previous environment."[64]

Evolving Institutions

As noted, beyond providing increased space for human rights activism, Middle Eastern governments would often develop human rights institutions – large and small – to maintain the appearance of a commitment to the human rights paradigm. However, according to constructivist analysis, as a result of the normative effects of their interactions with domestic and international human rights forces, state-sponsored human rights institutions or initiatives can increasingly gravitate toward adopting standard human rights discourses and even undertaking more and more meaningful and independent human rights activities. In other words, to "fit in" with global human rights protocols, they gradually step away from exclusively playing out scripted roles of presenting the government in the best light possible. Although many institutions retained their essentially token status, some demonstrated the type of incremental transformation detailed in constructivist accounts. Perhaps the most compelling example of this I encountered in my fieldwork was that of Jordan's National Center for Human Rights (NCHR). The NHRC emerged from a recommendation by the Royal Human Rights Commission and was instituted through a temporary law promulgated in 2003. Shaher Bak, who formerly served as Jordan's Foreign Minister, became the center's commissioner. The NCHR was charged with monitoring Jordan's human rights conditions, pushing the government to institute human rights–consistent policies and laws, taking human rights complaints and negotiating a resolution with the government on a victim's behalf, and promoting human rights through education and training. Created within the framework of the UN General Assembly's Paris Principles for Quasi-Governmental Human Rights Bodies, the center was to be supported by the state through resources and mandate but otherwise independent.

I was first alerted to the possibility that NCHR had come to function as something more than simply a promotional device of the Jordanian government in a meeting with Jordanian human rights advocates in which an activist who was otherwise highly outspoken in his criticism of the government's human rights practices praised the center's work, particularly its 2005 annual report. The NCHR began its work cautiously, inviting skepticism about its independence. Its first annual status report issued in 2004, however, demonstrated an inclination to treat Jordan's human rights issues

---

[64] *See* Mohamad al-Tayeb, *supra* note 45.

more seriously and professionally than its critics might have expected. Opting to go through the motions, the government formed ministerial committees to consider the report and its recommendations without taking significant steps toward implementing key recommendations. The government was nonetheless happy to showcase the NCHR to visiting foreign delegations, including a number of U.S. congressmen who paid the center a visit. The visit apparently made an impression on the American policymakers as the NCHR was specifically mentioned in a resolution introduced in the House of Representatives commending "the political and economic liberalization" undertaken by several Arab states, including Jordan.[65]

The NHRC's 2005 report was even more pointed in its challenge, reporting allegations of torture and unlawful detentions, calling for a fundamental revamping of election laws, and detailing restrictions and targeting of opposition political parties. This time the government chose not to play along, perhaps sensing it had lost its anticipated control over the process. By June 2006, the government had not put forth any official response or reaction to the report. The 2006 status report issued later that year continued the trend of notching up pressure on the government with an opening reference to findings of a controversial UN Special Rapporteur on Torture report, using the report as a vehicle to challenge the Jordanian government's claim that cases of torture are isolated and those who commit torture are properly prosecuted:

In October 2006, Mr. Nowak submitted an elaborate report to the UN General Assembly on the situation of torture in all countries of the world, including Jordan. . . . In reporting about the situation in Jordan, the Special Rapporteur said that "torture is systematically practiced at both the General Intelligence Department and the Criminal Investigation Department." He concluded that "cruelty and inhuman treatment" were "commonplace" at the correction and rehabilitation centers he had visited, with the exception of the Juwaideh women's center. He specifically referred to the situation at Al Jafr Reform and Rehabilitation Center (RCC).

On the 27th of December 2005, the NCHR submitted a recommendation in which it called upon the Government to amend certain provisions of the Penal Code, particularly Article 208, in a manner that makes this article harmonize with the provisions of the Convention against Torture and Other Cruel, Inhuman or Degrading Treatment or Punishment, which Jordan had ratified and published in the Official Gazette on the 15th of June 2006. But, until today, no steps have been taken in the direction of implementing this recommendation, even though the Center reiterated this recommendation on the 9th of July 2006 following the Government's publication of the Convention Against Torture.[66]

[65] H.RES.37, 109th Cong. (introduced January 6, 2005).
[66] 2006 Status Report, National Center for Human Rights, available at http://www.nchr.org
/jo/pages.php?menu_id=35&local_type=0&local_id=0&local_details=0&local_details1
=0&localsite_branchname=NCHR.

Here, the NCHR adroitly exploited what could only be viewed as an unprecedented Jordanian government concession borne out of international pressure: permission for a visit and investigation of Jordanian prisons by the UN Special Rapporteur on Torture, the first in the Arab world.

The NCHR's efforts have to date cultivated a number of victories in both expanding the institution's reach and imparting consequential change. Starting in 2004, the NCHR negotiated permission to carry out previously prohibited visits to and inspections of Jordan's prisons and it was the only human rights entity allowed inside the countries' general intelligence and security detention facilities. The center's 2005 and 2006 reports also detail some important gains in prison conditions including a royal directive to close down the Al Jafr prison widely known as a cite of torture and abuse for domestic detainees as well as a CIA detention facility to which tens of al-Qaeda suspects had been sent for interrogations. The NCHR also began conducting human rights trainings for police and security forces. Finally, on the day that I met with him in July 2006, Commissioner Shaher Bak was particularly encouraged by the government's announcement that it would publish into the Official Gazette five international human rights treaties it had signed but to which it had not given binding force through incorporation into domestic law. They consisted of the following:

- The International Convention on the Elimination of all Forms of Racial Discrimination (ICERD);
- The International Covenant on Civil and Political Rights (ICCPR);
- the International Covenant on Economic, Social and Cultural Rights (ICESCR);
- Convention against Torture and Other Cruel, Inhuman or Degrading Treatment or Punishment (CAT);
- Convention on the Rights of the Child (CRC);
- Optional Protocol to the Convention on the Rights of the Child on the involvement of children in armed conflict;
- Optional Protocol to the Convention on the Rights of the Child on the sale of children, child prostitution, and child pornography.

As Bak was clearly aware, having the international human rights instruments incorporated into domestic law opened up important legal and discursive channels for prompting greater compliance with international human rights norms, irrespective of the degree to which the concession was rooted in strategic motivations. "So, most probably we have a turning point in human rights in Jordan. Courts are obliged to take conventions into account and laws have to be changed and modified," Bak offered optimistically. The excerpt of the 2006 report cited above demonstrate how quickly the center was able to draw on the concession to call for legal reforms. The concession also pushed the governments' co-opting of human rights (i.e., by signing instruments without any sincere intent to fully implement them) further in the direction of more concrete institutionalization.

As this brief synopsis of the progression of its work indicates, the NHRC has increasingly become more independent from the government that brought it into being. Although in its first annual report the center complained of its limited governmental funding, by 2006 the NHRC had turned to other, readily available funds, including from Western governments and UNDP. A congenial lawyer from the complaints division wearing what seemed to be an Italian suit proudly informed me that very little of the center's funding now actually came from the Jordanian government. The NHRC had been created through a provisional law that was periodically extended. In its 2004 status report, the NHRC appeals for a law that would grant it permanent status. In 2006, after an extended battle in Parliament, legislation according the center permanent status was passed. The normative forces that had facilitated the Jordanian government's showcasing of the NHRC in visits by foreign government officials, including American congressman, also made it impossible for the government to simply dismantle the institution once it began transgressing into the governments' comfort zone, without incurring significant costs to its reputation. In announcing the government's decision to close the Al Jafr prison in a gathering held at the NHRC and attended by the Prime Minister, King Abdullah proclaimed his continued support for the NHRC and called on the government to deal with its reports in a "serious and transparent way."[67]

Instead of creating a national human rights body, as Jordan had, the Yemeni government opted to create a Human Rights Ministry in 2003, perhaps from an awareness that many national human rights bodies take the same path toward increasingly asserting autonomy as Jordan's NCHR had taken. Most of the human rights advocates I interviewed were emphatic in their disdain for the ministry, arguing that it served absolutely no useful human rights purpose. In fact, after the ministry's silence on a few high-profile cases, several human rights NGOs had called for the ministry's abolition and the creation of a national human rights body in its place. Nasser Arrabyee was a journalist who had accepted a position at the ministry between March 2004 and March 2005 out of respect for then-minister Amat al-Alim al-Soswa, who had asked him to join. I held an interview with him in a sun-filled office in his home. There was no paved road leading up to what seemed like a fairly new building. Wearing traditional Yemeni attire, Arrabyee was extremely welcoming and personable. Because we met in the afternoon he had already started chewing qat (a plant-based stimulant widely chewed in social settings in Yemen and parts of East Africa). He was eager to tell me about his experience with the Yemeni Human Rights

---

[67] Rana Husyni, *King Orders Jafr Prison Closed*, JORDAN TIMES, Dec. 18, 2006.

Ministry. Although he considered the former and current ministers as well as those who staffed the ministry to be "enthusiastic," he left out of frustration because "circumstances" prevented the ministry from being effective. At best, all they could do was write a letter on behalf of the complainant to the relevant ministry or agency, such as the General Prosecutor or the Ministry of Justice, he explained ("They want the Human Rights Ministry to be just a decoration to appease outside calls").[68] But when I probed further, he admitted that even within the one year he was at the institution, he did observe signs of the ministry slowly inching away from its decoration status, as well as socialization among the staff and even government officials approached by the ministry:

Learning from others was there. Getting affected by others was there also. When the Human Rights Ministry was writing letters to other ministries to complain, at the beginning they were surprised. What is this? But then they get familiar with it, especially the political security. Most of them did not think there was anyone who could say to them "Why are you doing this?" but then they got used to it. These are positive steps. I mean, there is education, cultural change, but it is not at the level of the ambition.[69]

Arrabyee's reference to "the level of ambition" touches on one of the biggest debates surrounding constructivist analysis of the impact of human rights norms: what level of reform or changes observed is to be considered consequential? Although the constant tension between co-option and actual transformations in the face of co-option is a real phenomenon, subtle changes are too often overlooked or discounted on evidence of co-option.

There were also indications of potentially greater movement to come. Both the UNDP Human Rights Initiative and the Danish Human Rights Partnership housed central offices steps away from the minister's office within the Human Rights Ministry. Sisse Bangolson, of the Danish Human Rights Partnership, was in the process of analyzing fourteen interviews from representatives of various Yemeni ministries surrounding human rights priorities to be taken up in upcoming dialogues and trainings. Neither the Danish nor the UNDP initiative was new to the region. I had encountered both efforts in Iran in separate collaborations with the Islamic Human Rights Commission, the University of Tehran, and Mofid University in Iran's seat of Shi'a seminaries, Qom. Although such efforts had little to do with the United States and predated September 11th, within the post–September 11th climate, they had better prospects of eliciting the attention and interest of Middle Eastern governments who purported heeding the American call for political reform. As we chatted in her office in the Ministry of Human Rights, Bangolson mentioned that she had only recently arrived in Yemen; previously, she had

---

[68] Interview with Nasser Arrabyee, Yemeni Journalist in Sana'a, Yemen (Jan. 15, 2007).
[69] *Id.*

been in Jordan working in the same capacity with the National Center for Human Rights.

Resources and Emerging Infrastructure

Middle Eastern NGOs benefited not only from their own regimes' human rights appropriations but to a large extent also from American human rights appropriations. Following September 11th, the same forces that prompted increased American pressure on Middle Eastern governments to institute reforms, propelled a substantial increase in the funding and institution of human rights initiatives in the region. Tremendous new resources poured in from a United States government eager to demonstrate its benevolent intentions in the region and human rights and development INGOs (themselves often funded through U.S. government grants). In contrast to the state-to-state-level pressure that proved unreliable, the funding and resources were for the most part consistent. Although funds such as the approximately $135 million spent on political reform and women's status projects by the United States' government's Middle Eastern Partnership Initiative (MEPI) between 2002 and 2005 pale in comparison to the hundreds of billions spent in the region to conduct the Iraq and Afghan wars and various security initiatives, it can hardly be denied that such assistance has provided considerable financial and institutional support for local human rights initiatives. Accordingly, the influx of resources has contributed to the development of a human rights infrastructure in parts of the region and spurred an unprecedented flood of activity and engagements around human rights in the form of public awareness campaigns, dialogs, legal reform, electoral reform, and women's participation initiatives.

Despite barriers such as licensing restrictions, requirements of explicit approval for receiving foreign funding, and efforts to delegitimize NGOs governments found most threatening, both in Jordan and Yemen, there was evidence of remarkable growth in the number of domestic human rights groups and their level of activity. According to Khalid al-Odah, seven new human rights organizations were inaugurated and granted government approval to operate in Kuwait in the post–September 11th era, whereas before 9/11 the groups had not been particularly active and their efforts had been informal because they lacked government approval.[70] As Nizam Assaf noted, "We have more organizations. We have more courses, conferences, publications, lectures, symposium. If you deal with these four, five years, and if you compare it with before September eleventh, you can see maybe twice [as much]."[71] Many of the activities have a technical training

---

[70] Telephone interview with Khaled al Odah, Founder, Kuwait Families' Committee (July 17, 2008).

[71] *See* Nezam Assaf, *supra* note 28.

dimension, such as how to use international human rights instruments in Egyptian courts or how to use information technology in human rights advocacy. Most, however, are more deliberative, encompassing precisely the type of argumentation, persuasion, and dialog around human rights norms so key to constructivist accounts of how international norms can gain domestic currency. In Yemen, Ali Seyf Hassan, the director of the Political Development Forum (PDF), hosts a weekly gathering of activists, members of various political parties, journalists, and academics. The forum is held on Tuesday afternoons in the *mafraj* of Seyf's home, a room in which family and friends typically gather to talk and chew *qat* for hours. The day I attended, there was a large contingency of Socialist Party members, a few Islamists, a journalist, and a human rights lawyer (who was also Seyf's son-in-law) in attendance. Sitting on cushions lining the floor along all four walls of the room, each had enough *qat* in front of them to last several hours of discussion. Seyf informed me that the PDF was also holding a more formal symposium in the coming weeks in which Mohammed Abdul Malik Al-Motawakel, a PDF advisor and Sana'a University professor specializing in human rights, would present a critical report on Yemen's compliance with international human rights treaty obligations, and a group of five lawyers and five political leaders would debate the report's findings. As constructivist accounts submit, it is through the era's repeated occasion for such formal and informal domestic interactions in which government officials, opposition forces, and civil society members are constantly forced to learn about, consider, and engage with international human rights norms on the one hand and justify contravening views and policies on the other, fostering consciousness-raising and internalization of the stigma associated with thwarting the framework.

Many of the countless conferences, capacity-building trainings, dialogs, publications, and so on, taking shape in the Middle East have been organized as regional efforts, both spurring and reflecting unprecedented levels of communication, exchange, and collaboration among Middle Eastern human rights activists and NGOs. At the time of my visit, the Amman Center for Human Rights Studies was hosting a training for Iraqi human rights activists, was in the midst of negotiating permission from the Jordanian government to host a training for Syrian human rights activists, and was holding its second annual conference on "Human Rights within Criminal Justice and the Required Strategies in the Arab World" with participants from throughout the region. Similarly, when I met with her in Sana'a, Amal Basha of the Arab Sisters' Forum for Human Rights had just returned from a conference in Libya. The Sisters' forum housed two regional women's networks on democratization and human rights and regularly either participated in or hosted conferences attended by activists from throughout the Middle East.

Still, according to Mohamad Naji Allaw of HOOD, activists are faced with persisting limits within these regional collaborations. As he explained, if he was as openly critical of the Egyptian government as he was of the American government, he would never be granted permission to enter Egypt to participate in a regional conference or training, and, conversely, a Moroccan, Jordanian, or Egyptian human rights advocate critical of the Yemeni government would be denied entry into the country for their criticism. In Allaw's view, this limitation has hampered regional cooperation and prompted him to focus his efforts on international cooperation.[72] Despite the existence of the dynamic Allaw described, within the tens of human rights networks that have been created and hundreds of regional conferences that have taken place, participants have mastered the art of pooling ideas, experiences, and effort in a way that more often than not just falls short of the red lines to which they are subject. Thus, although not ideal, regional cooperation serves as an important pillar for the region's burgeoning human rights infrastructure.

The increased flow of resources is not without other drawbacks and limitations. A number of interview participants expressed concern about mismanagement and even corruption in the rush by both American-based INGOs and local NGOs to claim their piece of the funds Western government donors were so intent on spending. For example, Khaled al-Anesi of HOOD offered this criticism:

Definitely those programs are important, but we feel they are not going to the right place. Unfortunately most funds go to workshops, conferences, and the people attending are people who already believe in human rights and they are the same people attending every conference and every workshop. Those people are talking to themselves and repeating themselves.... People just want to spend the money they spend regardless of the result. I could say there is a corruption in the system from the people involved on both sides, both in the West and those inside the country.[73]

Throughout the interviews, a related theme recurred whereby individuals with little experience, consciousness, or deep-seated commitment to human rights entered the human rights fray because it had all of a sudden become lucrative. This observation was confirmed particularly among activists familiar with human rights NGOs in Iraq. Although clearly problematic in some fundamental respects, such occurrences do not necessarily translate into absolute waste and zero achievement. As with local governments, the instrumental entry of individuals into the human rights field does not preclude an increasingly genuine embrace of the human rights agenda, in part facilitated by the socializing effects of the trainings, workshops, and forums Alanesi dismisses as redundant. The same general trends emerge among Islamists

[72] *See* Mohammad Naji Allaw, *supra* note 56.
[73] *See* Khaled Alanesi, *supra* note 14.

who have increasingly entered the human rights field in the post–September
11th era.

TRAVERSING THE RELIGIOUS AND THE SECULAR
IN/THROUGH HUMAN RIGHTS

Traditionally Islamist discourses have been infused with strong anti-
imperialist currents – aimed not only at direct Western political interventions and cultural productions but also at all entities and ideas that could be
considered heavily influenced by the Western tradition and Western politics.
Accordingly, Islamists often fashioned strict dichotomies between authentic/
Islamic norms and Western/foreign/imperialist norms. Human rights were
placed squarely in the latter category and portrayed as both a production and an instrument of the West and its cultural values and political
agendas. Islamic legal doctrine and key human rights prescriptions in the
realm of women's rights, minority rights, and torture were widely viewed as
largely irreconcilable. This Islamist stance resulted in secular human rights
forces construing Islamists as posing a significant obstacle to the realization of human rights in the region alongside the repressive governments in
power. The relationship between Islamists and human rights groups was
largely marked by mutual mistrust and conflict. Although a transformation
in both the Islamist stance on the international human rights framework and
Islamists relations' with human rights advocates began taking shape prior
to September 11, American human rights violations that disproportion-
ately targeted Islamists and American human rights promotion initiatives
that afforded them new avenues for challenging ruling elites, accelerated
the transformation dramatically in the post–September 11th era. As events
unfolded, Islamists and secular human rights forces inherited overlapping
priorities in areas such as the use of security prisons and courts, electoral
rights, and freedom of expression, paving the way for inroads toward bridging the religious/secular divide that had long plagued the Middle Eastern
human rights project.

The Domestic Human Rights Bargain

As described in Chapter 3, a press conference organized in Yemen to com-
memorate the first anniversary of the opening of the Guantanamo Bay detention facility. Beyond its significance for unsettling entrenched global human
rights scripts, what was remarkable about the event was the convergence
of secular and religious voices, symbols, and discourses it encompassed.
The event was hosted by HOOD. Both of the leading Yemeni NGO's central figures, Mohamad Najji Allaw and Khaled Alanesi, were affiliated with
Yemen's Islamist opposition party, Islah. Immediately outside of their main

office entrance was a large green prayer platform. At the time of my previous visit to the office, of the nearly dozen or so people I saw, the only woman was the secretary who wore a full *hijab*, including a *niqab* covering her face. As already noted, Allaw was widely recognized as one of the country's best attorneys and the NGO had gained great prominence for aggressively challenging both human rights violations committed by the Yemeni state and the United States government within its proclaimed "War on Terror." An extended interview with the two prior to the Guantanamo gathering indicated that after years of leading Yemen's most renowned human rights NGO, the group had largely adopted a universalist human rights disposition in the civil and political rights sphere, even vis-à-vis Islamist forces with which they identified politically. For example, when a leading member of Islah's radical faction brought forth a case against a journalist responsible for republishing the controversial cartoons of the prophet Mohammed that were first printed in a Danish newspaper, HOOD took up the journalist's defense. The opposing lawyers (with the assistance of the Government, according to Allaw) attempted to paint the HOOD team as foreign agents. "This is actually very dangerous because we were labeled as people defending the people who insulted the prophet. So if anyone would kill us, he would think he would kill us to get closer to God," Allaw had stated with a hint of satire.[74] It was revealing that Allaw found himself in the same precarious predicament as secular human rights activists and in response articulated the same complaint against Islamist action that secular rights activists in the region typically put forth.

At the Guantanamo gathering, the language employed by the handful of Human Rights NGO representatives (including HOOD) was for the most part confined to the standard fare of secular transnational human rights lexicon. Yet al-Asadi, the recently released Guantanamo detainee, and the detainee families present clearly did not conform to the secular, middle- to upper-class, elite profiles one is accustomed to seeing in such human rights gatherings in the Middle East. I was reminded of the religious worldview from which he entered the forum when I approached the former Guantanamo detainee to express regret for his five-year ordeal. I was somewhat caught off-guard when met with a bowed head, lowered gaze, and a murmured acknowledgment of my comment delivered indirectly through Khaled Alanesi, the HOOD lawyer overseeing the event. If distracted by the significance of the occasion and disoriented by the familiar transnational culture of the human rights NGO setting, I had forgotten about the bounds of prevailing gender rules to which those with al-Asadi's disposition ascribed, he had not. And yet, through his presence and various invocations of international norms, the twenty-four-year-old who had traveled to

---

[74] See Mohammad Naji Allaw, *supra* note 56.

Afghanistan "for jihad" prior to being detained by the Americans was mediating an entrenched religious grounding within a new secular terrain. This
was apparent, for example, in his characterization of the suffering taking
place at Guantanamo as a "violation of every law of men and God" and
his conclusion that the United States was not upholding the Geneva Conventions after accusing the prison's officials of hindering detainees' prayers,
cutting their beards, and stepping on the Quran.[75]

The impact of this melding of religious consciousness with human rights
tropes extends far beyond those directly affected, such as al-Asadi. Because
within religious circles the American "War on Terror" detainees came to
serve as the ultimate symbols of the injustice being endured by Muslims
in the post–September 11th era, a detainee's act of claiming and invoking
human rights norms lends legitimacy, authority, and a new emancipatory
air to the discourse, drawing in the larger religious communities. In the
same way that in the United States high-ranking military officers served
as compelling spokespeople for the human rights idea within conservative
circles, Guantanamo detainees served as compelling proponents for human
rights among Middle Eastern religious communities.

At the same time, increasingly closer interactions and ties between more
formal Islamist organizations such as the Islah Party and local, generally
secular, human rights actors and discourses constituted a significant emerging trend in Yemen. As Amal Basha of the Yemen-based Sisters Forum
for Human Rights explained, when the government crackdown on religious
groups first began after September 11th, human rights activists did not know
what to do because traditionally the two forces' had been in conflict, with
Islamists relegating many human rights provisions to the realm of the Western and un-Islamic and human rights defenders perceiving Islamist political
and legal gains as among the most formidable human rights challenges they
faced. In the end, to varying degrees, most Yemeni human rights advocates decided to openly condemn American and Yemeni rights violations
against religious forces and this allowed the two sides to coalesce around
post–September 11th rights issues. With the relationship's point of entry set
by a consensus surrounding torture and denials of due process as human
rights violations, human rights forces were able to forge dialogs and engage
Islamists on more contentious rights issues such as internationally recognized
women's rights. Basha drew a picture of the dynamic that emerged:

It's like a bargain. You need our support as women's groups in political rights or
civil rights, which we totally agree – whether you are religious, extremist, it's your
right to be protected, to have a fair trial. This is our belief. This is our principle. At
the same time, equality is also an issue and they started to see it that way. OK we

---

[75] Kawkab al-Thaibani, *HOOD, Families Demand Closure of Guantanamo*, YEMEN
OBSERVER, Jan. 19, 2007.

want the support of this group for our demands, our issues, our fights. To be on our side, we have to give them something.[76]

Whether borne out of a bargain, as Basha intimates, a gradual buildup of trust between the two forces, or their combination, nearly all Yemeni human rights activists interviewed referred to both the unprecedented Islamists presence in their workshops, trainings, and forums, and to Islamist forces new openness to engage with the very rights issues that previously rendered the two groups' encounters so contentious, particularly in the women's rights field. Receiving me in the NGO's spacious new Sana'a office, accented with ornate furniture and a large-screen television, Sa'ad al-Gedsi, director of the Women's Forum for Research and Training, describes the altered landscape for her women's rights activism vis-à-vis Yemeni Islamists:

> The other positive thing is that, as women's rights activists, we started to talk on topics we were not able to talk about. Last year we finished a three-year program called "women's human rights in Islam." In this project . . . we start talking about some topics that nobody would address before. Let's say *hijab*, people started saying its not *rokn* (pillar) of Islam. . . . Also, a researcher did a research for us entitled "Ten Obstacles for Women's Human Rights in Islam." They made a *fatwa* against this person and the youth within Islah posed a challenge to the older generation and they fought each other. We were not able to do that before – all the people were together against women's issues. Those people also began to listen. Before they don't listen and they don't come to our activities. They became less confrontational. We also started to invite them and there was good relations established with these groups which are not terrorist, but they thought that this is Islam. We started to bring them more in step with us.[77]

The picture painted by al-Gedsi's is further dissected by the UNDP's El Obaid El Obaid:

> You may be surprised, here in Yemen their [human rights forces] defending Guantanamo detainees is not necessarily ideological commitment to these who are there. It's a combination of both that and also having a safe opportunity to demonstrate a commitment to human rights . . . exploiting this opportunity to gain legitimacy and also not suffer any Western conspiracy or Eastern conspiracy by saying those rights have to be guaranteed by international conventions, because this was not an opportunity that was available to them before 9/11. On the contrary, the people who used to rely on that [international conventions] were called puppets of the West . . . or at least secular.[78]

From El Obaid and al-Gedesi's descriptions emerge a fundamental third dimension of human rights defenders' increased space. Not only have Yemeni human rights forces benefited from increased space for pursuing

---

[76] *See* Amal Basha, *supra* note 7.

[77] Interview with Sa'ad al Gedsi, director, Women's Forum for Research and Training, in Sana'a, Yemen (January, 17 2007).

[78] *See* El Obaid El Obaid, UNDP, *supra* note 34.

their human rights agenda as a result of international pressures on their governments and openings presented by the greater popular resonance of human rights as a result of American abuses, but also, through the new relationship with Islamists, advocates have secured the space to invoke human rights with less of a threat of being targeted or delegitimized as Western agents or un-Islamic by Islamists. At the same time, they achieved greater liberty to invoke international human rights norms or legal instruments without necessarily having to couch their arguments within Islamic discourses – something that was previously considered a prerequisite for promoting human rights by advocates in many parts of the region.

While taking advantage of their expanded space to employ human rights norms via secular, internationalist tropes, a number of Yemeni human rights groups also chose to pursue (or continue pursuing) engagements with Islamic discourses, symbols, and jurisprudential and textual interpretations, as well as enlist religious intermediaries. For example, Sa'ad Gedsi of the Women's Forum for Research and Training noted that the NGO often invites Islamic feminists and scholars rooting human rights and women's rights norms within the Islamic tradition from Tunisia, Egypt, and Morocco to help the group lead its seminars. In addition, through a Women's Human Rights in Islam Program, the group trained sixty imams in eight governorates to incorporate women's rights in their sermons at mosques. "Last year we reached 45,000 people through them," Gedsi is pleased to relay.[79]

The turn to (or continued engagement with) the Islamic framework are clearly borne out of a sense that this increased liberty to invoke international norms without resorting to Islamist discourses in relation to civil and political rights does not necessarily translate into an absolute liberty to do the same in the context of rights traditionally contested by Islamists. Further, now that they have finally attracted the attention of Islamist groups and religious communities, human rights (and particularly women's rights) advocates do not want to squander this rare opportunity to embark on a more rooted, cultural project. According to Amal Basha:

So we, the human rights groups in a country like Yemen, we try to base our arguments on Islamic discourses and interpretations. We say our Islamic legacy is like a basket. If you put your hand in you can bring out jewels or snakes. Just leave the snakes inside the basket and let's try to get out the jewels. Let's enhance human rights and base it on religion. This is development. This is modernization. You can't pursue fourteenth-century context. There are different issues. There are different challenges. We have to be up to the challenges as a Muslim society. You cannot ignore religion...you are still tied to the rules of your religion. If you say, "I'm not going to base my discussion on it," so you are alienated. You are not accepted. You are socially rejected. So we try to maneuver.[80]

---

[79] See Sa'ad al Gedsi, *supra* note 77.
[80] See Amal Basha, *supra* note 7.

Although, in a later section, I lay out how I believe the new associations
and interactions between Islamist groups and human rights forces (both
domestic and international) have spurred greater human rights consciousness among Islamists, here I would briefly note that there is undoubtedly a
flip side to the new relationship, one that its advocates acknowledge:

> But you know we become selective. If religion is supporting this, we have to use the
> religious discussion. But it's dangerous. If one case religion is going to support you,
> you use religion. You will get the support of the conservative society. If you don't use
> religion and you go to the rural areas promoting CEDAW and the rural women say,
> "what is CEDAW?" ... it's very challenging. It's like you are walking on landmines.
> You have to be careful where you put your foot and when to step and when to take
> it out.[81]

As Basha clearly recognizes, embedding human rights within an Islamic
framework is fraught with its own risks, limitations, and trappings. Clearly,
advocates cannot pursue theologically based frames and strategies to solidify
religious forces entry into the human rights tent without those human rights
discourses being in some way transformed in the process. Despite the obvious
benefits of, for example, having a human rights message heralded by an
imam in a mosque, it is likely that the message is still being delivered within
a context or alongside provisions that are inconsistent with the human
rights project. Perhaps more importantly, human rights forces risk ceding
considerable authority to religious laws, discourses, and figures in what
Anthony Chase has called, "the tail wagging the dog":

> Instead of whether the rights regime makes sense given the political and legal context
> of Muslim states, the question becomes whether or not there are convincing doctrinal
> arguments regarding the place of human rights. This accepts, in essence, the need
> for liberalist religious justification of human rights, making an argument for rights
> a dispute over religious doctrine – a dispute that takes place on an Islamic field of
> meaning on which reformers have little claim to institutional authority and human
> rights scant normative power.[82]

Yemeni human rights proponents, like their American counterparts who
invoke national security arguments and enlist military intermediaries, can
stretch their strategies so far that they risk stripping the human rights regime
of an autonomous moral authority and, as Chase argues, its normative

---

[81] Id.
[82] Anthony Chase, *The Tail and the Dog: Constructing Islam and Human Rights in Political
Context, in* HUMAN RIGHTS IN THE ARAB WORLD: INDEPENDENT VOICES (Anthony Chase
and Amr Hamzawi eds., 2007).

power.[83] In other words, the conversation becomes one of military strategy, foreign policy, or national interest in the American context, or one of furthering religious doctrine and prescriptions in the Middle Eastern context, rather than one firmly centered around upholding human dignity. In deriving justifications for human rights from Islamic sources, human rights advocates risk contributing to the hegemony of the politicoreligious establishment and its discourses surrounding gender, ethnic minorities, criminal sanctions, and sexual minorities, which, though evolving, remain unmistakably power laden and problematic from a human rights standpoint.

Chase also argues that theological arguments for human rights have not borne out their promise. This proposition is difficult to conclusively establish. In many instances, human rights arguments incorporating religious references succeed in promoting tolerance and challenging conservative orthodoxies. In fact, it is not uncommon to see reformers within Islamist parties positing the same arguments for human rights' compatibility with Islamic precepts that were first made by human rights or women's rights advocates. Two indicators may be key to how effective such efforts are. First, the more the relationship between human rights activists and religious forces is characterized by trust, mutual respect, and a sense of (at least some) common purpose rather than conflict and suspicion, the more persuasive human rights advocates framing can be. Second, the extent to which such efforts produce human rights results depends on the extent to which advocates are willing to challenge problematic orthodoxies rather than accommodate or avoid them. Finding the right balance between the two criteria is essential. As Sally Engle Merry has observed, "Rights need to be presented in local cultural terms to be persuasive, but they must challenge existing relationships of power in order to be effective."[84] Thus, instead of rejecting human rights advocates' engagement with Islamic frameworks categorically, it is perhaps more important to highlight the dangers of stretching the practice beyond its limits or relying on it too much, especially now that advocates enjoy greater liberty to step outside the bounds of the religious framework and can benefit from increased level of trust between the two forces. In the end, the fine line may simply be one of permitting a religious (or military) argument for human rights to take on center stage versus simply identifying common ground.

---

[83] This argument is complicated by the fact the contemporary human rights regime was borne in many ways out of a natural law tradition deeply rooted in religion and religious morality. However, since the regime's inception, religion, and particularly religious doctrine, has had less and less to do with the substantive development of human rights' contemporary legal regime. In fact, emerging areas, such as reproductive rights, directly challenge dominant Christian doctrine.

[84] SALLY ENGLE MERRY, HUMAN RIGHTS AND GENDER VIOLENCE 5 (2006).

I did not notice increased trust, engagement, or collaborations between Islamists and secular human rights forces in Jordan. One human rights advocate I interviewed appeared hostile to the Islamic Action Front (IAF) and even baffled by why Western researchers visiting Jordan were so intent on interviewing IAF members. Another activist said that her human rights organization's only interaction with Islamists stemmed from members seeking assistance in cases of abusive detentions or torture. In an article discussing the impact of IAF coalitions with secular opposition parties on the Islamist party's position of several women's rights initiatives proposed by the government, Janine A. Clark describes the IAF's continued hostility toward and disinterests in collaborating with human rights advocates:

What is interesting from the perspective of cooperation is that IAF opponents to the draft amendment also raised several important concerns that were shared by many secular lawyers and human rights activists in Jordan. Despite these commonalities, however, the IAF was unwilling to cooperate with these activists – precisely because their response was a secular one.... In public debates, the IAF pitted itself against human rights activists who similarly condemned Article 340 but were proponents of amendments to Articles 97 and 98. The IAF refused to engage with these secular laws, arguing that the problem of honor crimes could not be solved until Islam is applied in society and to the legal system.[85]

Although this demonstrates that the move toward greater alliance with local human rights actors and discourses has not materialized in Jordan the way it has in Yemen (and this can be attributed to the disparate social and political composition of the two states), it is not inconceivable that the IAF's increased turn to secular human rights discourses in the political and civil rights realm (discussed below) will move the group toward new bargains with human rights forces.

Shifting International Relationships

The same type of "bargain" and ensuing engagement that took shape in the Yemeni domestic realm also materialized between Islamist groups throughout the region and international human rights forces. Increasingly recognizing that foreign governments', NGOs', and international organizations' (IOs) calls for democratization provided them with vital protection and avenues through which to vie for political power, many Islamist groups revisited their stance on the human rights paradigm and altered the nature of their interactions with international human rights forces. Although Islamist engagements with these discourses are rooted in the adoption of a more pragmatic politics dating back to the 1990s, September 11th developments further underscored the strategy's imperative for Islamist groups. At the

---

[85] Janine A. Clark, *The Conditions of Islamist Moderation: Unpacking Cross-Ideological Cooperation*, 38 INT. J. MIDDLE EAST STUD. 539, at 553–554 (2006).

same time, United States' post–September 11th calls for democratization presented important opportunities for the strategy producing more concrete gains. As Mohammad al-Tayeb, chairman of the Human Rights, Liberties and Civic Organizations Committee in Yemen's Shura Council, observed:

Now let's go back to the Islamists, actually after September eleventh they experienced those ideas and they found that they can make the most of those ideas. If there is a democracy, they think they will win. That's what happened in Palestine and partially in Egypt and partially in Yemen. People are saying, "As long as democracy is going to help us get to power, so just embrace it." And they know the sensitivity of the international community to the idea of extremism. Most of them are trying to introduce themselves to the rest of the world as moderate, progressive.[86]

In the human rights realm this meant that Islamist criticism of the human rights paradigm, Western governments, and Western-based NGOs promoting liberalization became noticeably less pronounced and, in some moments, was even absent. Instead, Islamists demonstrated a greater willingness to legitimate, collaborate with, and engage in dialogs with American and other Western-based initiatives in the field of rights promotion.

A telling illustration of Islamists new reliance on and openness to Western-based INGOs took place in Jordan in June 2006. Several members of parliament (MPs) from Jordan's leading Islamist party, the IAF, were detained on charges of "fueling national discord and inciting sectarianism" after they offered condolences to the family of al Qaeda leader Abu Mussab al-Zarqawi and praised him as a martyr. Except for the Arab Organization for Human Rights (AOHR), local human rights groups generally declined to take up the case publicly. However, Human Rights Watch, which was in a position to take up the issue without fearing direct repercussions from the Jordanian government, clearly condemned the detentions as a violation of freedom of expression. Other than the Islamic Action Front's own objections, the Human Rights Watch rebuke was the primary challenge to the Jordanian government's actions reflected in the media. Indicative of Islamists' embrace of the INGOs backing, a report on the Muslim Brotherhood's Web site invoked the authority of the Human Rights Watch statement in the Zarqawi condolences case. The Human Rights Watch intervention was consistent with its 2007 World Report, which focused its coverage of rights violations in Jordan predominately on violations against Islamists.

Neither the existence of INGOs' objections to rights violations committed against Islamists nor the fact that Islamists availed themselves of international human rights groups' defense were unique to the post–September 11th era. However, previously these dynamics sat uneasily alongside the constant tension between Islamists and transnational human rights advocates.

---

[86] See Mohamad al-Tayeb, *supra* note 45.

INGOs were generally alarmed by the religious specificity claimed and privileged position accorded to Islamic jurisprudence by Islamists. Islamists were repelled by the secular commitment of the human rights project and INGOs' reifying and sensationalist accounts of their religious prescriptions. More often than not, it was the element of discord and its mutual apprehension that defined the two sides' relationship rather than the instances in which the two sides found common cause. In the post–September 11th era, human rights INGOs treated American and Middle Eastern abuses waged within the counterterrorism context with a new sense of urgency and placed them centrally within their Middle East agendas. This new emphasis on "War on Terror" abuses often overshadowed the Shari'a-based disputes that had been previously so contentious. Mirroring the dynamics transpiring between Islamists and domestic human rights forces, the new mutual focus on political and civil rights violations opened new, albeit still somewhat tentative, paths for collaboration and engagement.

Islamists also forged closer ties with Western-based and generally (U.S.-funded) political development INGOs who promoted rights agendas through training, education, and deliberations. In Yemen, Islah worked closely with the U.S. government–funded National Democratic Institute (NDI) in the run-up to the 2006 presidential elections, participating in the NGO's technical training courses in capacity building, platform development, candidate development, negotiation and conflict management, and election observing. Mohammad Kahtan, the Islah spokesman with whom I met, was unequivocal in maintaining that the programs were of great benefit to the party and had no complaints, even when prompted.

At the same time, Islamists also increased their participation in international debates and dialogs surrounding rights issues. For example, following a number of face-to-face dialogs and deliberations between Islamists and its analysts, the Carnegie Endowment for International Peace, a Washington-based think tank, put out a paper called "Islamist Movements and the Democratic Process in the Arab World: Exploring the Gray Zones." The paper identifies six areas in which mainstream Islamist parties displayed persistent ambiguities in their positions, despite their assertions of moderate stances: civil and political rights, women's rights, implementation of Shari'a law, religious minority rights, political pluralism, and the use of violence. Carnegie reports that it received considerable formal and informal feedback from Islamists throughout the region. Abdul Momen Abdul Futouh, a member of the Guidance Bureau of the Egyptian Muslim Brotherhood, provided a formal response that was placed both on the Carnegie and Brotherhood Web sites. In February 2007, the Carnegie team of Middle East analysts put out a subsequent paper in response to Islamist critiques of their initial publication in which they presented their case for continuing ambiguities and inconsistencies in Islamist positions through a case study of the Egyptian Muslim Brotherhood. As Mohammad al-Tayeb argued, Islamists who engaged in such international exchanges developed a consciousness and approach that diverged from those of Islamists who did not have such encounters:

Yes, I do see some changes. I personally have participated in several conferences – international conferences – to which some fundamentalist groups were invited. I could notice that the people coming to these conferences are people who are willing to learn. When they come back to their countries, they know exactly how to talk to the international community and it seems to me that this is very educative for them. They usually make use of this and they are different from those who do not have these interactions. Dr. Ariyani – head of Muslim Brotherhood in Egypt. Very nice guy, very open-minded. Very good interaction. He presented the Muslim group in a very moderate way. We usually see some of his other colleagues on the TV saying something different. This shows that those who do not interact with the world retain their previous extremism.[87]

Finally, traditionally Islamists put forth several reasons to justify their wholesale denunciation of American policies and interventions: the support of many of the regions' repressive regimes, overwhelming support for Israel, and the spread of morally corrupt cultural values, which they sometimes considered to be licensed via women's rights and freedom of expression rights. In the post–September 11th era where the United States demonstrated at least some willingness to pressure regional allies, some Islamists became more refined and strategic in their indictments of the United States. In Yemen, Islah's Mohammad Kahtan stated that although he regrets that the United States' always sides with Israel in the Palestinian/Israeli conflict and finds that the United States has failed in its fight against terrorism because it has abandoned its commitment to human rights, he considers American reform and democratization efforts in Yemen and elsewhere in the region to be positive. The intense tone of indignation and resentment of American hegemony I witnessed in the voices of many of the (predominately secular) NGO representatives I interviewed in both Jordan and Yemen was surprisingly absent in his voice. He simply called for continued American pressure on the Yemeni government to prevent the rolling back of the liberties that have been achieved. Although Kahtan's posture was likely tailored to me as an American researcher questioning him on Islah's human rights commitments and does not exactly match the populist rhetoric against American policies propagated by Islamists throughout the region (including Islah), it may nonetheless signal a fascinating new flexibility in Islamist dispositions.

[87] *See* Mohamad al-Tayeb, *supra* note 45.

The Impact of Post–September 11th Human Rights Engagements

In the post–September 11th era, some Islamist movements have inched away from questioning human rights and closer toward embracing important parts of the regime – even serving as the political force behind select human rights campaigns. In the battle over Jordan's new antiterrorism law, it was the IAF that stood against the measure along with local and international human rights groups. It was not the fact of their opposition that was of significance; rather, it was the fact that they overtly based their opposition on human rights grounds, even making direct references to international human rights law, which was exceptional. In the lengthy parliamentary debate that transpired, the IAF consistently referred to the legislation as contravening human rights, with IAF MP Nedal Abadi calling the measure a "violation of the country's agreements on human rights with the international community."[88] The Jordanian Bar Society, headed by an Islamist lawyer, had also been advocating extensively that the legislation contravened both the Jordanian constitution and international human rights treaty obligations. In June 2007, Ali Abul Sukkar, the head of the IAF's Public Freedoms Committee, announced that it would put out a report on the state of public freedoms and human rights in Jordan by the end of the year. He took the opportunity to call for the abolition of the state security courts, the preservation of Islamists' rights to compete in elections, the assessment of Jordan's prison conditions in response to concerns raised by human rights groups, and the release of IAF members being detained. Similarly in Yemen, activists and politicians affiliated with Islah stood with secular activists and journalists in weekly protests (sometimes incorporating prayers) organized in opposition to new government restrictions on press freedoms and pressure on journalists.

Despite the prevalent element of pragmatism and instrumentalism behind the Islamist gravitation toward the human rights project, as with the region's authoritarian leaders, the more Islamists have reached for and employed the language of human rights either to display "moderation" or to pose critiques of their rulers' or American policies and practices, the more they themselves became entangled in the human rights venture. Put differently, once leaders decided that they would engage the human rights framework rather than reject the regime's inherent legitimacy or universality with regard to traditional forms of torture, due process, freedom of political expression, or election rights – no matter how instrumental the move in the human rights direction was – they had to contend with inconsistencies and contradictions presented by their entry into the human rights field. Through

---

[88] IRIN, *Jordan: Parliament Endorses Anti-Terror Law*, Aug. 28, 2006, http://www.irinnews
.org/report.aspx?reportid=60568.

internal debates and contests, Islamist parties were forced to deliberate on which parts of the human rights corpus they would accept, which ones they would reject, and how they could justify their positions to both their traditional conservative constituencies and the international and local human rights, democratization, and reform partners with whom they forged new alliances. For example, when the IAF decided to support a restrictive press and publication law proposed by the government because it also contained provisions penalizing journalists for religious defamation, the move was criticized in an *al-Ghad* commentary as the movement's abandonment of its asserted commitment to reform.[89] Equally significant has been religious groups' potential acculturation of human rights norms through their entry into human rights processes (such as compiling reports) and development of their own human rights institutions (such as the IAF's Public Freedoms Committee). The outcome of the road some Islamists have traveled in the post–September 11th era has been a combination of concessions fostered by strategic considerations and genuine consciousness-raising, often in that order.

Carrie Wickham's interviews of Jordanian and Egyptian Islamists provide a glimpse into Islamists' increasingly complex and multifaceted new human rights consciousness. The Islamists she interviews condemn American human rights abuses in Guantanamo and Abu Ghraib, protest the introduction of human rights education in school curricula on grounds that they represent concessions to the United States and erosions of traditional values, and demonstrate a willingness to engage with and accept significant portions of the human rights framework – all at the same time.[90] Two of her interviewees had participated in a human rights seminar with the U.S.-based Carnegie Corporation. One of them, Abd al-Mun'em Abu-l-Futuh, states the following:

> The Carnegie delegation wanted us to accept all the provisions of global human rights documents. We agree with most points, but disagree on a few issues. Why do American analysts always focus on the few points of disagreement rather than on the 90% on which we agree?[91]

In asserting acceptance of substantial parts of the human rights paradigm while at the same time raising concerns about the erosion of traditional values (no doubt in reference to women's rights norms being introduced),

---

[89] Al-Ghad, *Arab Reform Bulletin*, Mar. 2007, http://www.alghad.jo/?article=5837.
[90] Carrie Wickham, *The Problem with Coercive Democratization: The Islamist Response to the U.S. Democracy Reform Initiative*, 1:1 MUSLIM WORLD J. HUM. RTS. (2004), http://www.bepress.com/mwjhr/vol1/iss1/art6.
[91] *Id.* at 7.

Islamists mediate between their traditional commitments and new forays into the human rights paradigm.

The human rights engagements of Yemen's Islah Party similarly illustrate both the complex human rights engagements the era has produced and Islamists' new openness to large segments of the human rights project. In an interview in the Islah Party headquarters in Sana'a, Mohammad Kahtan, the Islamist party's spokesperson, posits that most of Islah's activities are human rights–related in substance, although they may not always label them as such, except when they are discussing women's rights and international instruments. He points out that there are several chapters in the party platform dedicated to economic, political, and social rights and that, prior to our interview, the party had hosted two rights-centered conferences: one on the subject of achieving rights and freedom peacefully and one on women serving as members of Parliament and as ministers.

Within the party, forging a position on women's rights has proved particularly contentious. "We have a debate on women's rights, but on men's rights, we all agree," Kahtan offered.[92] The statement would fit squarely into darker feminist satire were it not for the additional (and somewhat redemptive) context lent by the rest of the picture Kahtan goes on to paint. Although the statement provides insight into the vast gulf between the human rights commitment to gender equality and the Islamist starting point and propensity to view women's rights as conceptually separate from "men's rights," it tends to obscure the party's complex and evolving encounter with international norms. Kahtan makes clear that the party rejects certain international women's rights prescriptions such as the prohibition of polygamy and provisions for equal inheritance for male and female heirs, the latter forming the basis for Islah's objection to the UN Women's Convention. However, after an extended internal deliberations and dialog on women's political participation, the party voted for women serving as MPs or ministers, announced it would have female candidates running in the next parliamentary election, and later elected thirteen women to serve on the party's central consultative committee. According to Kahtan, those who opposed women's political participation have ultimately come to comprise a small minority, although he also notes that it may take another seven years of dialog for the party to formally adopt a position that supports women's competency to serve as president.

When asked about previous Islamist convictions that human rights were un-Islamic or Western concepts, he argues that Islah will never accept something that is un-Islamic, but human rights and democracy are notions rooted

---

[92] Interview with Mohammad Kahtan, Islah Party spokesman, in Sana'a, Yemen (Jan. 20, 2007). It should be noted that the translation provided might be overly literalist and what is meant by "men's rights" is, in fact, "human rights."

within Islam. In response to a subsequent question regarding whether he views Islamic precepts as capable of adapting to changes in time and place, he justifies a qualified endorsement of dynamicism in interpretations of Islam by turning to a line of argument traditionally posited by Islamic reformists and human rights advocates – embedding the human rights framework within Islamic discourses as a means of extending the currency of their message:

Humanity is what unites us all. So absolutely there is space to move within Islam, within the basic principles. I am in Yemen and you are in America. Humanity unites us both. Justice unites us both. Freedom unites us both. So, Islam is an invitation to open up to the world, not for Muslims to be alone or a state on its own. Unfortunately, some Muslims have this vision that they should be isolated from the whole world.[93]

When asked if Western criticisms of Yemeni human rights violations are legitimate, Kahtan echoes the sentiment of Abd al-Mun'em Abu-l-Futuh cited above, stating that the areas of divergence are limited to issues such as polygamy and equal inheritance for men and women but that there is mutual agreement on the core. Again, it is telling what is considered the core and what is considered minor or peripheral, though that has long been a feminist critique of the international legal order and is not limited to Yemen's Islamists.

Political scientist Janine Clark describes earlier developments in Jordan's IAF party surrounding women's participation that seem to roughly parallel the course taken by Islah:

Relative to many other parties in Jordan, the IAF boasts a large female membership and a substantial number of women in leadership positions. The IAF has some 300 female members, which, according to the party leadership, constitutes approximately ten percent of the total membership. A women's sector, headed by a committee of ten women, represents women within the party and recruits new female members. To this end, it hosts educational programs on women's rights in Islam and organizes activities on political issues of concern to women.[94]

Clark's focus, however, is on the ways this progress is tempered by the fact that women's involvement is often linked with husbands' or fathers' associations to the party, that women are not represented in the party's highest decision-making body, that in practice women are discouraged from running for public office, and that in a rare case where a women was nominated as an MP candidate, it was for strategic reasons. Although these dynamics are clearly at play, they do not preclude the prospects of meaningful advances in women's rights and gender-consciousness stemming from women's increased presence in the party. In other words, regardless of the

[93] Id.
[94] See Janine A. Clark, supra note 85.

patriarchal and strategic reasons behind their entry into Islamist party politics and the political sphere within which they operate in general, as they
experience limitations from patriarchal structures while at the same time
being exposed to more emancipatory ideas about gender equality through
their interactions with local and international activists, their consciousness
can come to diverge from that of the party's male elite to whom they may
increasingly pose challenges. This is illustrated by Clark's own report that
although the IAF's male leadership rejected the implementation of quotas for
female members of Parliament, women inside the party embraced a quota
policy.

Whether it is in the realm of civil and political rights or to less acclaim in
the realm of women's rights and participation, the willingness of Islamists
to engage with the human rights framework and negotiate its terms is a
dramatic progression from previous positions that were more likely to take
the relativist stance as their starting point. Both because key Islamist leaders
have recognized the strategic importance of working with the framework
and because human rights' logic and underlying prescriptions of justice
increasingly converged with Islamists own worldview and contemporary
experiences, the Islamist view of the international human rights order as
unauthentic, imposed, or imperialist was to a significant extent unsettled.
Instead, Islamist discussions on human rights were marked by a new tone,
one that rendered human rights a subject of discussion and deliberation.
Such a shift, in turn, increased the concepts' internal presence, autonomy,
and legitimacy.

CONCLUSIONS

This chapter does not purport to present an assessment of the success or
failure of the human rights project in the Middle East following September
11th. Instead it attempts to highlight the many layers of the Middle Eastern encounter with human rights in the post–September 11th era. American
human rights violations in Iraq and beyond, as well as the tremendous
human suffering directly or indirectly attributed to the American military
intervention in Iraq, were seen as indicative of both Middle Eastern disempowerment, dispossession, and tragedy vis-à-vis American hegemony and
human rights powerlessness to meaningfully challenge it. At the same time,
"the Iraqi theater" led to an unprecedented resonance of the human rights
ideal, which gave expression to their plight and aspirations for justice even
as its realization and practice lagged behind. At the same time, outside the
Iraqi context, American human rights promotion initiatives provided important (though often circumspect or unintended) openings for the furtherance
of the human rights project. Consequently, the post–September 11th era

has offered a unique moment in contemporary Middle Eastern history in which Middle Eastern governments, populations, and Islamists simultaneously adopted and engaged with human rights discourses to varying degrees. Even those who invoked the norms instrumentally were not entirely immune from also being either attracted by its promise or gripped by its normative and evaluative influences, resulting in a transformed knowledge, consciousness, and discourse.

FIVE

From the Ashes of the Post–September 11th Era: Lessons for the Human Rights Project

In the post–September 11th era, the international human rights project has been faced with formidable challenges, arguably even crises. Although linkages between human rights and hegemonic discourses can hardly be considered unique to this era, their manifestations have rarely been so transparent and centrally positioned in global affairs. Middle Eastern governments' violations of a full array of internationally recognized rights persist. American violations have included torture, egregious denials of due process, and, even more troubling the suffering and denials of human dignity stemming from war that often do not even appear on global human rights radars.[1]

Despite these concerning trends, developments since September 11th demonstrate that power dynamics can hardly be reduced to a simple one-dimensional calculus of domination and resistance. They can also be subverted and entrapped by their own confines. Accordingly, the post–September 11th era has also seen Arabs and Muslims returning the human rights gaze after Abu Ghraib, a Yemeni human rights nongovernmental organization (NGO) calling on the U.S. Supreme Court to restore American adherence to the rule of law, Americans seeking refuge in relativism and Middle Easterners seeking refuge in universalism, and both societies engaging with human rights in new and unprecedented ways. Perhaps more importantly, it has provided key lessons for rights advocates about how emancipatory and hegemonic human rights currents are intertwined and revealed the need for the interrogation of old assumptions and strategies. Thus, this last chapter is devoted to a final assessment of the question: "What are the era's key lessons for moving human rights advocacy forward?"

---

[1] Amid all of this, larger-scale global crises such as the AIDS epidemic and genocide in Darfur have been overshadowed.

REVISITING THE EAST/WEST GEOGRAPHY OF HUMAN RIGHTS: RECOGNIZING AMERICAN RELATIVISMS AND MIDDLE EASTERN UNIVERSALISMS

Although the contentious debates surrounding cultural relativism versus universalism that consumed global human rights politics and theory in the 1980s and 1990s have evolved (even died down to a large degree), the demarcation has endured, structuring post–September 11th human rights dynamics through a firm embeddedness within the confines of the East/West geography of human rights. In other words, even as the relativism/universalism labels have fallen into relative disuse and many have in theory accepted the need for more nuanced analytical tools, the binary's core divisions and assumptions survive. Taking an anthropological view, Jane Cowan, Marie-Benedicte Dembour, and Richard Wilson contend that "universalism and relativism cannot in themselves do justice to reality. The two terms are umbrella terms for a range of different and changing political, moral and legal positions."[2] Moreover, quoting Abdullahi An-Naim, the prominent Western-based scholar of human rights in the Muslim world, "no country either fully accepts or fully rejects the universality of human rights."[3] Accordingly, this section's focus on "American relativisms" and "Middle Eastern universalisms" does not stem from any notion that either label can be applied exclusively to one context or the other; rather, it is an attempt to shed light on the inaccuracy of traditional assignment of universalism to the United States and relativism to the Middle East. A second reason the universalism/relativism dichotomy is invoked here is to argue for a reassessment of prevailing distinctions between justifications for human rights contingency and noncompliance based on who invokes them and how they are packaged. The vastly differing treatment of justification for rights violations viewed as stemming from culture and religion in the Eastern context and justifications for rights violations presented as security and political imperatives recognized by Western states requires thorough reexamination. Put differently, a crucial lesson emerging from the post–September 11th era is that much of what passes as universalism or a temporary aberration from universalism is, in actuality, indistinguishable from what is considered relativism in other contexts or the distinctions that are put forth and largely accepted are often difficult to justify.

---

[2] Jane K. Cowan, Marie Benedicte Dembour, and Richard Wilson, *Introduction, in* CULTURE AND RIGHTS 30 (Jane K. Cowan, Marie Benedicte Dembour, and Richard Wilson eds., 2001).

[3] Abdullahi A. An-Naim, *Introduction: "Area Expressions" and the Universality of Human Rights: Mediating a Contingent Relationship, in* HUMAN RIGHTS AND DIVERSITY: AREA STUDIES REVISITED 3 (David P. Forsythe and Patrice C. MacMahon eds., 2003).

The contention that American adherence to human rights can be highly contingent, not universal, has been made by numerous scholars. Noted human rights scholar David Forsythe has commented that "the U.S. endorses international human rights in the abstract but practices a human rights policy that reflects cultural relativism and national particularity."[4] Equally, An-Naim has cited U.S. assertions of national sovereignty as just as relativistic as those posited by China or Iran.[5] It is the post–September 11th era's whirlwind of human rights violations, legal contests, and American/Middle Eastern interactions, however, that have brought out the perceptiveness of these contentions. When the United States' posture toward human rights–related international legal obligations so closely resembles that of more repressive states, it can hardly be surprising that American human right practices can come to mirror those of repressive states, given conducive leadership and circumstances. This is precisely what has transpired in the post–September 11th era. A preexisting contingent legal disposition gives way to increasingly contingent human rights practices.

The following two news accounts, one of American complaints to Saudi Arabia regarding the imprisonment of three individuals who had urged the Saudi government to adopt a constitutional system and the second detailing Kuwaiti complaints of American Guantanamo detentions, demonstrate just how much American and Middle Eastern human rights discourses and practices converge. The first account is of an exchange following a June 2005 speech in Cairo in which the U.S. secretary of state had criticized the Saudi action through a universalist premise that the acts prompting arrests of local activists "should not be a crime in any country."[6] *The Washington Post* reports:

In Riyadh, the Saudi capital, Rice met with Crown Prince Abdullah, the kingdom's de facto ruler, and other officials. She later told reporters that she had raised the issue of the three jailed petitioners with the crown prince, reiterating that their actions "should not be a crime." But the foreign minister, Prince Saud Faisal, responded that they had broken Saudi laws and that the matter was therefore in the "hands of the court." Saud, who said he had not read a transcript of Rice's Cairo speech, asserted that Saudi Arabia would undertake reform at its own pace and in accordance with its traditions.[7]

[4] David P. Forsythe, *U.S. Foreign Policy and Human Rights in an Era of Insecurity: The Bush Administration and Human Rights after September 11th, in* WARS ON TERRORISM AND IRAQ: HUMAN RIGHTS, UNILATERALISM AND U.S. FOREIGN POLICY 91 (Thomas G. Weiss et al. eds., 2004).
[5] See Abdullahi A. An-Naim, *supra* note 4, at 3.
[6] Glenn Kessler, *Rice Criticizes Allies in Call for Democracy,* WASHINGTON POST, Jun. 21, 2005, at A01 http://www.washingtonpost.com/wpdyn/content/article/2005/06/20/AR2005062000468.html?referrer=emailarticle.
[7] *Id.*

The second account is of an exchange that takes place just three months later between the Kuwaiti and American foreign ministers following reports of widespread hunger strikes among Guantanamo detainees and subsequent forced feedings by prison authorities. Here, an AFP article reports

Kuwait's foreign minister has urged the United States to resolve the issue of hundreds of Muslim detainees imprisoned at Guantanamo Bay, Cuba. Sheikh Mohammad al-Sabah said he told U.S. Secretary of State Condoleezza Rice that "Guantanamo represents a moral and legal challenge to the United States."

. . . .

I told Secretary Rice about reports on the health condition and the hunger strike by the inmates and that this was unacceptable to GCC (Gulf Cooperation Council) states.[8]

When coupled with repeated assertions by Bush administration officials that Guantanamo detainees are dangerous men who have committed war crimes and will be tried accordingly, it is difficult to qualitatively distinguish between American and Middle Eastern charges of human rights violations against each other and corresponding defenses rooted in relativism.

An exchange between the International Court of Justice's Roslyn Higgins and U.S. Secretary of State Condoleezza Rice at the 2006 American Society of International Law annual meeting provides further parallels between the American disposition and the type of relativism ascribed to Middle Eastern contexts. When confronted with the contradictions between the United States' asserted universalist stance and its thwarting of the international human rights legal framework in practice, Rice directly invokes cultural relativism. The exchange is cited at length because, when dissected, it provides a wealth of material relevant to the current discussion:

Roslyn Higgins: I think it is very important to try and avoid, if it's at all possible, the impression in international relations that one is keen on human rights and other people being made accountable but not opening oneself up to scrutiny. [*Applause*] And most of the great allies of the United States have found these treaties quite livable with and put up with the periodic investigations on their behavior under them. And of course in my country it's absolutely routine to be told by the Strasburg Court you've got it wrong, that was not lawful, kindly change something, and it's no big deal. We do so. The culture is profoundly different.

Condoleezza Rice: Well, that's the point, though. The culture is profoundly different. The United States is a very different entity. With all due respect, we broke from Europe. So the United States is different. [*Applause*] And the United States, of course, has a very, very free press so it's not as if human rights issues in the United States and American behavior and behavior of the government is not very often up to scrutiny. We also do have a separation of powers . . . there is congressional scrutiny of what is

---

[8] *Kuwait Chastises US over Guantanamo*, AGENCE FRANCE PRESSE, Sept. 21, 2005, at XX.

done, there is legislative scrutiny through the judicial branch at all levels of the United States. So it's not as if the United States can somehow hide in a corner what we are doing. But we have a very different culture, we have a very different history, and I think that has to be respected. I would never say to Europe don't pursue incitement laws because we think that that would be a problem for freedom of speech. You have a different tradition. And so we have to recognize that countries with different traditions are going to view these things differently and I don't think that it is the purpose of international law or of international relations to simply agree for the sake of comity.[9]

Again, this is an extremely rich exchange. Higgins is clearly troubled by the impression of insincerity, hierarchy, and double standards in the West's application of international human rights norms left by U.S. policies, but, at the same time, her concern comes across as being more focused on the appearance of these elements than with their actual existence. Nonetheless, she engages in the type of shaming American government officials have encountered throughout the post–September 11th era, and as a result, Rice is forced to stray from the official universalist script and admit to subscribing to a contingent conception of human rights. The exchange provides the perfect occasion for a reevaluation of the ingrained categories and assumptions within mainstream human rights discourses, namely, by revealing that countries cannot be so neatly placed into relativist or universalist camps and that there is a lot missed by starting out with assumptions of relativism in Eastern contexts and universalism in Western contexts.

The series of exchanges also bring to light the overlapping terrains and gray zones between cultural relativism and politically rooted motivations for not adhering to human rights norms. In the Middle Eastern context, much of what is labeled as cultural or religious relativism has less to do with culture or religion and more to do with political and ideological agendas expressed through cultural or religious discourses. In other words, appropriation of culture and cultural relativism have been a fixture of Middle Eastern human rights violations and the appropriations have traditionally been frequently obliged and accepted at face value by global human rights forces anticipating the formulation. In the same manner American human rights relativisms display intertwined political and cultural dimensions. Militarism, glorification of violence as the inevitable blunt instrument of those fighting the good fight, and constructions of masculinity and sexuality combine with neoconservative ideology and political power struggles to produce the post–September 11th era's array of human rights violations.

Ultimately, the outcome is that in their human rights dispositions American and Middle Eastern governments come to share many habits of human rights relativism and contingency. The United States invokes the sufficiency

---

[9] Conversation with U.S. Secretary of State Condoleezza Rice, American Society of International Law Annual Meeting (Mar. 29, 2006).

of "American values" and its constitutional tradition of rights to place the United States' actions above international human rights law. Middle Eastern governments or Islamist leaders may similarly contend that Muslims are answerable only to God, not a secular international order, and that the moral guidance provided by the Islamic tradition is sufficient safeguard against injustice. Both have traditionally had a reluctance to take on international legal obligations beyond abstract odes to freedom and human dignity; when they have taken on international legal obligations, both American and Middle Eastern governments have constructed their obligations such that they amount to little more than a commitment to obey existing domestic laws. Finally, as the post–September 11th era has made abundantly clear, Middle Eastern and American governments have demonstrated a contingent adherence to rights in practice, through a shared willingness to deprive particular individuals labeled as "the enemy" of due process rights and subject them to torture or cruel, inhumane, and degrading treatment.

Many would consider it a stretch to compare American human rights practices with those of Middle Eastern contexts. In fact, it can hardly be denied that the United States has a strong tradition of protecting rights. I was reminded of the rooted nature and substance of the American commitment to observing rights in perhaps the most unlikely of places – a restroom at the American embassy in Yemen that was fully accessible to people with disabilities, an observance of rights that was far removed from what I would otherwise encounter in Yemen. Moreover, there clearly are greater levels of civil and political rights, such as freedom from torture and arbitrary detention, accorded to an American citizen who seeks to exercise speech and association rights from within. Thus, in comparing traditional political and civil rights practices toward citizens, the United States can be seen as relatively, though by no means absolutely, freer than many other countries in the world. Yet, like almost any other country, American rights guarantees have holes, contradictions, and inconsistencies and some of the United States' biggest rights achievements have emerged from decades of struggle and oppression. More importantly, the American tradition and practice of rights internally cannot capture the entire picture of American approaches to human rights – past or present. In fact, a comparison of American treatment of its own citizens with repressive Middle Eastern countries' treatment of their citizens is full of distortions if one takes the notion of human rights seriously. Instead, it is imperative to juxtapose each country's treatment of human beings, regardless of nationality or citizenship. Once one considers American treatment of noncitizens to that of Middle Eastern states' treatment of their citizens, American human rights violations in the post–September 11th period are easily comparable and arguably worse, given the human toll and impact of the war in Iraq, cases of torture or rendition to torture, and the deprivations of liberty among the untold innocents among the more than 83,000-plus individuals detained. As rendition victim Maher Arar powerfully concludes in his testimony before American Congress, the distance between human rights adherence and egregious human rights violations by those who espouse human rights commitments can be much shorter than many have come to expect:

> In sharing my story and experiences with you today, I hope that the effects of torturing a human being will be better understood. I also hope to convey how fragile our human rights have become and how easily they can be taken away from us by the same governments that have sworn to protect them.[10]

Middle Eastern universalisms are equally important to recognize. The Middle East is often imagined as a third-world locale mired in cultural and religious relativisms and inherently prone to violence and political dysfunctionality. Yet a closer look reveals that, in many respects, Middle Eastern popular aspirations lie in the realization of some form of universal rights and not the exceptionalism and denial of internationally recognized rights that has marked their history. In fact, because it emerges from their own lived experiences of local and international abuses of power, the yearning for the genuine achievement of human rights is quite arguably – at specific moments throughout the post–September 11th era, at least – more widely and deeply felt by Middle Easterners than by the Americans mired in social and political debates over when it is appropriate to dispense with human rights guarantees. Polls gauging American views during the post–September 11th era have repeatedly shown that a sizable number of Americans oppose the absolute prohibition of torture mandated under international human rights law.[11] Perhaps most fascinating is a 2006 BBC poll that surveyed citizens of twenty-seven countries and found that in the United States 58 percent of those polled believed there should be clear rules against torture while 36 percent believed some degree of torture should be allowed. The same survey found that, in Iraq, the numbers were 55 percent for strict rules against torture to 42 percent for some allowance of torture and in Egypt they were 65 percent for strict rules against torture and 25 percent for some allowance of torture.[12] The fact that the percentage of Americans willing to accept some practice of torture is lower than the percentage of Egyptians with the same view and not leaps and bounds higher than the percentage of Iraqis with the same view, despite the level of insecurity and chaos in Iraq, is telling.

---

[10] Rendition to Torture: The Case of Maher Arar, Testimony before House Subcomm. on International Organizations, Human Rights, and Oversight and House Subcom. on the Constitution, Civil Rights, and Civil Liberties, 110th Cong. 1 (2007). (Oct. 18, 2007) http://judiciary.house.gov/hearings/hear_101807.html.

[11] See, for example: *Poll Finds Broad Approval of Terrorist Torture*, THE ASSOCIATED PRESS, Dec. 9, 2005, http://www.msnbc.msn.com/id/10345320.

[12] World Public Opinion.org, *World Citizens Reject Torture, BBC Global Poll Reveals*, Oct. 18, 2006, http://www.worldpublicopinion.org/pipa/articles/btjusticehuman_rightsra/261.php?nid=&id=&pnt=261&lb=bthr.

Given these parameters, the post–September 11th era brings out an acute need for the reconceptualization of the definitions of culture, relativism, and universalism adopted within the human rights paradigm. To the extent that relativism (particularly in its most opportunistic and co-opting forms) is to be stigmatized and countered as an unacceptable form of violating international human rights norms, all of its manifestations should be treated with the same level of skepticism and scrutiny. There should be a conscious effort on the part of human rights advocates to avoid the tendency to emphasize deviations attributed to Eastern culture or religion and in fact tolerate their invocation as rationales for outside intervention while using less damning criteria in assessments of "national security" and "fight for freedom" rationales for thwarting international law. If universalism is understood as the ideal human rights behavior occupying the opposite end of the spectrum, then the understanding of the bar for recognizing universalism should also be expanded, such that it encompasses not just the violations emphasized by Western "human rights promoters," including the United States, but those more comprehensively correlating with the lived experiences of populations on the other end of global and local power dynamics. As a later section will take up, within the current discussions this means seeing and challenging the profound human rights consequents of American wars and militarism.

Beyond the need for reconceptualized visions of relativism and universalism, a broadened and more complex understanding of culture must be adopted. There is now a strong case to be made for understanding culture as Sally Engel Merry and other anthropologists have described it: dynamic, unbounded, contested, multifaceted, intertwined with power relations, and equally present in Eastern and Western contexts.[13] Key to considerations of culture and its compatibility with rights in the Eastern as well as Western contexts is moving beyond equating culture with long-standing traditions and customs thought to be stagnant. Such a disposition allows for activists to focus on the cultural roots of violence and patriarchy and its linkages to post–September 11th human rights developments not only in the Middle Eastern context but also in the American context.

This process of linking American human rights violations and culture briefly surfaced in both liberal and conservative media outlets in the immediate aftermath of Abu Ghraib. This commentary in the conservative American magazine *The National Review* is quoted at length because of its elaborate engagement with the rights and culture nexus in the American context:

So it is that in Abu Ghraib and its aftermath we see some of the seamy undercurrents of America magnified in a horrifying fashion – in particular, the celebration of cruelty, the ubiquity of pornography, and a cult of victimhood. Any society, of course, will

---

[13] Sally Engle Merry, *Human Rights Law and the Demonizing of Culture (and Anthropology along the Way)*, 26:1 POL.LEGAL ANTHROPOLOGY REV. 55 (2003).

produce weak and malicious people, and prison abuses are nothing new.... But the distinct echoes of Abu Ghraib in our culture are unmistakable.

Consider the iconic film of the 1990s, Quentin Tarantino's *Pulp Fiction*. It includes a scene of the rape of a man imprisoned and kept as a sexual slave, which prompted laughs in theaters. The victim, "The Gimp," became a figure of fun. Tarantino's latest, the *Kill Bill* movies, present the same romance of power and violence, arbitrarily and stylishly wielded. Cruelty, Tarantino tells us, can be fun.

This is not to say that the filmmaker, or anyone besides those who committed and condoned the acts, is in any way responsible for Abu Ghraib. It's just that Tarantino – and he's not the only one – touches something within us that enjoys exalting the strong and humiliating the weak. And not just on movie screens. Large men forcibly sodomizing smaller men in U.S. prisons is widely made light of in America.

So, it was shocking to see a large gloved man smiling in a picture with his arms crossed as he stood over a pile of naked Iraqi detainees, but there was something familiar about it too. The apotheosis of the strong. There was something familiar in the picture of Lynndie England, with a cigarette dangling from her lips, pointing her finger at the genitals of a naked detainee. We know what she's doing in that picture – she's trying to seem cool. She thinks that cruelty is a game, that the strong engage in it casually.

Then, there is the very fact of the pictures. The American jailers, who live in a country where pornography is a $10 billion-a-year business, became amateur pornographers. They videotaped themselves having sex with one another. One of the officers disciplined at Abu Ghraib allegedly took pictures of female soldiers showering. The Americans sexually humiliated Iraqi prisoners, forcing them to masturbate, to wear women's underwear, and to commit (or feign committing) unnatural acts, and captured it on film. If they had done this stateside in different circumstances, they might be very rich and perhaps even up for an Adult Video Award.[14]

Similarly, a column in *The New York Times* entitled "Jesus and Jihad" made a connection between widely popular evangelical literature that glorifies the demise and torture of "infidels" and rights violations against Muslims:

No I don't think the readers of "Glorious Appearing" will ram planes into buildings. But we did imprison thousands of Muslims here and abroad after 9/11, and ordinary

[14] Rich Lowry, *Abu Ghraib and US: Don't Judge Us by Those Photos*, NATIONAL REVIEW, May 11, 2004, http://www.nationalreview.com/lowry/lowry200405110847.asp. *See also* Karin Chenoweth, *Fallout from Abu Ghraib*, N.Y. TIMES May 7, 2004, at A32, in which a reader writes:

The treatment of the prisoners at Abu Ghraib raises the question of how much pornography has permeated our culture. We as a society have turned a blind eye to the $4 billion industry that turns mostly on sexual humiliation, because most of us consider it to be a private matter that involves consenting adults. But when pornography is so pervasive that I receive it unbidden in my e-mail, it has become part of what the late senator Daniel Patrick Moynihan (D-N.Y.) described as "defining deviancy down." Photographing and videotaping the sexual torture and humiliation of prisoners is a new twist. We must at least consider the possibility that widespread, unutterably crude pornography has altered the norms of behavior governing some Americans.

Americans joined in the torture of prisoners at Abu Ghraib in part because of a lack of empathy for the prisoners. It's harder to feel empathy for such people if we regard them as infidels and expect Jesus to dissolve their tongues and eyes any day now.[15]

Although neither an indictment of violence and pornography within American society in a conservative publications such as *The National Review* nor an indictment of evangelical extremism in a more liberal publication like *The New York Times* are new, the linkages between American cultural and religious phenomenon and the human rights violations they encompass arguably are.

Beyond this initial foray into human rights and culture analysis among a handful of columnists in the media following Abu Ghraib, American human rights advocates came to recognize that a key dimension of their strategy to combat "War on Terror" human rights violations necessarily had to be cultural. With the most highly rated and acclaimed television dramas regularly depicting and glorifying torture on American television and sales of t-shirts that say, "I'D RATHER BE WATERBOARDING" in the post–September 11th era, human rights was as much of a cultural transplant to the United States as it was to the Middle East. As noted in Chapter 2, once American advocates recognized this, they began to embark on cultural initiatives such as Human Rights First's pioneering "Primetime Culture" project that targeted the damaging depictions of torture in popular American television dramas.

Advocates also increasingly began to contemplate coalition-building and engagement with religious figures and institutions. When a discussion of human rights activists' strategies in countering Bush administration policies erupted in November 2007 on one of many listservs subscribed to by American human rights and civil rights advocates who consider questions of post–September 11th detainee rights and torture issues, one of the group's leading voices suggested enlisting the aid of religious institutions. "I do think there is one thing that could turn the debate around: churches," he writes.[16] He contends that if religious institutions such as the country's churches, synagogues, and mosques added the torture issue to their sermons in the manner in which some of these religious institutions take on issues like abortion, public opinion on the matter could be moved. This would in turn create the impetus for the type of unequivocal action banning torture by CIA interrogators American politicians are currently reluctant to take. "Unless and until this becomes an outrage in religious communities nationwide and the broader implications for treaty-compliance generally are appreciated, I'm afraid there will be no inclination in Congress to bring a halt to the

---

[15] Nicholas Kristof, *Jesus and Jihad*, N.Y. TIMES, Jul. 17, 2004.
[16] Entry by American civil rights lawyer on listserv on post–September 11th torture policies (Nov. 11, 2007; quoted with permission of the author).

program" he concludes.[17] The parallel to the Women's Forum for Research and Training initiative to train sixty imams to educate mosque attendees on women's rights in Yemen (detailed in Chapter 4) is striking. Although recourse to such strategies of religious engagement remained minimal in the post–September 11th campaigns waged to date in the United States, that they *are* considered signals an increased awareness of the various interconnections between religion and human rights not thousands of miles away but in American human rights advocates' own backyards.

Thus, the lessons to be drawn in the relativism/universalism realm that has so occupied the international human rights project since its inception are clear. In the final analysis, if it is to achieve greater success, advocates have to reexamine the contours of the framework's engrained dichotomous discourses – rights versus culture, East versus West, and relativism versus universalism. Instead of obliging governments' various appropriations of culture, human rights, relativism, and universalism in the pursuit of political agendas, human rights discourses should more effectively unveil and dissect them.

REFINING HUMAN RIGHTS FRAMES

As Chapter 1 laid out, in the post–September 11th era, ontological rights-based identity constructions were widely deployed by the Bush administration to justify both American military interventions in the Middle East and human rights violations committed within those interventions. Accordingly, "America as leader of the free world and destined purveyor of rights and democracy" comes to occupy the fore of the administration's rhetoric justifying post–September 11th interventions. At the same time, American human rights advocates often adopted variations of the same ontological formulations in their efforts to challenge existing American human rights violations and compel American political pressure on Middle Eastern allies responsible for egregious human rights practices. Calls for the United States to reassume its human rights leadership position, frames of human rights violations as inherently un-American, and deployments of "it's about us, not about them" carried strong undercurrents of predestined East/West hierarchy. The same was true of widespread constructions of the harm of post–September 11th American violations as primarily rooted in the global precedents they set and the ways in which they undermined the work of human rights advocates worldwide. Thus, for much of the post–September 11th era, many of the identity and role constructions deployed by Bush administration officials and human rights advocates overlapped. For instance, both the U.S. Defense Secretary Donald Rumsfeld and human rights advocates called Abu Ghraib

[17] *Id.*

"un-American" and inconsistent with American values.[18] Both George W. Bush and human rights advocates framed global human rights promotion as an essential American role. In each instance, the argument being made started from the premise that the United States has an inherent commitment to universalism and human rights promotion.

It is not difficult to understand how calling on the United States to resume its "natural" leadership role in the human rights field or return to its essential rights-promoting self is an attractive option for advocates attempting to challenge American human rights practices within the precarious post–September 11th climate. Linking human rights to existing norms and identity constructions is a key strategy employed by activists worldwide and fits squarely within the constructivist framework. Such frames undoubtedly hold tremendous promise of fostering the internalization of human rights norms and limiting the range of acceptable behavior by tapping into existing domestic discourses. This is particularly important in cases where international human rights discourses have little domestic resonance or have been affectively delegitimized through a rise in domestic discourses such as nationalism or, in third-world contexts, anti-imperialism. Certainly in the first few years of the era, it seemed that human rights advocates had few available avenues for challenging the legal interpretations, policies, and discourses being put forth in the name of "national security" and "protecting freedom" in a way that made substantial impact other than posing their arguments in terms of essential American values and leadership. Further, although American-based international nongovernmental organizations (INGOs) are likely to dispel Middle Eastern identity constructions that justify human rights violations in the name of Islamic values, they are less willing to really dissect American identity constructions and assertions of "distinctive values." Again, the tendency cannot be summed up in Orientalism. It is easy to see how human rights NGOs would intuitively gravitate toward identity constructions built around adherence to human rights.

However, there is ample reason to consider refining such constructions. Consider an exchange between Dana Rohrabacher, the ranking Republican on the Subcommittee for International Organizations, Human Rights, and Oversight of the House Committee on International Relations, and Maher Arar, the Syrian-Canadian victim of an American rendition, during a U.S. House of Representatives hearing held on the topic of extraordinary renditions and Arar's case. After having likened the Arar case to a wide array of incidents of unfortunate but inevitable "human errors," including medical mistakes and friendly fire, and recounting the extraordinary circumstances presented by the September 11th attacks, Rohrabacher seeks an affirmation

---

[18] United States Senate, *Testimony of Secretary of Defense Donald H. Rumsfeld before the Senate and House Armed Services Comittees*, May 7, 2004, http://armed-services.senate .gov/statemnt/2004/May/Rumsfeld.pdf.

that essential American values mitigate American culpability in cases like Arar's:

Rohrabacher: Do you think that what you went through reflects the values of the American and Canadian people or do you accept the fact that this was a mistake – the Canadians have already apologized, a lot of Americans have apologized, but our government has yet to apologize. Do you accept that as a reflection that we as a people really do not go along with the type of treatment that you went through...for someone who is an innocent person and someone who is not engaged in terrorism?

Arar: I would have believed this was an innocent mistake if this was not happening to others. There seems to be a pattern where other – the number we heard was 100 – where people are being sent to other countries to be tortured, and this is regardless of whether those people are true terrorists or not. To send people to torture under any circumstances is wrong. We now know that most of the information the Americans had was inaccurate or false, but even, even if all this information was true, it does not justify sending me to Syria. I should have been sent back to Canada.

And what is troubling, even if you assumed that it was a mistake, a civilized country like the United States, they should take action to try to remedy the situation. They should not take the position they have been taking in courts to try to dismiss my case, using state secrets claims. I call that abuse [that is] ongoing. They have not allowed me to pursue justice in courts. When a person is wronged, the best place to go is courts. But so far, unfortunately, I have not been able to establish trust in the system.[19]

Throughout Arar's testimony one gets the sense that he at one time believed and would like to be able to continue to believe in the "America as the civilized beacon of human rights" narrative. Yet his own experience with nearly a year of torture after rendition to Syria, an American government that admits no wrongdoing in his or the slew of other rendition cases, and his inability to achieve justice within the American judicial system leave him little choice but to recognize its unreliability. Arar is accordingly forced to challenge the American congressman's attempt to justify a contingent application of human rights by invoking essential American values as a substitute for human rights–consistent action. Arar's response is tangential to the immediate discussion. Rohrabacher's attempt to erase American culpability by invoking essential American identity constructions suggests that human rights advocates' use of similar ontologically based arguments for American human rights compliance may have serious limitations and counterproductive outcomes. In other words, advocate's construction of calls for a resumption of essential American human rights identity often too closely resemble, feed, or reinforce the nationalism, exceptionalism, and hierarchy from which Rohrabacher's and similar arguments justifying rights violations flow. This is particularly true when such calls are not constructed carefully

[19] See Maher Arar, supra note 10.

enough to compel human rights promotion and adherence while foreclosing avenues for human rights appropriations.

In addition to explicitly making ontological "human rights violations are un-American" claims, many human rights advocates' calls for the resumption of American human rights leadership roles are firmly rooted in the same underlying constructions. Consider, for example, this statement by Human Rights First Washington director Elissa Massimino at a Georgetown Law Center forum titled "War, Terror, and Human Rights":

And as a human rights activist, I also have to say that the bigger reason for us that is so critical: these policies undermine U.S. leadership in the world on human rights and so I'm often asked, when I am in meetings with government officials, "Why are you focusing so much on these few problems that we've had when the U.S. is a leader on human rights and all hell is breaking loose in Darfur. Look at North Korea. Don't you have something better to do?" And I wish with all of my heart that I could spend more of my time like I used to, which was working on what the U.S. could do to get Robert Mogabe in Zimbabwe back treating his citizens with respect for human rights. But what we hear nearly every day from our colleagues from these countries around the world . . . is "get your damn country back on track because it's killing us and we can't do what we are trying to do on our own societies when our government uses the example of the United States as cover for what they are doing." But to solve any of those problems, Darfur among them, we have to have the United States at its most powerful in terms of its leadership on human rights. And if we can't fix these problems, we can't get there and those problems can't be solved. So this motivates groups like me to spend so much time trying to make this better. Because until we do, the United States won't be able to play the role it's been playing.[20]

Although, as Chapter 4 lays out, it is true that American disregard for international standards presented tremendous challenges to the advancement of human rights worldwide, viewing this fact as a primary rationale for human rights advocates' American campaign reflects a vision that at its core, the human rights project is meant to correct the behavior of other, mainly third world, countries and that the United States' destined role is to lead not follow. It can accordingly enjoy greater prerogative in determining when it is necessary to intervene militarily based on human rights rationales. In other words, as Amy Bartholomew has suggested, such prescriptions are akin to calls for the United States to resume its role as "benevolent hegemon."[21]

[20] Presentation by Elisa Massimino at the 1st Annual Samuel Dash Conference on Human Rights, Georgetown Law Center (Apr. 10, 2006).

[21] Amy Bartholomew, *Introduction, in* EMPIRE'S LAW: THE AMERICAN IMPERIAL PROJECT AND THE WAR TO REMAKE THE WORLD 8 (Amy Bartholomew ed., 2006). Bartholomew cites the following passage from an Amnesty International press release (*Report 2005: A Dangerous New Agenda*, May 25, 2005):

The USA as the unrivalled political, military and economic hyper-power, sets the tone for governmental behaviour worldwide. When the most powerful country in the world thumbs its nose at the rule of law and human rights, it grants a license for others to commit abuse with impunity and audacity. From Israel to Uzbekistan, Egypt or Nepal, governments have openly defied humanitarian law in the name of national security and 'counter-terrorism'.

The form of power in operation is key to the argument. The use of military force, imprisonment of tens of thousands of "War on Terror" detainees, commission of acts of abuse and torture, and maintenance of close ties with governments with egregious human rights practices are the more outwardly apparent manifestations of American power. However, in many respects it is the more constitutive manifestation of power that sets the stage for much of these more overt exercises of power. The United States as *inherent* human rights observer or inherent human rights leader is a powerful construction that facilitates the more conventional forms of military and economic power deployed. The inaccurate portrayals of American human rights practices and commitments within prevailing identity and role constructions are dangerous because the more the construction is internalized, the greater the chance that violations will be overlooked or dismissed and denials or justifications accepted. The more they have internalized the identity and role construction, the less vigilant or predisposed human rights advocates (much less an American public on whose consent American military interventions would depend) will be to identifying human rights violations or appropriations. If ontologically based identity constructions are used uniformly by human rights advocates and detractors alike, when the president declares freedom and human rights to be America's calling, governmental and nongovernmental actors as well as a less than skeptical public will be more inclined to accept it. The constructions can thus enable the American governments to exercise power in the name of human rights and democracy as the Bush administration has in Iraq while obscuring American's ability to see the violence and denials of human dignity committed in their names and allowing them to take comfort in their identities constructed as human rights champions. As Cyra Choudhury observes:

Even in opposing the war, so eminent a statesman as Robert Byrd reiterated this identity describing America as "a country which believes in justice, the rule of law, freedom and liberty."[22] Such patriotic and wholesome formulations of who we are leave little space to examine how we can fall far short of and act if not *be* exactly the opposite of what we claim to be. And the reification of this identity forecloses the possibility of considering our culpability in any serious manner. The converse side of this identity equation, then, is the "Other."[23]

In other words, placing the United States as the world's a priori human rights devotee or leader distorts the true image of American exercises of power – whether military interventions or human rights violations – permitting them to be more readily viewed as rooted in good intentions, benign, or

[22] Cyra A. Choudhury, *Comprehending "Our" Violence: Reflections on the Liberal Universalist Tradition, National Identity and the War on Iraq*, 3:1 MUSLIM WORLD J. HUM. RTS, 9 (2006), available at: http://www.bepress.com/mwjhr/vol3/iss1/art2.

[23] *Id.*

aberrant. In a related manner, when Americans and their values are portrayed as inherently compatible with human rights, they are accorded greater authority and legitimacy to determine that they do not require international human rights safeguards at home or abroad.

Because of the negative effects of invoking ontologically rooted American human rights identity constructions and roles, human rights advocates should make every effort to link identity-based frames not to something essential or ordained but to actual commitments, practice, and even asserted values and history. The frames should be constructed such that in highlighting traditions, behaviors, or values consistent with the upholding of rights and human dignity, they do not wipe out inconsistent behavior and values – both past and present. In other words, American human rights forces should move away from arguments surrounding America's essence and focus on American behavior. Although American history and asserted values remains relevant, they are not determinative. Simply put, American advocates need not necessarily abandon all invocations of American identity and traditions of recognizing rights; rather, they should take great pains to avoid perpetuating the fiction of a destined and spotless American commitment to human rights. Further, American human rights actors should make every effort to not replicate U.S. government presentations of American values as universal and synonymous with the international human rights order; instead they should present convergences and divergences between the American experience and global human rights principles. Finally, American human rights proponents must take on the challenge of framing their arguments for American compliance in a way that does not rely on or reify the East/West human rights hierarchies. In the end, the distinctions that should be made are extremely subtle and often hinge more on tone and context than what is being actually articulated. The difference may lie in framing the human rights issues involved as presenting questions of "who we want to be," "who we should be," or "who we have been" at a particular moment in time rather than "who we are" intrinsically.

Many of these prescriptions are captured in an ACLU video commemorating the 60th Anniversary of the Universal Declaration of Human Rights (UDHR) in 2008. The video begins by introducing the declaration and Eleanor Roosevelt's instrumental role in its coming into being. Clips of her speeches at the United Nations and pictures of her engaged in the drafting of the declaration are accompanied by commentary describing her pivotal role and noble motivations. Mary Robinson, the former UN High Commissioner for Human Rights, states:

It's much more than a declaration; it's a breakthrough for humanity. It happened in a very fearful world in 1948 and it happened in the context of a relatively new United Nations, a new Commission on Human Rights, chaired by an American woman, Eleanor Roosevelt, who worked with a number of eminent jurists and knew how to bus them into writing the Universal Declaration in straightforward language.[24]

The video, however, does not simply project an idealized picture of Eleanor Roosevelt and, by extension, the United States' importance in the creation of the UDHR to make a case for the international instrument's relevance to the United States. Two minutes into the piece, human rights scholar Catherine Powel injects another layer into the message being developed: "One of Eleanor Roosevelt's less celebrated roles is the fact that she worked against enforcement of the Universal Declaration of Human Rights to assuage the concerns of segregationists in the South," she explains.[25] From there, the video focuses primarily on the United States' history of exceptionalism in its treatment of human rights and the way activists are attempting to implement international human rights standards at home.

Overall, because the promotional video is produced by the ACLU, which has a long tradition of openly criticizing U.S. government action, the "UDHR at 60" video tilts more toward highlighting American shortcomings and exceptionalism than American linkages or commitments to rights. Other human rights organizations may opt for a different balance between the various aspects of the complex American encounter with the international human rights regime. The point in highlighting this particular video, however, is not to endorse its approach entirely but to put forth an intriguing example of an attempt to present a more multidimensional and accurate portrayal of the American relationship with the human rights paradigm than the one that emerged in the Gonzales confirmation and McCain amendment initiatives presented in Chapter 2.

Similarly, the post–September 11th era has crystallized the imperative of premising calls for American human rights leadership on the United States' actual compliance with international norms at home and abroad, not any ascribed essence. As laid out in Chapter 4, although riddled with inconsistencies and double standards, American diplomatic interventions and promotion initiatives are not without the potential for tangible positive impact. Whether it is out of an internalization of the identity constructions being reinforced or out of the normative pressure to square American behavior with human rights appropriations, the United States' involvement with human rights in the region has opened up new avenues for the strengthening of the regime in many parts of the Middle East. Continued American interventions in the form of diplomatic pressure, and to a lesser degree, funding and resources can be of much needed assistance to local movements. Thus, while it is often overstated, when it does actually take-on principled and consistent policies, American human rights advocacy can have a uniquely

---

[24] American Civil Liberties Union, *60th Anniversary of the Universal Declaration of Human Rights*, http://www.udhr60.org/ (last visited Aug. 6, 2008).
[25] *Id.*

positive impact. In fact, there seems to be something highly persuasive in the world's only superpower abiding by human rights constraints. After September 11th, one of the few instances in which American human rights commitments were discussed positively in the Middle East was in relation to the fact that it was American journalists who uncovered the Abu Ghraib story and that was made possible by virtue of American freedom of expression. Even El Obaid El Obaid, the UN human rights program director in Sana'a and Sudanese-Canadian legal scholar who argues that American leadership is not necessary and currently counterproductive, concludes, "If the Americans applied their own principles consistently I think the world would be a better place."[26] Consequently, it is not only important, it is arguably inevitable, given current political realities, to think in terms of American political intervention or leadership in the human rights realm. Even so, proponents should strive to ensure American human rights leadership is treated as an earned status not simply an ontological attribute. What makes this argument most pressing is of course the United States' overwhelming military and economic power and demonstrated willingness to enlist human rights to the aid of that power. Human rights INGOs are responsible for the consequences of the way they formulate their arguments for American human rights leadership and compliance. They must formulate their arguments in a way that challenges, not propels, the constructions leading to post–September 11th military interventions. What distinguishes American human rights advocates' use of identity constructions and frames from similar efforts by human rights advocates throughout the world is that the consequences of American human rights activists' constructions extend far beyond their borders, as they are fundamentally built on global hierarchies – that is, the United States is granted a status superior to other, primarily non-Western, states vis-à-vis human rights. Though it can be fraught with a myriad of its own trappings, Islamic feminists' forays into contests over what rights or status of women are Islamic or un-Islamic rarely affect actors other than themselves and the local women whose rights they seek to elevate. Thus, if there is one overarching and glaring lesson to be learned from the post–September 11th era, it is that the United States can neither be viewed nor portrayed as human rights compliant simply because it is the United States. Instead, human rights advocates must attempt to link their frames more closely to American actions.

AMERICAN MILITARY INTERVENTIONS AND HUMAN RIGHTS

From the Middle Eastern perspective, U.S. military interventions in Afghanistan and particularly Iraq lied at the heart of the region's post–September

---

[26] Interview with El Obaid El Obaid, UNDP, Chief Technical Advisor, UNDP Human Rights Project in Yemen in Sana'a, Yemen (Jan. 24, 2007).

11th human rights tragedies. The faces of Iraqi children with bloody bandages wrapped around their heads, the rubble of Iraqi houses, the despairing screams and weeping of Iraqis losing a family member, accounts of lack of electricity, sanitation, and medical facilities by humanitarian workers, and the stories of the estimated one to two million Iraqi refugees fleeing the violence in Iraq were a constant fixture of Middle Eastern news coverage and public consciousness. In Jordan and Yemen, the human rights advocates I met uniformly condemned American military interventions in the region, viewing both specific American actions and the violence spurred by the American use of force as exacting an astounding human toll. As a result, most of the Middle Eastern human rights advocates I met were just as vocal about the Iraq War, occupation, and policies affecting civilians as they were about torture, Abu Ghraib, and Guantanamo.

In Yemen, however, I came across indications that arriving at this stance was often a more complex undertaking than it may appear. In two interviews I encountered a perception that although traditional normative routes of dialog, shaming, and framing had some impact, it was ultimately the threat of force by the United States that had served as the biggest impetus for numerous Middle Eastern states' willingness to present initial openings for human rights and democratic reforms – openings that advocates were then able to exploit.

An interview with Mohammad al-Tayeb, the former minister and current chairman of the committee for Human Rights, Liberties and Civic Organizations of the Shura Council (Upper House of the Yemeni Parliament), drew out the dilemma faced by rights proponents in the region. He began by explaining that although Yemen, Jordan, and Morocco were Middle Eastern countries that had embarked on processes of democratization and human rights improvements before September 11th, in Saudi Arabia and other parts of the gulf region, human rights were labeled as Western ideas meant "to colonize us." After 9/11, when the United States began to preach human rights and democratization, these countries began to "shake." Then, when the Iraqi invasion unfolded, many countries were "waiting to see who was next," thinking Iraq was only "the beginning."[27] This propelled them to institute limited reforms. However, when later in the interview I asked him what he thought of the United States' designation as the world's human rights model, he was quick to criticize the American use of force in the region, prompting a fascinating exchange:

A: The United States is not the model, but what we live in this part of the world is far worse than anything one can imagine. So we are not looking for the ideal. The mistake the United States is making is that they do not use the proper reference and

---

[27] Interview with Mohamad al-Tayeb, chairman of the Human Rights, Liberties and Civic Organizations Committee in Yemen's Shura Council and former Yemeni minister, in Sana'a, Yemen (Jan. 21, 2007).

way of introducing themselves. For example, they are now fighting in Iraq. This is costing them almost $2 billion a week. Can you imagine if they used this money to help these principles, these governments, these people. They can achieve so much without spilling blood, without destruction.

Q: But you said these changes were triggered by U.S. involvement.

A: Yes, it was triggered, but I'll tell you something... when they misused their power...

Q: But if [there was] no threat [of the use of force], just this money [for human rights promotion]..?

A: The money plus the threat, but not the invasion would have...

Q: But you think the threat is necessary?

A: Yes, this part of the world is most resistant to democracy on the whole Earth. I mean, if you look at our history, the openness came when the Turks came and French came to Egypt.... I don't know why we are resistant to these principles. It does seem to me that this part of the world does need some shaking.

Q: But it wouldn't work with the economic incentives?

A: Economic incentives are very important for Yemen or Morocco. So the Americans can use this money to pursue these ideas and principles.

Q: And if you get the reform in a few countries, it wouldn't spread?

A: Of course, if you set a model in the region, then the others will follow.[28]

Al-Tayeb's instinct to condemn the violence of American military action due to its clear human costs but at the same time view the threat of such military intervention as necessary for prompting reforms – taking what is essentially an impossible and incoherent position – speaks to the dilemma faced by at least some rights proponents in the region.

The discussion of the United States military interventions also figured prominently in my interview with Amal Basha of the Sisters Forum for Human Rights. Like al-Tayeb, she also initially seemed at a loss in reconciling the devastating human rights outcomes produced in Iraq with her sense that American interventions had opened up new possibilities for human rights advances in the region, including Yemen:

Without this vigorous American intervention for democracy, those systems are not going to allow democracy. We need the intervention because these leaders have been resisting democracy... they are not going to allow real transformation. But at the same time, there is this conduct [the American intervention in Iraq]. It's really a dilemma.[29]

---

[28] *Id.*

[29] Interview with Amal Basha, director, Sister's Forum for Human Rights in Sana'a, Yemen (Jan. 22, 2007). Manar Rishwani had made a similar point in Jordan, asserting that "If the United States decided to stop talking about democracy, everything will vanish." Interview with Manar Rishwani, columnist for Al Qad Newspaper in Amman, Jordan (Jun. 6, 2006).

When I asked Basha what she thought would be the effect of the United States stepping out of the picture and local human rights advocates being left with human rights and civil society initiatives from countries like Denmark and Canada, she speculated that the pace of reform and civil society development would be significantly slower.[30]

However, in the end, although she recognized that a large part of the Yemeni government's responsiveness to American calls for reform stemmed, at least to some degree, from the post–September 11th threat of force, Basha simply could not validate the American use of force in the region:

We need the support of the U.S. and the West for building our capacities. By having this dialog with the government, we need Western pressure. But when it comes to military interventions, we are against military intervention, because in the end the cost is too high. As civil society, human rights organizations we are against any type of violence and any military intervention; it will come with it. We are not ready to bargain with (inaudible) ... we have to have a civil start, with all the support from the outside.[31]

Taken together al-Tayeb and Basha's reflections are quite revealing. At the same time that they are instinctively critical of American exercises of power through force and violence, their post–September 11th experiences seem to provide evidence that these same *realpolitik* prescriptions have aided the advancement of human rights goals in much of the region. However, in the end neither can endorse American military action. Al-Tayeb, who is not a human rights advocate but a politician with an apparent desire to see the human rights project advanced in the region, attempts to sidestep the difficult choice posed by opting for only the threat of American force. Basha, who is a seasoned human rights advocate, ultimately chooses an unequivocal rejection of American military interventions and is clear about the consistency of that position with her human rights agenda. Once she considers alternative paths (albeit promising less dramatic results) and weighs the costs of relying on American uses of force, she simply cannot justify condoning American military interventions such as the Iraq War.

El Obaid El Obaid expands on the stance of Middle Eastern human rights advocates:

Most of the positive effects of this [American military threat as catalyst for reform] are offset by the very strong reaffirmation of what I think in an eternal truth now. That is, you cannot spread human rights through the use of force. So in that sense, in an immediate country you may have a degree of change but in the normative sense, the negative effect is a lot more in terms of actually to the extent that the average person may associate any talk of human rights with an incredible, excessive, arrogant use of force.[32]

[30] *See* Amal Basha, *supra* note 29.
[31] *Id.*
[32] *See* El Obaid El Obaid, *supra* note 32.

Put differently, there is an ultimate recognition that the more human rights are imbued with power the less persuasive they become. Despite the yearning for American leadership on all sides and recognition of the mixed effects of American military interventions, in the final analysis it is not the American human rights package (whether through military interventions or co-opting of the language of rights) that is able to sell the human rights project in the Middle East. Instead, human rights is embraced because of its emanicpatory potential and the avenues for challenging local and international impositions of power it presents.

A final observation by Mohammad al-Tayeb speaks further to the pitfalls of relying on American power through force:

Frankly speaking, those countries who did this [instituted reforms] against their internal will, they are happy with what is happening now in Iraq, with the American big dilemma in Iraq. So now the American government has already lowered their rhetoric or their support to those ideas. They are no longer saying it as they used to say as strongly as in the past. So this puts those governments at ease. Now some of them are betting on the American failure in Iraq...some Arab countries who feel that it's better to have the Americans out with total failure than to have them succeeding. So this is the problem. The problem is that it is the superpower that ignited these ideas.[33]

Thus, as al-Tayeb articulates, a further problem with reliance on American "human rights leadership" through force is that, in addition to sometimes being hollow, it can disappear as quickly as it appeared.

The primary point brought out by these series of interviews is that although American military interventions have had contradictory human rights outcomes – producing devastating results in Iraq but potentially contributing to some openings in other parts of the region – the immense human toll and larger implications of such mass-scale violence set off by the war simply cannot justify support for such military operations that are, at their core, not humanitarian or otherwise legitimately grounded in the letter or spirit of international norms and in fact provide the grounds for openly challenging such military action.

In the United States the human toll of the Iraq War to Iraqi civilians has hardly made a dent in American public consciousness or political discourses. The little mainstream media coverage of the humanitarian crisis in Iraq that has been produced has largely been limited to sanitized or embedded forms that rarely provide a true sense of the war's considerable humanitarian toll. But perhaps most troubling for the purposes of this study has been the leading U.S.-based human rights INGOs' treatment of American military interventions and their human costs in the post–September 11th era. Despite the repeated blurring of American military action and a human rights, women's rights, and humanitarian mission in Afghanistan as well

[33] See Mohamad al-Tayeb, *supra* note 33.

as important cues that human rights and humanitarian discourses could be deployed to (at least in part) legitimate the American military intervention in Iraq, American human rights INGOs challenged neither the questionable international law grounds on which the intervention lied nor the insertion of human rights and humanitarian discourses into the mix of rationales provided for the intervention in the wake of the Iraq War. Instead, they took the route of maintaining a neutral position on the war while insisting on American adherence to international humanitarian law within the conflict.

Here I take a limited look at the leading American INGO, Human Rights Watch's stance vis-à-vis the Iraq War and its human rights dimension by presenting (1) an interview with Joe Stork, the Deputy Director of Human Rights Watch's Middle East Division, in August 2008 and (2) a 2004 Human Rights Watch statement on the subject. I first lay out the organization's position as I discern it from these two sources and leave my analysis of the position and its implications for the end.

My interview with Stork was revealing in the contrast in tone and perspective to those of activists in the Middle East it brought to the fore. When I asked him about how the Iraq War has affected discussions of human rights in the Middle East, Stork offered what is in part a critique of Middle Eastern advocates' inability to pose a well-developed human rights challenge to the war and in part a dismissal of the general Middle Eastern view of the war and its human rights connections:

Of course, the rights groups in the region – to the extent that they say anything at all about this – it tends to be pretty abstract and rhetorical and demagogic, frankly, and so, it's sort of "all the problems are the occupation" and "it's a human rights violation," which is not how we see it. It's all very black and white. I mean, I am exaggerating slightly. I mean, I don't know of any group in the region that in any serious way has taken up the war . . . or the occupation for that matter . . . some of them have exposed the massacres and so forth. I don't know of any that have done thinking about positioning themselves or trying to address it in a systematic way. "Occupation bad," full stop.[34]

Stork also indicates that there was never any serious consideration given to opposing the Iraq War at Human Rights Watch:

There are always discussions, but our organizational position is that it is beyond our mandate, so I wouldn't say this war represented any particular strong push to kind of modify that mandate. Most of us think it is pretty convincing. Now individuals in the organization are free to – and certainly did – voice their own concerns but not as Human Rights Watch.[35]

Elsewhere he provides further insight: "Look, there were people within our organization who were not opposed to the war and some of us, and I include

---

[34] Interview with Joe Stork, deputy middle director, Human Rights Watch, in Washington, DC (Aug. 4, 2008).

[35] Id.

myself here, who had spent some time working on Iraq ... I've got to say it's a tough call when you are looking at that particular government."[36]

When asked whether there had been any discussions within the organization about countering American appropriations of human rights discourses as justification for the Iraq War, Stork submitted that Human Rights Watch did speak out against such appropriations, referring to the 2004 statement I discuss in considerable detail below. He also added the following:

We did actually put out a couple of reports on Iraq during the Saddam era in the period just before the war and these are things that had kind of been in the making. ... so these could be read and I'm sure some people did read them as at least providing the intellectual underpinning or whatever you want to call it. I don't think it's true. That is not why the war was fought, and I don't think – look, we don't hold things back just because of the political conjecture that we fear things may be misused or used for purposes which we are certainly not intending.[37]

Human Rights Watch cannot control what different political parties, factions, or interests make of their work, he concluded. The organization's job was to put out information about violations "as factually, as dispassionately, as honestly" as they could.[38]

The next set of questions I posed to Stork surrounded the level of Human Rights Watch's advocacy and efforts relating to the humanitarian conditions arising from the Iraq War compared to the organization's efforts in relation to Guantanamo, secret prisons, and torture issues. Stork's answer was that the organization had done as much reporting and investigating of human rights and humanitarian conditions as had been possible given the safety constrains with which it was faced. Because their methodology was based on interviewing victims in the field and, for most of the duration of the Iraqi War, it was impossible for the organization to visit Iraq safely, the organization's engagement with the Iraq War was inevitably more limited in scope compared with their coverage of detainee rights and torture issues.[39] This lack of access to the field and reporting in turn prevented the organization from taking on greater efforts to pressure the United States government in relation to human rights violations stemming from the war in a comparable manner:

We don't lobby except where we have done work and done investigations. So it's not like we lobby on abstract issues. We lobby on the issues we researched and documented and published on. So, for instance, we've done a lot of lobbying on the issue of detainees, the legitimacy of certain kinds of detentions of Iraqis and so forth. Probably that is the issue since 2004 we've had the most to say and we also did a big report on abuses by the armed groups in Iraq targeting civilians. Again, that was

[36] *Id.*
[37] *Id.*
[38] *Id.*
[39] *Id.*

based on statements of the groups and so forth and to some extent getting testimony from people who have left Iraq...but I'd say in terms of the occupier side of it, probably the detainee issue has been [inaudible] because those are matters of law.[40]

When I clarified that I was interested in their work in Iraq beyond detainee issues, such as conditions faced by Iraqi civilians, Stork provided this response:

Well, that's the area – we are not out there. What do we have to say that we can use our authority on? We look for opportunities. Particularly back in the '04–'05 period, we did raise certain issues, for instance, the siege of Falluja, but, you know, again, when we are not there...we have to be able to answer the line of, in this case the U.S. government, which is saying "we took every precaution...and there is this going on and that going on and we don't really know" and it's true, we don't really know what's going on and we are not in a position to do an investigation. And when we do, for instance, the report we did on checkpoint casualties in Baghdad...we showed a pattern of a serious problem – sort of "shoot first, ask questions later" – but we couldn't go back and do that again....When we can, we would certainly like to get back in there and take up these issues. But when there is a bombing or an air assault or whatever kind of an assault out there in Haditha or wherever, and there are reports of civilians killed, the most we can do is say we are concerned by these reports and the warring parties have to take all precautions to protect civilians...that doesn't add too much. We are not in a position to say this was an indiscriminate attack.[41]

A number of the arguments put forth by Stork in his interview were developed several years earlier in Human Rights Watch's statement on the topic.

First, it is worth noting that it was not until 2004 that the leading American human rights organization addressed the issue of humanitarian justifications for the Iraq War. Early in the policy statement, Kenneth Roth, Human Rights Watch's executive director, iterated the INGO's general policy on wars. Like Stork, Roth began by stating that Human Rights Watch takes no position on questions of whether a state should go to war because "the issues involved usually extend beyond our mandate, and a position of neutrality maximizes our ability to press all parties to a conflict to avoid harming non-combatants."[42] The only exception he pointed to is the instance in which the INGO will affirmatively support or advocate for military intervention for humanitarian purposes.

Roth then went on to explain that the reason Human Rights Watch did not advocate for the Iraqi intervention was that "the Iraq war was not mainly about saving the Iraqi people from mass slaughter and because no such slaughter was then ongoing or imminent":[43]

40 Id.
41 Id.
42 Ken Roth, War in Iraq Not a Humanitarian Intervention, HUMAN RIGHTS WATCH WORLD REPORT (2004).
43 Id.

A humanitarian rationale was occasionally offered for the war, but it was so plainly subsidiary to other reasons that we felt no need to address it. Indeed, if Saddam Hussein had been overthrown and the issue of weapons of mass destruction reliably dealt with, there clearly would have been no war, even if the successor government were just as repressive. Some argued that Human Rights Watch should support a war launched on other grounds if it would arguably lead to significant human rights improvements. But the substantial risk that wars guided by nonhumanitarian goals will endanger human rights keeps us from adopting that position.[44]

He also clearly develops the case for Bush administration policies being appropriations of the human rights and humanitarian lexicon, far removed from the administration's primary motivations:

Over time, the principal justifications originally given for the Iraq War lost much of their force. More than seven months after the declared end of major hostilities, weapons of mass destruction have not been found. No significant prewar link between Saddam Hussein and international terrorism has been discovered. The difficulty of establishing stable institutions in Iraq is making the country an increasingly unlikely staging ground for promoting democracy in the Middle East. As time elapses, the Bush administration's dominant remaining justification for the war is that Saddam Hussein was a tyrant who deserved to be overthrown – an argument of humanitarian intervention. The administration is now citing this rationale not simply as a side benefit of the war but also as a prime justification for it. Other reasons are still regularly mentioned, but the humanitarian one has gained prominence.[45]

Thus, as the leading American human rights INGO reads it, the Iraqi war was never a legitimate humanitarian intervention and the use of human rights rationales was overwhelmingly instrumental.

The statement is primarily concerned with the impact of the military intervention in Iraq on the legitimacy and credibility of the humanitarian interventions in the future. "[A]t a time of renewed interest in humanitarian intervention, the Iraq War and the effort to justify it even in part in humanitarian terms risk giving humanitarian intervention a bad name. If that breeds cynicism about the use of military force for humanitarian purposes, it could be devastating for people in need of future rescue," Roth laments.[46] The statement goes on to outline a set of criteria for determining whether a war can be considered a humanitarian intervention. These criteria include (1) whether humanitarian intervention is the last available option, (2) whether the intervention is guided primarily by a humanitarian purpose, (3) whether every effort is made to respect international human rights and humanitarian law within the intervention, (4) whether it is reasonably likely that the humanitarian intervention will do more good than harm, and (5) whether the preferred route of seeking UN Security Council or other multilateral

[44] *Id.*
[45] *Id.*
[46] *Id.*

support was taken. The report concludes that the Iraqi military intervention fails to meet the bar on all counts.

Post–September 11th events provide an important opportunity to more closely examine the response of a U.S.-based human rights INGO like Human Rights Watch toward American militarism. This topic was not initially a central focus of the research and emerged only as the project progressed. Thus, I do not lay any claim to either dealing with the subject in any kind of a comprehensive or conclusive way or presenting the full scope of either Middle Eastern or American perspectives. Instead, I bring to the fore only a number of questions pertaining to American human rights INGOs' treatment of the Iraq War and occupation that emerge from the research but that I believe have to date been largely absent from post–September 11th human rights discussions. Should American human rights INGOs ever challenge their government's military interventions? Should American human rights INGOs challenge their government's appropriations of human rights or humanitarian rationales for military interventions? What kind of responsibility should an American human rights organization have for investigating, publicizing, and lobbying the U.S. government with regard to abuses stemming from an American war? Finally, is it time for a broader conception of human rights that better incorporates the human costs of wars? In briefly taking up each of these questions in turn, I offer only my thoughts on the Human Rights Watch position laid out above, cognizant of the limited and preliminary nature of the research on which they are based but hopeful that the discussion may provoke more extensive debate, research, and introspection on the topic.

Answering the question of whether a human rights organization should ever take up the task of designating particular military actions as unjust or unjustifiable in relation to their potential human toll is clearly not an easy undertaking. The rationale behind the Human Rights Watch position that entering the fray of military strategy and decision making should be beyond a human rights NGO's mandate is understandable. Human rights advocates may not always be qualified to make such determinations and, if they do, they risk being completely shut out by the government they seek to influence. However, the most central feature of a human rights NGO's mandate is monitoring, publicizing, and *preventing* human rights violations and, as the Human Rights Watch statement acknowledges, much of the human rights costs of war are largely foreseeable. Moreover, there was a near international consensus that American orchestration of the war was not justified and, as a preemptive war not authorized by the Security Council, violated established use of force doctrines under international law. Accordingly, American human rights INGOs had ample grounds to depart from their mandate and challenge the Iraq War as the drumbeats for war grew louder and louder.

Given the countervailing considerations presented, the official Human Rights Watch position is not in and of itself at the crux of this critique. What I find more problematic is the level of serious deliberation given to the course of opposing the Iraq War by the organization in the lead up to the war and the soundness of the decision thereafter. There seems to have been few occasions before or after the Iraqi invasion at which the organization seriously considered modifying its position that taking a stance on wars (or American wars) should always remain beyond its mandate. The 2004 statement addressed only criticism that Human Rights Watch should have endorsed the war, and its primary indictment of the Iraq War was that the war risked giving humanitarian intervention "a bad name." Neither the questionable international legal underpinnings nor potential/actual human costs appear to have triggered a more potentially course-changing discussion. The Iraq War experience should at least raise the question of whether it still makes sense for American INGOs to maintain "neutrality" (effectively silence) on American military interventions unless they are affirmatively advocating for what they consider to be a genuine humanitarian intervention.

The second question, that of whether American human rights organizations should take on U.S. government appropriations of human rights discourses to justify military action, is, I would contend, more straightforward. After September 11th, the American government (and particularly the Bush administration) deployed undefined notions of freedom and liberty to justify American foreign policy while using tyranny, stoning, and rape rooms to demonize and dehumanize its enemies. Although the Bush administration did increase its reliance on human rights rationales for the Iraq War as the weapons of mass destruction rationale fell apart, given the United States' history (and, in the case of "Operation Enduring Freedom" in Afghanistan, very recent history) of entwining human rights and humanitarian rationales with national security or geopolitical motivations for its interventions, U.S.-based INGOs could have been looking for more than just exclusive assertions of a humanitarian mission to place the American war under scrutiny.

Simply identifying the Bush administration's various human rights appropriations in relation to the Iraq War a year and a half after the invasion is not enough. The case can easily be made that the human rights cause would have been better served by U.S.-based INGOs actively challenging, even the most "subsidiary" deployments of human rights justifications for war. This does not mean staying silent on Iraqi human rights violations because they may be co-opted, as Stork suggests. It does, however, entail making every effort to give voice to the argument that although the Iraqi violations in question are deplorable and require various forms of action and response, they should not be used to further the case for military action.

The third question posed revolves around U.S.-based INGOs' coverage of human rights violations stemming from U.S. military action in Iraq. Although the Human Rights Watch statement refers generally to the high human toll of war (as reason to limit humanitarian interventions to only the most dire humanitarian crisis), and specifically to the profound human toll of the American war in Iraq several times, the organization's coverage of and activism surrounding the humanitarian crisis faced by Iraqis as a result of the American military action displays a deficiency in emphasis and tone. Throughout the post–September 11th period while elaborate mobilizations brought the detainee rights and torture policies to the fore of American political contests and public consciousness, initiatives highlighting the human rights and humanitarian costs of the U.S. military intervention in Iraq were relatively few and far between.

Further, although adhering to a methodology that requires firsthand accounts and spotless field research to maintain its credibility and effectiveness is vital, it is not difficult to envision such a formidable international human rights organization demonstrating greater resourcefulness and flexibility, namely, by seeking out alternative ways of verifying human rights conditions in Iraq and then more aggressively pressing for changes in U.S. policies accordingly. Certainly, the organization did not have open access to secret CIA prisons but was able to uncover important information nonetheless. Given all that was known about conditions in Iraq, perhaps Human Rights Watch and other INGOs could have been more aggressive in finding avenues to hold the American government accountable and less inclined to give it the benefit of the doubt in relation to the war.

Addressing the fourth question may also shed further light on the discrepancy in coverage and emphasis on the various American policies in the post–September 11th era. Much of the impetus for the post–September 11th era American human rights mobilizations surrounding torture and detainee rights was a sense that the United States was taking part in acts traditionally associated with repressive Eastern/Southern states' behavior – a clear step backward in its human rights commitments. However, while mobilizing in response to patterns of what they associated with Eastern forms of violence materializing in a Western context, they continued to largely decenter the military violence being committed by their own government, further illuminating Western blind spots in conceptions of human rights relativism and universalism discussed above. Cyra Choudhury provides a useful description of what a more universalist outlook would entail in the post–September 11th context:

To put it simply, the discussion should not be limited to whether or not torture is legal and should be undertaken in the "ticking bomb" context or any other scenario or to what constitutes torture, how much "pressure" ought to be placed on the "bad people" during interrogation. But rather it should be expanded to include critical appraisals of our bombings, detention, the lack of security, the demolition of houses, collective punishment, and it ought to take into consideration the fact that civilians in Iraq are suffering physical and psychological harms that may rival torture in their magnitude. Ultimately, it must account for the fact that Iraqis are losing their lives. Without such an expansion of the discussion, the resulting failure to encompass all violence against Iraqi civilians will continue to cut sharply against liberals' claims of support for *universal* human rights.[47]

In other words, as Middle Eastern activists and populations (as well as a number of domestic American rights NGOs) clearly saw, the human toll of the Iraq War, including those cited by Choudhury, and reported death tolls of over 100,000 Iraqi civilians and four million displaced refugees should be viewed as grave human rights violations and treated with the same level of urgency, mobilization, and outrage as American detention and torture policies. Dismissing Middle Eastern conceptions of what has transpired throughout the Iraq War as human rights violations by designating them as "abstract" or "not law" may betray a constrained vision of the human rights project.

Again, although American INGOs frequently do report on and wage campaigns on the civilian toll of specific American operations within the war by invoking international humanitarian law, there is a glaring deficiency in their emphasis and tone.[48] Further, as international lawyer Naz Modirzadeh remarked at the closing session of the 2006 American Society of International Law Annual Meeting, there is a lot the United States has done in Iraq that is deeply problematic yet perfectly legal under international humanitarian law. Although a discussion of reforming international humanitarian law is well beyond the scope of this study, it is important to ask whether American INGOs' stance reflects a human rights outlook that is confined and overly legalistic – conceptually divorced from broader, more integrated, views of the project of advancing human dignity.

It could be that there is more to the disposition of Middle Eastern human rights groups than abstractness and demagogy and an inability to grasp what is and what is not law. At least one example, that of Amal Basha's struggle with and ultimate resolution of the contradictions posed by U.S. use of force in Iraq, would suggest so.

Each of the four areas briefly explored here coupled with U.S.-based human rights INGOs' engagements with national security discourses and the enlistment of top-ranking military generals in their post–September 11th campaigns, as detailed in Chapter 2, raise important questions about

---

[47] See Cyra A. Choudhury, *supra* note 22.
[48] At least one notable exception to this trend has been Human Rights Firsts' elaborate campaign to highlight the plight of Iraqi refugees.

whether these INGOs have taken an overly accepting position toward American militarism during the era. They should now take the opportunity presented by post–September 11th developments to begin a conversation about whether a new approach to American militarism is in order.

ARE INTERNATIONAL HUMAN RIGHTS CAPTIVE TO POWER?

Through the composite of the American campaign to counter the United States' "War on Terror" human rights violations presented in Chapter 2, it becomes apparent that American power is not beyond the influence of the international human rights regime in any absolute sense. The human rights proponents involved simultaneously added to and drew from the legitimacy of international human rights norms. Eventually, the campaign was successful both in posing constraints on American power and policy options and in disturbing the mainstream American narrative about the United States' relationship to the international human rights order. Several of the campaign's participants elaborated on how specifically the presence of an international legal framework aided their efforts. In response to a question regarding the importance of international law as a tool in the development and passage of the McCain amendment, one Congressional staffer provided the following observation:

I think it's critical because it gives everybody something to look at and say, "Here is the standard and we're not following it . . ." rather than saying we have no standards and we are just going to make it up. The fact that we could say, all we're trying to do, is close a loophole, done by the CAT, that was already ratified by the Senate, it has meaning under the Constitution, it's from a United States reservation under the CAT, all these other countries have signed up to it, no other country claims a legal right to engage in cruel, degrading, and inhumane treatment except the United States and the Europeans can sort of push the same way. It provides a semiclear framework that you can try to converge toward. Basically, you'd have to invent it, if it didn't already exist.[49]

A human rights advocate otherwise highly skeptical of the ability of international human rights norms to constrain American behavior during the era did find that at some level the existence of international legal norms aided their human rights agenda:

That's where it [international law] did make a difference. We had the starting point of the Geneva Conventions, we had the starting point of the Convention Against Torture. It meant something that we were parties to those treaties. It meant something that we had embraced those obligations. It meant that we had promised. It meant that we had evaluated ourselves and that we would hold ourselves to those

---

[49] Interview with congressional staffer, in Washington, DC (Feb. 24, 2006).

standards – that those values were our values. The existence of international law and treaties was the prerequisite to having those obligations.[50]

In this account, the advocate often conflates how international law was more widely understood (i.e., what U.S. policymakers understood their international legal obligations to mean) with the types of arguments advocates could make by referencing the international human rights regime (i.e., what U.S. obligations should mean to American policymakers). Nonetheless, this account, like the one presented before it, sheds light on a fundamental point: despite the fact that existing American identity constructions marginalized international law through nationalist discourses and a sense of American preeminence and power, when an opening was presented, international human rights norms entered American civil society/governmental contests over human rights policy and proved effective both as a key frame of reference and a normative influence.

Although the types of international challenges and mobilizations against American human rights practices in the post–September 11th era were not without significant impact, in the end, it was the domestic initiative that made the most headway in challenging American attempts to thwart international human rights norms. Compliance (or movement in the direction of compliance) with international human rights law was clearly less a matter of vertical enforcement from above and beyond American borders than a product of domestic contests and mediation in overlapping legal, political, and social terrains. This is true not only when enforcement is conceived in traditional terms but also when enforcement is thought of as rooted in normative influences. Thus, although the case study demonstrates the potential impact and effectiveness of international human rights norms when channeled through constructivist processes of shaming, framing, and persuasion, these processes bare their greatest fruits as they play out inside the United States.

In the Middle Eastern context, human rights also frequently served as a tool for checking both American and local rulers' exercise of power. It was in relation to its proclaimed mission to spread liberty and democracy that the United States encountered some of its greatest obstacles. Although invoking a "human rights guardian" identity construction allowed the United States to legitimate its exercises of power, the certitude of the legitimacy was not a given. First, it became increasingly clear that United States could not determine the legitimacy of its actions alone; the legitimacy it sought was ultimately a product of its interactions with global (and, for the purposes of the present analysis, Middle Eastern) leaders, journalists, human rights activists, and populations. The key to greater license to pursue its agendas through appropriating human rights was perpetually proving a genuine commitment to spreading human rights norms through its actions to a skeptical

Middle Eastern and global audience – in essence a catch-22 and near impossible feat. As Nico Krisch has explained, "International law is important to powerful states as a source of legitimacy. But in order to provide legitimacy, it needs to distance itself from power and has to resist its mere translation into law."[51] This is in line with constructivist assertions that at some point actors appropriating human rights norms, no matter how instrumentally, will feel compelled to either conform to the norms or take steps to resolve its inconsistencies. They do so to avoid stigmatized charges of hypocrisy and deployment of raw power. This in effect is the power of morally rooted norms such as human rights. The point has also been aptly made by Andrew Arato in the democratization context:

> The language of democratization, though mobilized for an imperial purpose, thus lands the bearers of the discourse in an international legal field that does not allow democracy to be openly replaced by its opposite. The democratic justification binds, at least to some extent, even those who use it in bad faith.[52]

In the post–September 11th period, domestic and international human rights proponents have frequently made use of this phenomenon and demanded the United States government live up to its assumed identity construction as the promoter of democracy, freedom, and human rights. Overlooking the ways in which such pressure has impacted human rights outcomes in the Middle East would be to leave out a key dimension of post–September 11th human rights dynamics. At various junctures, the Bush administration has been moved to put some pressure on its authoritarian allies in the Middle East to adopt democratic measures, uphold rights, and open space for local rights advocates to operate. Although it can certainly be argued that such progress is inadequate or incomplete, particularly given the magnitude of the human rights challenges at hand, it is important to recognize that American human rights appropriations are not without their own trappings and can sometimes be subverted.

In Yemen, I attended a ceremony celebrating the conclusion of a U.S.-funded girls' leadership project that had offered young Yemeni women an opportunity to work in various Yemeni government ministries. I learned at the ceremony that the Girls' World Communication Center (the local NGO facilitating the project) also conducted a year-long human rights training introducing international human rights instruments to Yemeni women. In a conversation with Iman al-Tawqi the Coordinator of the NGO's human rights program, I inquired about the challenges the group faced in conducting the trainings. She told me that when the trainers are presenting the international instruments, they constantly have students ask, "What is the

---

[51] Nico Krisch, *International Law in Times of Hegemony*, 16:3 Eur. J. Int'l L. 369, 369 (2005).

[52] Andrew Arato, *Empire's Democracy, Ours and Theirs, supra* note 21, at 223.

point? These instruments are not implemented, especially when it comes to the powerful." The answer she said she gives in these instances is "Well, it's better to have them (international human rights instruments) than to not have them. Like our constitution, it is not always implemented, but it's better to have one than not at all."[53] Although it is not articulated in this way, the answer reveals a recognition that not unlike the operation of domestic law in the Middle East (and indeed everywhere), international law's ability to constrain power is partial and less than guaranteed. Yet, at the same time, its emancipatory potential makes its worth clinging to. In the final analysis, it is the principles of universal human dignity as well as the equality of states, cultures, races, religions and individuals enshrined in international human rights norms which give expression to Middle Eastern aspirations, and hold out the promise of challenging abuses of power by American and local rulers alike. In essence, the increased Middle Eastern turn to human rights in the post–September 11th era is testament to this recognition. Were it not understood as an emancipatory force that can be used to hold the powerful to account, it would not have any appeal or legitimacy. It was through the aid of the legitimacy of international human rights discourses that American/Middle Eastern power relations were, from time to time, turned on their heads. Even if the reversals were momentary or miniscule in their scale, they were frequently not without consequence. The point is made eloquently by Amy Bartholomew, referencing the March 2005 Department of Defense National Defense Strategy and finding that American strength "will continue to be challenged by those who employ a strategy of the weak using international fora, judicial processes, and terrorism."[54] As she elaborates:

All of this goes some way towards bolstering the contention that the defense and reform of law's empire and the further legalization of international and global relations may hold the promise – even if it is distant – of 'constraining' and possibly even 'attacking' imperial power. In this one regard, the Bush administration is right, not deluded, international and cosmopolitan law are strategies of and for "the weak."[55]

Beyond the Middle Eastern response to American power detailed in this book, the global move to reclaim human rights and its egalitarian tenets is notable. The more the Bush administration assaulted human rights norms, the more the emancipatory embodiment of human rights was claimed, furthered, and embraced globally. There was in fact a global movement to reclaim the emancipatory essence of the regime and reject the transparent

---

[53] Interview with Iman al-Tawqi, coordinator, Girl's World Communication Center, in Sana'a, Yemen (Jan. 22, 2007).

[54] United States Department of Defense, National Defense Strategy of the United States of America, (Mar. 2005), http://www.defenselink.mil/news/Mar2005/d20050318nds1.pdf.

[55] Amy 21 Bartholomew, *Empire's Law and the Contradictory Politics of Human Rights*, *supra* note, at 178.

infusion of power the United States was attempting. This was accomplished in virtually every demonstration, sit-in, and letter-writing campaign carried out. Pressure on local governments to resist American human rights violations spanned from Indonesia to Europe to Ecuador.

The significance of the global protest and backlash against both the United States' instrumental uses of notions of human rights and freedom to justify the Iraq War, and its rights violations of Arab and Muslim detainees held in conjunction with the War on Terrorism cannot be discounted. The protests suggest that even when American officials go to extensive lengths to appropriate human rights discourses, many people are equipped with the tools and consciousness to see through such appropriations or that the essentially emancipatory tenets of the discourse itself provide the tools and consciousness to evaluate such appropriations, particularly when they are so blatant.

Along the same lines, Anthony Chase has argued that post–September 11th developments have reshaped expectations of state obligations, noting that Abu Ghraib–style torture is "historically unexceptional" in terms of "its general violence," but "now causes general revulsion." As he explains, the recent trend

epitomizes a shifting normative environment; analogous acts in previous eras were either taken as inevitable or, even, celebrated, but in today's normative environment publicity over such events is a substantive defeat, reducing an actor's ideological legitimacy and, hence, ability to pursue its agenda. Bush, as well as his top generals, explicitly term abu Ghraib the U.S.'s biggest defeat in Iraq. There are, in other words, strong political-normative incentives to abide by human rights law. Just as the Bush administration paid a *realpolitik* price for flouting human rights (and humanitarian) law, states that act within the constraints of the rights regime reap tangible benefits. More generally, these sorts of normative shifts are what have both constituted and further stimulated the legal-political construction of the human rights regime, creating the sorts of incentives that have made it a viable part of contemporary politics, rather than just an idealistic sideshow.[56]

The normative shift of which Chase speaks is more fitting when viewing global developments rather than developments in the United States where the shift has simultaneously gone in the direction of human rights promotion and its opposite – toward increased acceptance of torture and war as a means of safeguarding American interests and "freedom." Still, his larger contention that human rights have been deployed to check American power and have served as a barrier to unfettered American power is apt. It is also important to recognize that part of the reason Abu Ghraib and Guantanamo garnered such a large-scale global reaction to human rights violations that do occur throughout the globe regularly was the conducts' roots in American

[56] Anthony Chase, *The Transnational Muslim World, the Foundations and Origins of Human Rights, and Their Ongoing Intersections*, 4:1 Muslim World Journal of Human Rights, 8 (2007), http://www.bepress.com/mwjhr/vol4/iss1/art1.

power – both in the form of unapologetic contraventions of international human rights law and its appropriations of human rights discourses.

All of these facets of the unfolding of post–September 11th era events belie the point that international human rights law cannot be viewed as intrinsically captive to power, a tendency Fuyuki Karasawa has called "anti-imperialist absolutism" within the context of humanitarian and human rights interventions.[57] It frequently maintains some dimension of autonomous emancipatory presence with the potential to challenge power, even as power attempts to co-opt it and strip it of its potential. As Kurasawa contends, and the case studies undertaken in this text demonstrate, assessments of the extent to which human rights either manifests or transcends power must be circumstantial, an admittedly difficult undertaking particularly when the two conditions are as intertwined as they have been in the post–September 11th era. Amy Bartholomew's contention that "empire's law" and "law's empire" should be viewed as "points on a spectrum rather than distinctly separate entities" is also helpful. Ultimately it is a relative and shifting conception of human rights' relationship to power that best captures all of the internal, intercultural, and transnational American and Middle Eastern interactions revolving around human rights policies, practices, and discourses that have transpired in the post–September 11th era.

CONCLUSION

This book has put forth the argument that the contemporary human rights project simultaneously constrains and manifests power. Yet recognizing that contemporary human rights dynamics lie between hegemony and emancipation should not prevent advocates from actively pursuing a course that pushes the human rights project farther away from the former and closer to the later.

In his inaugural address, Barack Obama, the successor to George Bush, declared "we reject as false the choice between our safety and our ideals," signaling a departure from the eight years that preceded his ascendance to power. He also affirmed that "America is a friend of each nation and every man, woman, and child who seeks a future of peace and dignity, and that we are ready to lead once more." From this declaration, it was difficult to know how precisely Obama envisioned American leadership, as inherent or earned? Another statement coupled with a slew of new policies two days into his administration was encouraging. After signing three executive orders revoking Bush administration Guantanamo, torture and detainee treatment

[57] Fuyuki Kurasawa, *The Uses and Abuses of Humanitarian Intervention in the Wake of Empire, supra* note 21.

policies, Obama stated "America's moral example must be the bedrock and the beacon of our global leadership." As promising as some of Obama's stances may be, it would be a mistake for human rights advocates to view Barack Obama's presidency as simply the end of a nightmare or aberration in American history. From within the crushing human rights crises of the post–September 11th era and the myriad of civil society attempts to challenge them, important lessons for American human rights advocacy emerged, foremost among them, that neither American human rights compliance nor leadership can be viewed as a given. Human rights advocates should take every opportunity to engage with and incorporate these lessons in their work. Obama may have stronger human rights commitments than his predecessor, but even under an Obama administration innumerable American human rights struggles remain to be won- both domestically and internationally. Just one early example of this has been Obama's reluctance to endorse prosecutions or investigation commissions to hold those responsible for post-September 11th era human rights violations accountable for their actions. More importantly, human rights advocates must take advantage of any openings from an administration relatively more inclined toward upholding human rights and taking on international legal obligations in order to build a stronger foundation for human rights norms' regulation of the actions of future American leaders more inclined towards the Bush administration's worldview. The lessons of the post–September 11th era are crucial to both endeavors. Thus, if those committed to human rights seize on its opportunities for introspection and change, the dwindling era will be left with a legacy of human rights' enrichment alongside its various human rights tragedies.

Conclusion

It is difficult to give a semblance of coherence to the storm of human rights contests that have raged in the post–September 11th era. The era's human rights story was one of glaring failings, formidable challenges, unending contradictions, unprecedented mobilizations, and new opportunities – all unfolding simultaneously. The deluge of stunning human rights developments came in such rapid succession and in such sheer volume that throughout most of the era advocates would leave one crisis only to tend to the next. There was virtually no time to step back and take a broader view of all that had transpired – the winding and crossing paths taken by American and Middle Eastern forces, the ground forfeited and ground gained, and the interconnections between actors and actions traditionally viewed as standing worlds apart. The juxtaposition of three key human rights struggles of the era provides the opportunity for precisely such a global view and pause for reflection.

Most visibly, the era stood stained by its array of human rights violations – renditions to torture, sexual humiliation, hoods, dogs, cages, sensory deprivation, waterboarding, black sites, indefinite detentions without trial, patent racial and religious inscriptions, legal memos justifying and political rhetoric euphemizing torture, categories invoking rights-based rationales to justify the withholding of rights, and military air strikes made in the name of furthering rights and freedom. Moreover, all of this played out amid the backdrop of American policymakers and Middle Eastern autocrats shaking hands and proclaiming a shared unwavering commitment to both fighting the War on Terrorism and bringing human rights and democracy to the Middle East. Each news report unveiling a new batch of human rights transgressions, a new convoluted legal doctrine paving the way for abuses, or a new link to the government officials, lawyers, and military officers firmly seated at the top of existing power structures gave rise to a greater sense that the emancipatory promise of the human rights paradigm was fading – that it had become once and for all apparent that the framework simply could not withstand the weight of state power and especially of powerful states determined to undermine and co-opt it.

The era was also marked by its innumerable contradictions. Middle Eastern adversaries referred to American human rights abuses, violations of international law, and media capitulation to state rhetoric. At the same time, American government officials highlighted repression and denials of freedom in places like Iran while the Bush administration fought domestically to reserve its right to torture detainees in U.S. custody. Neither seemed troubled by the inconsistencies of their position. The element of truth in each assertion served to veil the abuses of power being justified and the abuses of power served to corrupt the calls of human rights adherence being made. And yet although these effects were realized to a considerable extent, they were never quite realized absolutely. This was due to the era's remarkable mobilizations and campaigns designed to unveil American and Middle Eastern governments' human rights appropriations and preserve the essence of the human rights idea.

In the Middle East, because they did not derive legitimacy from their populations, authoritarian governments were compelled to respond to American pressure and take up both liberal reforms and illiberal "War on Terror" detainee treatment policies as a means of ensuring their survival. Such double-edged American pressure created both important openings and new challenges for Middle Eastern human rights advocates. At the same time, activists, intellectuals, and governments had to reconcile their condemnations of American interventions with the reality that they relied on and in some cases actively sought those very interventions. Finally, both Western and Middle Eastern advocates soon came to realize that in many spots in the Middle East, it was Islamists with their long history of eschewing human rights prescriptions who had become one of the most formidable forces for resisting authoritarianism in the region.

Contradictions also abounded in the American context. Taking on the role of the human rights teacher, American government officials promoted secular human rights prescriptions for Middle Eastern ills notwithstanding their own proclivities to mix rights, religion, and politics and, more critically, their own unwillingness to uphold key international human rights obligations. Accordingly the American government funded and visited Middle Eastern human rights initiatives as it continued to flout both the letter and spirit of the international human rights legal regime. In the process, it was repeatedly confronted with and forced to contend with the very human rights norms it espoused, recognizing that it faced obstacles if it failed to present itself as something more virtuous than the embodiment of raw power. Emerging from the dynamic was a firm rhetorical embrace of the morally engrained language of human rights. However, the language had the potential to constrain American action as much as it could enable American action, revealing the ultimate vulnerability of power built on the co-opting of morally based norms. Faced with mounting challenges from within and without, the world's sole superpower often found itself trapped and often trapped itself. The predicament stemmed predictably from the vast gap between its morally based rhetoric and its overt thwarting of the international human rights project.

Perhaps just as remarkable as the era's dizzying array of contradictions have been the numerous parallels between Middle Eastern and American human rights dynamics it has unearthed and the converging paths of Middle Eastern and American human rights advocacy it has produced. In each of their separate contexts, advocates began with international human rights law lacking legitimacy amid political and social discourses imbued with nationalist sentiments. They faced governments that alternated between portrayals of human rights as foreign impositions and idealistic prescriptions born out of naiveté. As a result American and Middle Eastern advocates pursued (often strikingly similar) avenues for pushing the boundaries of prevailing discourses and creating expanded space to bring human rights into mainstream political contests and consciousness. The era's successive human rights failings created critical openings from which the argument for human rights compliance could emerge. Abu Ghraib with its inescapable visual representation of denials of human dignity reigned foremost among them. As the era unfolded, American advocates also found themselves embarking on cultural projects and contemplating religious engagements with striking parallels to those long pursued by their Middle Eastern colleagues. Finally, in both contexts, advocates found themselves soliciting the aid and authoritative voices of powerful domestic intermediaries – the military brass in the American case and religious forces in the Middle Eastern case. Although the collaborations were understandably coveted, they also posed critical questions about the trade-offs encompassed and the hazards involved. As they moved through the era, both American and Middle Eastern advocates took significant strides toward making the human rights project more compelling and pressing to their respective audiences, gradually transforming human rights from a widely dismissed and marginalized paradigm eyed with suspicion to a framework increasingly understood as having real political, social, and legal clout and relevance. At the same time, a domestic human rights infrastructure slowly took shape around them that in spite of its considerable shortcomings was more than what human rights forces had to work with before the era began.

Despite their parallels and converging paths, in both American and Middle Eastern discourses, the case for human rights compliance was frequently made by some contrasting reference to the actions of the Other.

Embedded within the debates erupting on both sides was a sometimes implicit, sometimes explicit, argument that there must be a change in course because otherwise "We will have become like them." However, even as a distancing from the other's actions served as a catalyzing force for an increased turn to human rights (the regime being disregarded by the other), strides were simultaneously made in the opposite direction – toward displacing the hierarchies of cultures and peoples long entwined with the human rights project. Witnessing the overt commission of human rights violations by the United States often left activists and observers disoriented, feeling like they had stepped into a strange new reality they barely recognized and nostalgic for the days in which they could confidently know that the U.S. government would not commit torture and, if it did, the American legal system would put an immediate stop to it. Yet they were eventually forced to adopt new parameters to make sense of the era's unfolding human rights contests. This often meant slowly moving away from engrained assumptions that Western action would generally correlate with the progress and achievement of rights and that American human rights transgressions (including violence through war) would generally encompass an element of calculated rationality or justified means to liberal ends. Thus, as the post–September 11th era progressed, it became increasingly apparent that human rights could not be neatly tied to a particular geography, place, or locale with the same degree of certainty it had been in the past. It was now much more conceivable that torture, denials of due process, and, by extension, other human rights violations could take place anywhere. The once seemingly reliable demarcations of the East/West geography of human rights now looked skewed and unreliable. At the same time, the Middle Eastern eye on American human rights transgressions in the post–September 11th era offered an alternative configuration and mapping of the flow of global human rights dynamics. The creation of this altered terrain was less attributable to any conscious decision to reassess traditional human rights equations on the part of advocates and observers alike than to what may be more accurately understood as the consonant dissonance produced by the Guantanamos, CIA black sites, and torture memos of the era.

EMERGING OUT OF THE ERA

Some potentially promising consequences flow from the transformed human rights landscape taking shape as the post–September 11th era winds down. First, although a time of tremendous international conflict, the post–September 11th era has provided important opportunities for bridging global divides between civil society forces. In many respects, American and

Middle Eastern journalists, lawyers, and NGOs took important strides toward greater dialog, exchange, and collaboration on more equal terms during the era. This comes through in a comment on the cooperation between Yemeni and American lawyers on Guantanamo cases by HOOD's Khaled Alanesi:

And our American friends, they always contact us and in every accomplishment, they say without you, we couldn't have done it. We also say that without them we couldn't do anything. Guantanamo detainees' cases showed that we unite on the basis of freedoms and rights. In the case of the Guantanamo detainees, it shows that we all agree on freedom and human rights because the people working on the case are Muslims, Jews, Christians, rightist and leftist, believers and non-believers. They belong to different groups. So this shows the idea of freedom and human rights.[1]

Second, the new human rights outlook may enable a greater inclination on the part of both American and Middle Eastern populations to look inward and rediscover the many overlooked denials of human dignity taking place at their footsteps. Most important, however, has been the increased possibility that co-opting human rights as license for military interventions not genuinely rooted in humanitarian considerations will prove a more arduous task than it was at the onset of the post–September 11th era. This potential advance could be seen in the relative absence of emphasis on Iranian human rights practices in discussions of military action against Iran in the United States in 2008. As Trita Parsi of the National Iranian-American Council, who has been involved lobbying efforts against U.S. military action in Iran, observed:

There seems to be a deliberate attempt for U.S. advocates of military action in Iran to not use human rights justifications. It is not an argument the American public finds attractive. There are two reasons for this: the failed experience in Iraq and the lack of U.S. credibility on human rights after Abu Ghraib and Guantanamo.[2]

Two final episodes provide insight into the state of the human rights project as the post–September 11th era draws to a close. On September 24, 2007, the scandal-prone Iranian president, Mahmood Ahmadinejad, was invited to speak at Columbia University in New York City. The occasion attracted an unusual mix of protestors. They included American Jewish groups objecting to what they considered a major American university's inappropriate welcoming of a holocaust denier, free-speech supporters challenging the assertion that Ahmadinejad should not be allowed to address the university, women's rights and gay rights supporters highlighting the

---

[1] Interview with Khaled Alanesi, executive director, HOOD, in Sana'a, Yemen (Jan. 15, 2007).
[2] Telephone interview with Trita Parsi, president of the National Iranian-American Council (Aug. 1, 2008).

repression suffered by women and homosexuals in Iran, and antiwar protestors implicitly challenging the use of Ahmadinejad's rhetoric and Iranian human rights conditions as devices for advancing a war agenda with Iran. Among the many handmade signs displayed by the disparate voices assembled on the Columbia University campus was one that simply read "Protecting Human Rights Begins at Home." Six years after September 11th, the sign displayed was as perplexing and multifaceted as the era to which it belonged. On one reading, the slogan could be interpreted as a message to Americans fixated on Iranian human rights violations while turning a blind eye to their own human rights deficiencies – freedom of speech at this forum, gay rights in the United States, or Abu Ghraib and Guantanamo. Alternatively, the same sign could have been directed at Ahmadinejad, who is apt to cite American human rights violations to obscure deplorable rights conditions in Iran. The anecdote's significance lies not in which of the two interpretations served as the sign's original inspiration; rather, its significance lies in the fact that either (or both) interpretation is now widely imaginable. In this way, the sign comes to epitomize the evolution of human rights equations at the end of the post–September 11th era.

Another event that took place three months earlier was equally notable. On June 25, 2007, a group of graduating high school students selected as Presidential Scholars was invited to the White House for a photo-op and gathering with the U.S. president in honor of the prestigious award. They took the occasion to pass George W. Bush a letter that was signed by 50 of the 140 young awardees. The letter the president was forced to read silently, as the students watched, stated the following:

Mr. President.

As members of the Presidential Scholars class of 2007, we have been told that we represent the best and brightest of our nation. Therefore, we believe we have a responsibility to voice our convictions. We do not want America to represent torture. We urge you to do all in your power to stop violations of the human rights of detainees, to cease illegal renditions and to apply the Geneva Convention to all detainees, including those designated enemy combatants.

Signed, . . .

The American students' initiative mirrors the efforts of Yemeni youth who posed direct challenges to American embassy officials regarding the United States' human rights policies recounted in Chapter 3 and similar efforts by the same group to promote human rights in their own way within Yemen. Thus, despite the utter failure of so many of the era's leaders (including those of the "free world") to apply international human rights norms in good faith, these are promising signs that in the United States as in the Middle East and beyond, a generation of future leaders has emerged from this tragic era with a commitment to carry the human rights project forward. In other words, as the era begins to burn out, emerging from the ashes of its many human rights tragedies and tribulations is an affirmation of much of what lies at the core of the human rights ideal. Such episodes provide considerable promise that the emancipatory spirit of the human rights paradigm will remain a formidable force for challenging the power-laden spirit of its co-option.

Bibliography

Jean Allain, "Orientalism and International Law: The Middle East as the Underclass of the International Legal Order." 17 Leiden J. Int'l L. 391 (2004).

Abdullahi An-Naim, "Introduction: Area Expressions" and the "Universality of Human Rights: Mediating a Contingent Relationship," in David P. Forsythe and Patrice C. MacMahon, eds. *Human Rights and Diversity: Area Studies Revisited*, University of Nebraska Press, pp. 1–21 (2003).

Andrew Arato, "Empire's Democracy, Ours, and Theirs," in Amy Bartholomew, ed. *Empire's Law: The American Imperial Project and the "War to Remake the World*," Pluto Press and Between the Lines, pp. 217–244 (2006).

Michael Barnett and Raymond Duvall, "Power in International Politics." 59 Int'l Org. 39 (2005).

Michael Barnett and Shibley Telhami, eds., *Identity and Foreign Policy in the Middle East*, Cornell University Press (2002).

Amy Bartholomew, "Empire's Law and the Contradictory Politics of Human Rights," in Amy Bartholomew ed. *Empire's Law, The American Imperial Project and the "War to Remake the World*," Pluto Press and Between the Lines (2006).

Henning Boekle, Volker Rittberger, and Wolfgang Wagner, "Norms and Foreign Policy: Constructivist Foreign Policy Theory," University of Tubingen Center for International Relations/Peace and Conflict Studies TAP 34A (1999).

Jutta Brunnee and Stephan Toope, "International Law and Constructivism: Elements of an Interactional Theory of International Law." 39 Colum. J. Transnat'l L. 19 (2000).

Micheal Byers, ed., *United States Hegemony and the Foundations of International Law*, Cambridge University Press (2003).

Anthony Chase, "The Transnational Muslim World, the Foundations and Origins of Human Rights, and Their Ongoing Intersections." 4:1 Muslim World J. Hum Rts. 8 (2007). Available at: http://www.bepress.com/mwjhr/vol4/iss1/art1.

Anthony Chase and Amr Hamzawi, eds., *Human Rights in the Arab World: Independent Voices*, University of Pennsylvania Press (2007).

Jeffrey Checkel, "Why Comply? Constructivism, Social Norms, and the Study of International Institutions." ARENA Working Papers WP 99/24 (1999).

Cyra A. Choudhury, "Comprehending 'Our' Violence: Reflections on the Liberal Universalist Tradition, National Identity and the War on Iraq." 3:1 Muslim

World J. Human Rts. (2006). Available at: http://www.bepress.com/mwjhr/vol3/iss1/art2.

Janine A. Clark, "The Conditions of Islamist Moderation: Unpacking Cross-Ideological Cooperation." 38 Int. J. Middle East Stud. 539–560 (2006).

Andrew Cortell and James Davis, "Understanding the Domestic Impact of International Norms: A Research Agenda." 2 Int'l Stud. Rev. 65 (2000).

Jane K. Cowan, Marie Benedicte Dembour, and Richard Wilson eds., *Culture and Rights: Anthropological Perspectives*, Cambridge University Press (2001).

Ken Cunningham, "Permanent War? The Domestic Hegemony of the New American Militarism." 26:4 New Pol. Sci. (2004).

Jack Donnelly, "International Human Rights: Unintended Consequences of the War on Terrorism," in Thomas G. Weiss et al, eds. *Wars on Terrorism and Iraq: Human Rights, Unilateralism, and U.S. Foreign Policy*, Routledge, pp. 98–112 (2004).

Susan G. Drummond, *Mapping Marriage Law in Spanish Gitano Communities*, University of British Columbia Press (2006).

Martha Finnemore and Kathryn Sikkink, "Taking Stock: The Constructivist Research Program in International Relations and Comparative Politics." 4 Am. Rev. Pol. Sci. 391 (2001).

———, "International Norm Dynamics and Political Change." 52 Int.'l Org. 887 (1998).

Martha Finnemore and Stephen Toope, "Alternatives to 'Legalization': Richer Views of Law and Politics." 55:3 Int'l Org. 743 (2001).

David P. Forsythe, "U.S. Foreign Policy and Human Rights in an Era of Insecurity: the Bush Administration and Human Rights after September 11th," in Thomas G. Weiss et al., eds. *Wars on Terrorism and Iraq: Human Rights, Unilateralism and U.S. Foreign Policy*, Routledge (2004).

Thomas Franck, *The Power of Legitimacy among Nations*, Oxford University Press (1990).

Branwen Gruffydd Jones, *Decolonizing International Relations*, Rowman & Littlefield (2006).

Karen J. Greenberg, ed., *The Torture Debate in America*, Cambridge University Press (2006).

Stanley Hoffman, *Chaos and Violence: What Globalization, Failed States, and Terrorism Mean for U.S. Foreign Policy*, Rowman & Littlefield (2006).

Michael Ignatieff, "Introduction: American Exceptionalism and Human Rights," in Michael Ignatieff ed. *American Exceptionalism and Human Rights*, Princeton University Press (2005).

Ian Johnstone, "US-UN Relations after Iraq: The End of the World (Order) as We Know It?" 15 Eur. J. Int'l. L 813 (2004).

Ratna Kapur, "The Tragedy of Victimization Rhetoric: Resurrecting the 'Native' Subject in International/ Post-Colonial Feminist Legal Politics." 15 Harv. Hum Rts. J. (2002). Available at: http://www.law.harvard.edu/students/orgs/hrj/iss15/kapur.shtml.

Robert Keohane, "International Relations and International Law: Two Optics." 38 Harv. Int'l L.J. 487 (1999).

Fuyuki Kurasawa, "The Uses and Abuses of Humanitarian Intervention in the Wake of Empire," in Amy Bartholomew, ed. *Empire's Law, The American Imperial Project and the "War to Remake the World,"* Pluto Press and Between the Lines (2006).

Harold Koh, "Why Do Nations Obey International Law?" 106 Yale L.J. 2599 (1997).

Nico Krisch, "International Law in Times of Hegemony: Unequal Power and the Shaping of the International Legal Order." 16:3 Eur. J. Int'l L. 369–408 (2005).

George E. Marcus, "Ethnography in/of World System: The Emergence of Multi-Sited Ethnography." 24 Ann. Rev. Anthropology 95–117 (1995).

Jamie Mayerfeld, "Playing by Our Own Rules: How U.S. Marginalization of Human Rights Led to Torture." 20 Harv. Hum. Rts. J. 89 (2007).

Sally Engle Merry, *Human Rights and Gender Violence*, University of Chicago Press (2006).

———, "Human Rights Law and the Demonizing of Culture (and Anthropology along the Way)." 26:1 Pol. Legal Anthropology Rev. 55 (2003).

Julie Mertus, "Human Rights and Civil Society in a New Age of American Exceptionalism," in Richard A. Wilson, ed. *Human Rights in the "War on Terror,"* Cambridge University Press (2005).

———, *Bait and Switch: Human Rights and U.S. Foreign Policy*, Routledge (2004).

Naz K. Modirzadeh, "Taking Islamic Law Seriously: INGOs and the Battle for Muslim Hearts and Minds." 19 Harv. Hum. Rts. J. (2006). Available at http://www.law.harvard.edu/students/orgs/hrj/iss19/modirzadeh.shtml.

Shadi Mokhtari, "A Constructivist Analysis of the Impact of International Human Rights Norms: The Case of Women's Rights under Islamic Law in Iran" (2005) (unpublished LLM thesis, York University).

Makau Mutua, "Savages, Victims, and Saviors: the Metaphor of Human Rights." 42 Harv. Int'l. L.J. 201 (2001).

Obiora Chinedu Okafor, *The African Human Rights System, Activist Forces and International Institutions*, Cambridge University Press (2007).

Obiora Chinedu Okafor and Shedrack C. Agbakwa, "Re-Imagining International Human Rights Education in Our Time: Beyond Three Constitutive Orthodoxies," 14 Leiden J. Int'l L. 563 (2001).

Catherine Powell, "Locating Culture, Identity, and Human Rights," 30 Colum. Hum. Rts. L. Rev. 201 (1999).

Balakrishnan Rajagopal, "The Role of Law in Counter-Hegemonic Globalization and Global Legal Pluralism: Lessons from the Normada Valley Struggle in India." 18 Leiden J. Int'l L. 345–387 (2005).

Thomas Risse, "'Let's Argue!': Communicative Action in World Politics." 54:1 Int'l Org. 1 (2000).

Thomas Risse and Katheryn Sikkink, "The Socialization of International Human Rights Norms into Domestic Practices: Introduction," in Thomas Risse, Stephen Ropp, and Kathryn Sikkink, eds. *The Power of Human Rights*, Cambridge University Press (1999).

Anthea Roberts, "Righting Wrongs or Wronging Rights? The United States and Human Rights Post-September 11." 15 Eur. J. Int'l L. 721 (2004).

Loretta J. Ross, "Beyond Civil Rights: A New Vision for Social Justice in the United States." 2:1 Hum. Rts. Dialogue (1999). Available at: http://www.cceia.org/resources/publications/dialogue/2_01/articles/607.html.

Larbi Sadiki, *The Search for Arab Democracy: Discourses and Counter-Discourses*, Columbia University Press (2004).

Edward Said, *Orientalism*, Vintage (1979).

———, "Saving Amina Lawal: Human Rights Symbolism and the Dangers of Colonialism." 117 Harv. L. Rev. 2365–2386 (2004).

Anthony Shadid, *Night Draws Near: Iraqi People in the Shadow of America's War*, Henry Holt (2005).

Deborah Weissman, "The Human Rights Dilemma: Rethinking the Humanitarian Project." 35 Colum. Hum. Rts. L. Rev. 259 (2004).

Carrie Wickham, "The Problem with Coercive Democratization: The Islamist Response to the U.S. Democracy Reform Initiative." 1:1 Muslim World J. Hum. Rts. 6 (2004). Available at: http://www.bepress.com/mwjhr/vol1/iss1/art6.

Quintan Wiktorowicz, *Islamic Activism: A Social Movement Theory Approach*, Indiana University Press (2004).

Richard A. Wilson, ed., *Human Rights in the "War on Terror,"* Cambridge University Press (2005).

Andreas Wittel, "Ethnography on the Move: From Field to Net to Internet." 1:1 Qualitative Soc. Res. (2000).

Mai Yamani, ed., *Feminism and Islam*, New York University Press (1996).

Haifa Zangana, "The Three Cyclops of Empire-Building: Targeting the Fabric of Iraqi Society," Amy Bartholomew, ed. *Empire's Law: the American Imperial Project and the "War to Remake the World,"* Pluto Press and Between the Lines, pp. 254–255 (2006).

Index

Paths to International Justice
Social and Legal Perspectives
Edited by Marie-Bénédicte Dembour and Tobias Kelly

Law and Society in Vietnam
The Transition from Socialism in Comparative Perspective
Mark Sidel

Constitutionalizing Economic Globalization
Investment Rules and Democracy's Promise
David Schneiderman

The New World Trade Organization Agreements: 2nd Edition
Globalizing Law Through Intellectual Property and Services (2nd Edition)
Christopher Arup

Justice and Reconciliation in Post-Apartheid South Africa
Edited by François du Bois, Antje du Bois-Pedain

Militarization and Violence against Women in Conflict Zones in the
    Middle East
A Palestinian Case-Study
Nadera Shalhoub-Kevorkian

Child Pornography and Sexual Grooming
Legal and Societal Responses
Suzanne Ost

Darfur and the Crime of Genocide
John Hagan and Wenona Rymond-Richmond

Planted Flags: Trees, Land, and Law in Israel/Palestine
Irus Braverman

Fictions of Justice: the International Criminal Court and the Challenge of Legal
    Pluralism in Sub-Saharan Africa
Kamari Maxine Clarke

Conducting Law and Society Research: Reflections on Methods and Practices
Simon Halliday and Patrick Schmidt

After Abu Ghraib: Exploring Human Rights in America and the Middle East
Shadi Mokhtari